Wild Plants
of the
Eastern Caribbean

Sean Carrington

Senior Lecturer in Plant Biology,
University of the West Indies,
Barbados

CARIBBEAN

© Copyright text Sean Carrington 1998
© Copyright illustrations Macmillan Education Ltd 1998

All rights reserved. No reproduction, copy or transmission of this publication may be made without written permission.

No paragraph of this publication may be reproduced, copied or transmitted save with written permission or in accordance with the provisions of the Copyright, Designs and Patents Act 1988, or under the terms of any licence permitting limited copying issued by the Copyright Licensing Agency, 90 Tottenham Court Road, London W1P 9HE.

Any person who does any unauthorised act in relation to this publication may be liable to criminal prosecution and civil claims for damages.

First published 1998 by
MACMILLAN EDUCATION LTD
London and Basingstoke
Companies and representatives throughout the world

ISBN 0–333–67443–X

10 9 8 7 6 5 4 3 2 1
07 06 05 04 03 02 01 00 99 98

This book is printed on paper suitable for recycling and made from fully managed and sustained forest sources.

Typeset by EXPO Holdings, Malaysia

Printed in Hong Kong

A catalogue record for this book is available from the British Library.

Illustrations by Cecilia Fitzsimons

All photographs courtesy of the author
Back cover photograph courtesy of Andrew Collymore

Contents

Dedication	iv
Preface	v
Introduction	1
Monocotyledons	13
Dicotyledons	25
Glossary of botanical terms	103
Glossary of creole and French common names	106
References	114
Index	116

To Richard A. Howard, who dedicated his life to the study of our plants

Preface

This book aims to describe the more common flowering plants, both native and naturalised, found in the Eastern Caribbean. It has evolved out of a previous effort, *Wild Plants of Barbados*, and not surprisingly (for those of you who know the topography of Barbados) the focus is on plants found at lower elevations. With a flora of the Lesser Antilles of over two thousand species, it is clear that such a book must be selective. The photographs are essentially the same as those used in the Barbados book, although the number has been increased, a few new plant descriptions have been added and new snippets of plant lore incorporated. Information on traditional medicinal uses of plants is for interest only and the reader is advised not to experiment with these herbal remedies. For this reason, I have intentionally kept them vague, but for those who are particularly interested there are several publications from the French islands which provide detailed information.[9], [45] The given distribution of each species is based largely on Richard Howard's authoritative *Flora of the Lesser Antilles*.[30]

Probably the greatest challenge faced in preparing this book was to provide for each plant a list of common names, representative of the entire island chain. Each island has its own vernacular names for these plants and it is no easy task to compile them. I took the combined approach of collecting names from the literature and also of writing to experts in each island and asking them to provide common names, using the scientific names and photographs from the Barbados book as a guide. The response was overwhelming and there are a number of people I must thank: Cynthra Persad, Reginald Andall, Curtis Mitchell (Grenada); Clive Bishop, Kenrick Johnson, Earle Kirby, Amos Glascow, Fitzgerald Providence (St Vincent); Steve Gamble (Mustique); Roger Graveson (St Lucia); Arlington James (Dominica); Jacques Fournet (Guadeloupe); Kevel Lindsay (Antigua) and Nigel Carty and Milton Whittaker (St Kitts). Besides consulting the publications listed under References at the end of the book, I also made use of a list of St Lucian plant names compiled by Verna Slane and Laurent Jn-Pierre some years ago for a forestry workshop I attended. I would appreciate being informed of any errors in the common names I have listed and accept full responsibility for these. The spelling of French creole names has been standardised according to rules for creole in the English-speaking islands and was undertaken by Jacques Fournet of Guadeloupe and Lawrence Carrington of Trinidad. For this I am most grateful. Most of the French creole names are from Martinique and Guadeloupe but many are from St Lucia, Dominica and Grenada. A few common names in standard French have also been included, generally when no creole name was available for that island.

Arlington James of Dominica thoughtfully provided me with interesting explanations of some of the creole names he sent me and this gave me the idea to expand this into a glossary of all the creole names listed in the book. Jacques Fournet translated and explained most of these and Jeanette Allsopp also helped. I would like to thank them both.

Last, but by no means least, I would like to record my debt to the following, who taught me much of what I know about the flora of the region: Richard Howard, Dennis Adams, Bernard Rollet and the late Graham Gooding.

I hope this book will stimulate others to appreciate and protect the plants with which we share these islands.

Dry coastal forest, Antigua

Introduction

The Flora of the Lesser Antilles

The flora of the Lesser Antilles numbers almost 3000 species of native, naturalised and commonly cultivated flowering plants.[32] If one ignores cultivated plants and simply considers wild flowering plants, those that are native or naturalised, the tally falls to about 2100 species.[48] These plants are fully described by Howard (1974–1989) in his multi-volume *Flora of the Lesser Antilles*[30] which is the definitive work that has been referred to in compiling this book.

Our flora reached our shores on wind and ocean currents and with the help of birds. In addition, some of our wild plants are deliberate introductions which have since become self-seeding and naturalised. These exotic species amount to no more than 9 per cent of our flora.[48] Of more interest are those plants which are unique or endemic to the Lesser Antilles, species that have evolved here with isolation over time. Some 13 per cent of our flowering plants fit into this category.[32] Some of these are unique to single islands, others span the whole archipelago and, at least for the trees, most are found in the rain forest and montane vegetation.[7] It is crucial that we conserve these endemic species which are uniquely ours by preserving their habitats.

Plant communities of the Lesser Antilles

The island archipelago can be conveniently divided into mountainous volcanic islands, typically higher than 500 m, and low-lying islands. The main arc of islands from Saba down to Grenada comprises these mountainous islands, most of which are potentially volcanically active. The low-lying islands to the north-east of this main arc, Anguilla to Marie Galante, constitute a second category geologically and were formed from extinct submerged volcanoes, now topped by limestone. Low-lying Barbados is in a third and unique class. This island, with its coraline limestone cap, was uplifted by earth movements during the past 600 000 years and part of its limestone cap has been lost in one area, exposing the underlying oceanic and sedimentary deposits.

Plants form recognisable communities determined by climatic features such as rainfall as well as by factors such as soil type, salinity, exposure and temperature. Only in the mountainous islands is the widest range of such vegetation types evident. Complex systems of classifying these have been devised, the most accepted being that proposed in the 1940s by the forester J.S. Beard,[7] but for our purposes a simple, purely descriptive approach will suffice. We can divide these islands into a coastal zone where the saline influence predominates, dry, intermediate and wet zones where water availability predominates and, finally, a montane zone where extreme conditions of low temperature, wind exposure and cloudiness come into play. Within each zone several plant communities are found. It should be realised that all these islands have been greatly altered since colonisation. An extreme example is Barbados, which was almost entirely deforested within 60 years of European settlement.[11] The main plant communities described represent what are considered optimal or climax communities that would predominate in each zone were these islands left entirely to themselves. The situation today is far from this, with many plant communities representing degraded and recovering versions of those described.

All islands have **coastal** vegetation. Where sandy beaches occur this may take the form of certain pioneer plants like ***Ipomoea pescaprae*** colonising bare sand, which in turn give way to strand vegetation above the high tide mark. In this area, shrubs like the sea grape, ***Coccoloba uvifera***, are found and as one goes further inland a littoral forest with trees like the manchineel, ***Hippomane mancinella***, and white cedar, ***Tabebuia*** spp., may be evident. Where the sea abuts rocks and sheer cliffs, a rock pavement vegetation of mat-forming, succulent plants like ***Sesuvium portulacastrum*** and even shrubs and stunted trees are found which are able to survive in mere pockets of soil and tolerate the salt-laden air. The discharge of fresh water at the coast may support some form of swamp community. Mangroves are the most common of such communities, typically developing on leeward shores. The typical shore-front dominant here is the red mangrove, ***Rhizophora mangle***, with its prop roots acting as a baffle against tide action, trapping run-off and providing an important rearing ground for near-shore fisheries. A second, less common, swamp community is freshwater swamp forest, dominated by ***Pterocarpus officinalis***, a large tree with striking buttress roots. This may lie inshore from a mangrove or occur quite independently, along river banks.

In the Eastern Caribbean, at elevations of less than 100 m, there is a marked dry season of five months stretching from February–June. These low-lying areas constitute a **dry zone** in which non-availability of water at this time limits the kind of plant communities that can survive. In most islands, these areas have been cleared of the original plant cover and what natural vegetation there is today is secondary. The littoral forest intergrades with this type of dry forest of open canopies, some trees of which are deciduous, such as ***Bursera simaruba***. Thorny shrubs and cacti are typical and often recovery from past clearance is incomplete so that a treeless thorn scrub community of ***Agave***, cacti and various shrubs may predominate.

At **intermediate** or mid elevations, 100–300 m, the dry season is still felt but the period of drought is shorter. Under such conditions more stratified and luxuriant forests are seen, with a dense canopy of evergreens 10–20 m high and an incomplete emergent layer at twice this height. Understorey palms and evergreen shrubs along with abundant lianas, mosses, ferns and some epiphytes complete this summary. Such forests still exist at Turner's Hall (Barbados), Walling's (Antigua) and King's Hill (St Vincent), to name a few examples. For the low-lying islands, this covers the main natural plant communities found and most of the plants described in this book are restricted to these plant communities and degraded forms of them.

In the mountainous islands, further ascent brings one into a **wet zone** where a period of reduced rainfall is still experienced but where there is always an excess of supply over water loss and use. These conditions support the most luxuriant of forest types – locally termed rain forest, although this is quite different from the rain forests of Asia and South America.[32] This is the most species-rich community and it is here that the highest number of endemic species is found. Three tree strata are found and the highest, at 30 m, comprises a dense canopy in which *gommier*, ***Dacryodes excelsa***, is dominant.[7] Epiphytic ferns, aroids and bromeliads clothe the branches of the trees. The two lower tree layers are discontinuous and each has its own distinctive species composition. The shrub layer is variable and may even be absent. Such rain forests may be found as high as 1000 m if there is shelter but typically at about 500 m they give way to montane vegetation.

As for the wet zone, water is in abundance in the **montane zone**. Mist and dim light prevail, and from the swirling clouds water condenses on the vegetation, creating sodden conditions. Strong winds sweeping over the summit result in a single stratum of dwarfed, gnarled, wind-raked trees, laden with mosses and epiphytes. Below this and in areas where the rain forest is degraded, groves of palms or tree ferns may occur. Mount Qua Qua in the Grand Etang Forest Reserve of Grenada is an accessible example of this elfin woodland community.

It must be emphasised that the plant communities just described are but single points along a continuum of vegetation types. This is only a superficial overview of what is in effect a wide and complex array of plant communities.

Plant classification

Plants are the cornerstone of life on earth, converting the sun's energy into food, as well as providing material for shelter, clothing, medicines and most other human needs. The immense plant diversity on earth is organised (classified) by arranging the different plants into groups according to shared characteristics. The plants which bear flowers (flowering plants) are the dominant plants today and worldwide they probably number over a quarter of a million species. Within the flowering plants, the structure of the flower itself is a major consideration in this process of classification. Plants which look decidedly different to the layman may be considered closely related by botanists because of similarities in the finer details of flower structure. Such related flowering plants are grouped into families, with over 300 families being recognised. These families are arranged in a particular sequence, where closely related families are placed side by side. There are several such schemes differing slightly according to the views of the botanists who developed them. The system used in this book is based on one developed by the German botanists Adolf Engler and Karl von Prantl about 100 years ago but which is still widely used.

Plant classification is perhaps best introduced using familiar examples:

Family	Genus and species	Common name
Malvaceae	*Hibiscus rosa-sinensis*	Hibiscus
Malvaceae	*Hibiscus sabdariffa*	Sorrel or roselle
Malvaceae	*Gossypium barbadense*	Cotton

Although hibiscus, sorrel and cotton at first sight may not seem to resemble each other, they have remarkably similar flower characteristics and so are placed in the same family, the Malvaceae. Furthermore, botanists consider the hibiscus and sorrel plants to be sufficiently similar that they are placed together in a sub-group of the family called a genus. Hibiscus and sorrel are placed in the genus *Hibiscus*, while cotton is distinct enough to be placed in another genus, *Gossypium*. All plants are described scientifically by their genus and species names, a binomial (two-word) system which is universally accepted and has been in use for two centuries. While these scientific names have the disadvantage of being in Latin, they do not vary from place to place as is the case with common names.

Variant forms of a recognised species can also be distinguished. A subspecies (ssp.) is where the variant form differs in a number of important ways and a variety (var.) is where the difference(s) is (are) relatively minor. The variety of the agriculturist or horticulturist is called a cultivar (cv.), a term used exclusively for cultivated plants. How different must plants be to be considered different species, or to be classified in different genera or different families? Which families are most closely related? These are difficult questions which can only be answered by the experts and even they often disagree!

How to use this book

Family characteristics

In a book of this sort, space does not permit a description of each of the families you will encounter. Detailed illustrated accounts of these can be found elsewhere.[26],[58] Recognising family characteristics is, however, the first step in being able to identify a plant. In the next section, therefore, some of the large, key families in the region are introduced, along with short cut means of identifying them. In this book the families of flowering plants are arranged in a particular sequence based on their apparent relatedness, monocotyledons first followed by dicotyledons. The family to which a plant belongs is given at the top of each entry.

Plant entries

At this stage it is important to understand what information is provided in this book and how it is organised. Each plant entry is based on the ground plan indicated in Figure 1. Entries are grouped under a family heading. This is usually a scientific family name as well as a more easily remembered family name, based on a well-known member of the family. For each individual plant entry the scientific name and the authority for the name are given. The authority (which can be ignored by the general reader) lists the name(s) of the botanist(s) who ascribed this name to the plant and it is usually provided in an abbreviated form. This information becomes important when different botanists have given the same scientific name to different plants: it is really saying, *this* scientific name as used by *this* botanist. In addition, it is an unfortunate fact that a single plant may have been given different scientific names by different botanists, based on their perception of how the plant should be classified. Throughout this book I have used the scientific name that appears in

Malvaceae – ← Flowering plant family
Hibiscus family

Scientific name
Sida acuta Burm. f. ← Authority

broom(weed); sweet broom; wire weed; *balyé midi/onzè/savann*
← Common names

Bushy herb to 1 m tall, stem usually hairless. Stipules linear, 7 mm long. Leaves alternate, lanceolate to elliptic, 2–6 cm long, margin toothed above the base. Flowers yellow, 1 cm across, occurring singly or a few to each axillary cluster. Fruit round and flattened, to 5 mm across, of 8–10 spike-topped segments.
← Description

Habitat → Wayside weed.
The pounded stem and root serve as a poultice for sprains.[28]
← General information
← Reference source

Distribution in the eastern Caribbean →

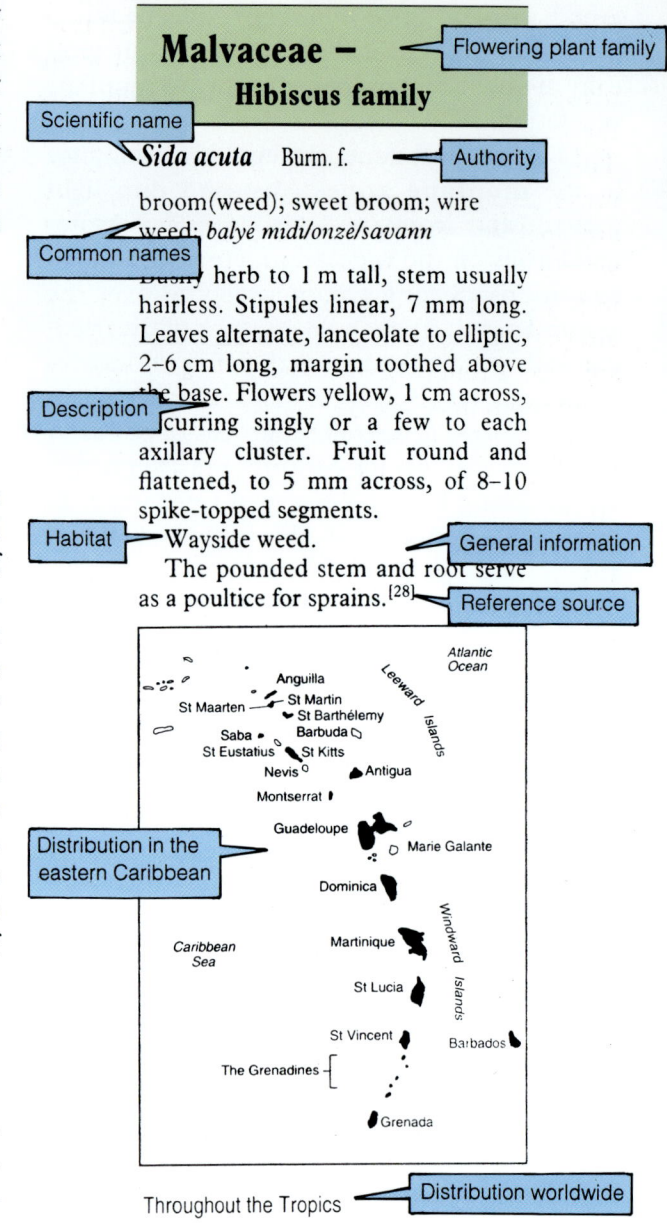

(map showing: Anguilla, St Maarten, St Martin, St Barthélemy, Saba, Barbuda, St Eustatius, St Kitts, Nevis, Antigua, Montserrat, Guadeloupe, Marie Galante, Dominica, Martinique, St Lucia, St Vincent, Barbados, The Grenadines, Grenada; Atlantic Ocean, Leeward Islands, Windward Islands, Caribbean Sea)

Throughout the Tropics ← Distribution worldwide

Figure 1 Layout of information for each plant entry in this book

Flora of the Lesser Antilles[30] but be aware that other names or synonyms may exist for each plant. The vernacular or common names for the plant in the Lesser Antilles then follow. This is not an exhaustive list but gives the most popular names from throughout the archipelago. Some names comprise several words and are quite variable. Optional parts of these names are given in parentheses, while alternative words are separated by a slash or solidus. French creole (*kwéyòl*) and French common names are italicised. *Kwéyòl* is a language spoken in the French islands as well as in English-speaking islands which were at one stage French, such as Dominica, St Lucia and Grenada. Its vocabulary relies heavily on French but the syntax is African. A glossary explaining the meaning of *kwéyòl* and French common names is provided at the back of the book. Some of these names, however, defy translation.

Description of plants

The plant description within each entry does not necessarily detail every feature of the plant but, in conjunction with the photograph, it is certainly sufficient to make a positive identification. While technical terms are kept to a minimum, the Glossary of Botanical Terms at the back of the book explains those used and some of these terms, describing the basics of flower, inflorescence and leaf form, are also illustrated in Figures 2, 3 and 4.

After the description, the plant's typical habitat is listed, followed by additional facts, folklore and information on that plant. This is information I have gathered myself or, where it comes from the literature, the sources are indicated by numbers which correspond to references listed in the Reference section at the end of the book. A word of caution is necessary with regard to medicinal uses of plants. While there is little doubt of the potential of some wild plants as sources of drugs for medicinal use, be warned that herbal medicine is not to be experimented with nor practised by novices. A survey of the literature will reveal a bewildering array of medicinal uses for some plants. I have only reported reputed properties which keep

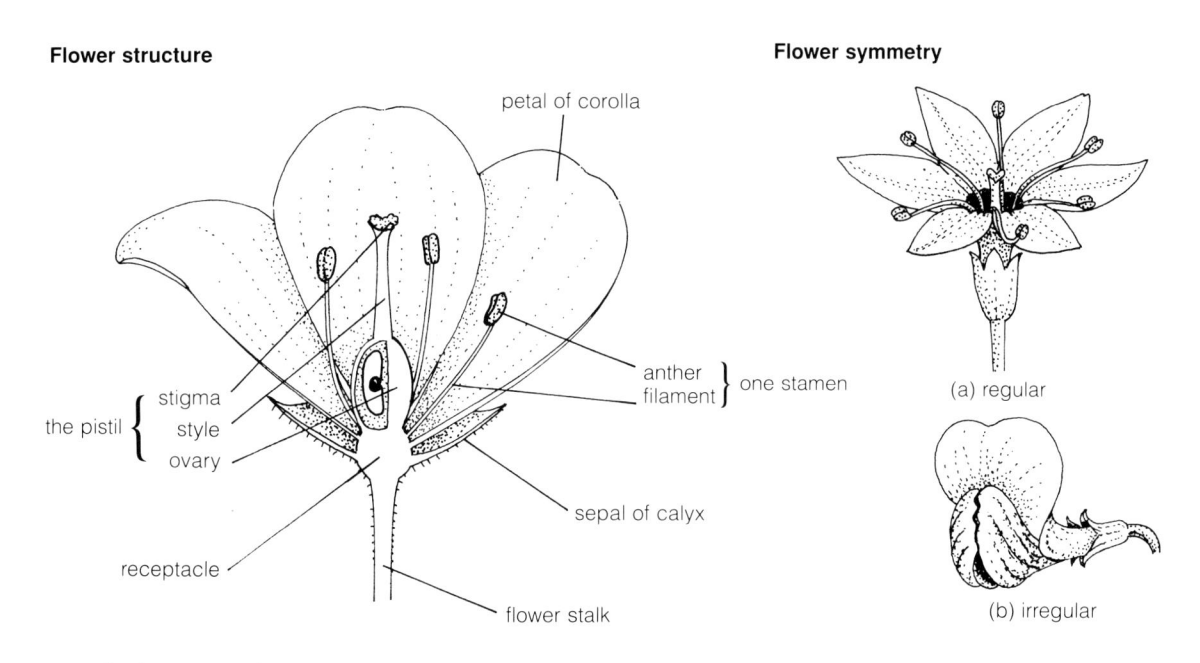

Figure 2 The flower – botanical terms

(a) Cymose

- simple cyme
- scorpioid cyme

◆ youngest flower   ✿ oldest flower

(b) Racemose

- simple raceme
- spike
- umbel
- corymb
- panicle
- head

Figure 3   The inflorescence – botanical terms

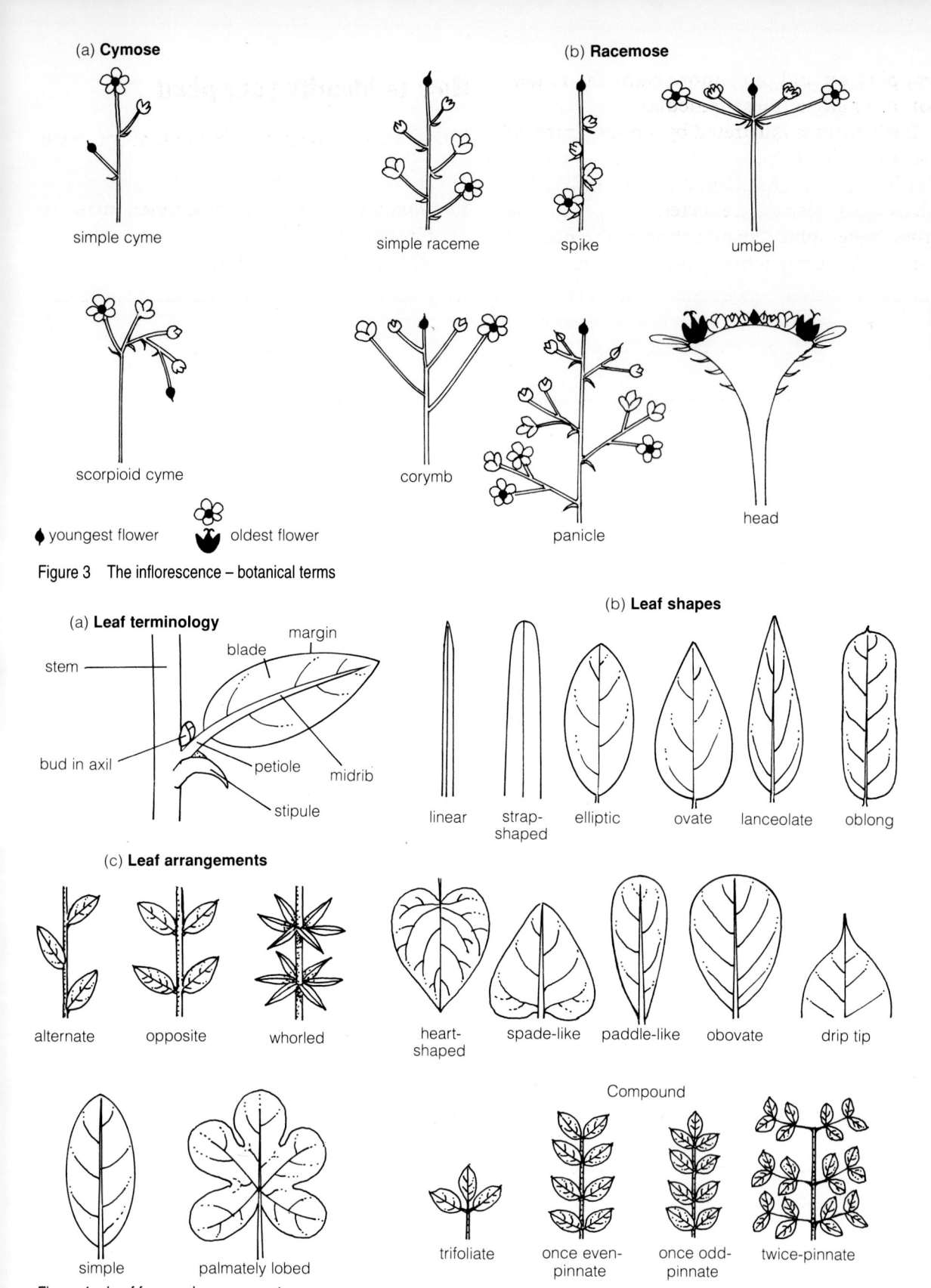

(a) Leaf terminology

stem, bud in axil, blade, margin, petiole, midrib, stipule

(b) Leaf shapes

linear, strap-shaped, elliptic, ovate, lanceolate, oblong, heart-shaped, spade-like, paddle-like, obovate, drip tip

(c) Leaf arrangements

alternate, opposite, whorled

simple, palmately lobed

Compound

trifoliate, once even-pinnate, once odd-pinnate, twice-pinnate

Figure 4   Leaf form and arrangement

cropping up and once more warn the reader not to try any of these remedies.

Each entry is illustrated by a photograph of the plant and by a map of the Eastern Caribbean with the shaded islands indicating where that plant is reported to occur. The broad geographical distribution of the plant is then listed, using zones defined in Figure 5.

How to identify your plant

When faced with an unknown plant you must decide:

1. whether it is a monocotyledon or a dicotyledon
2. what family the plant belongs to

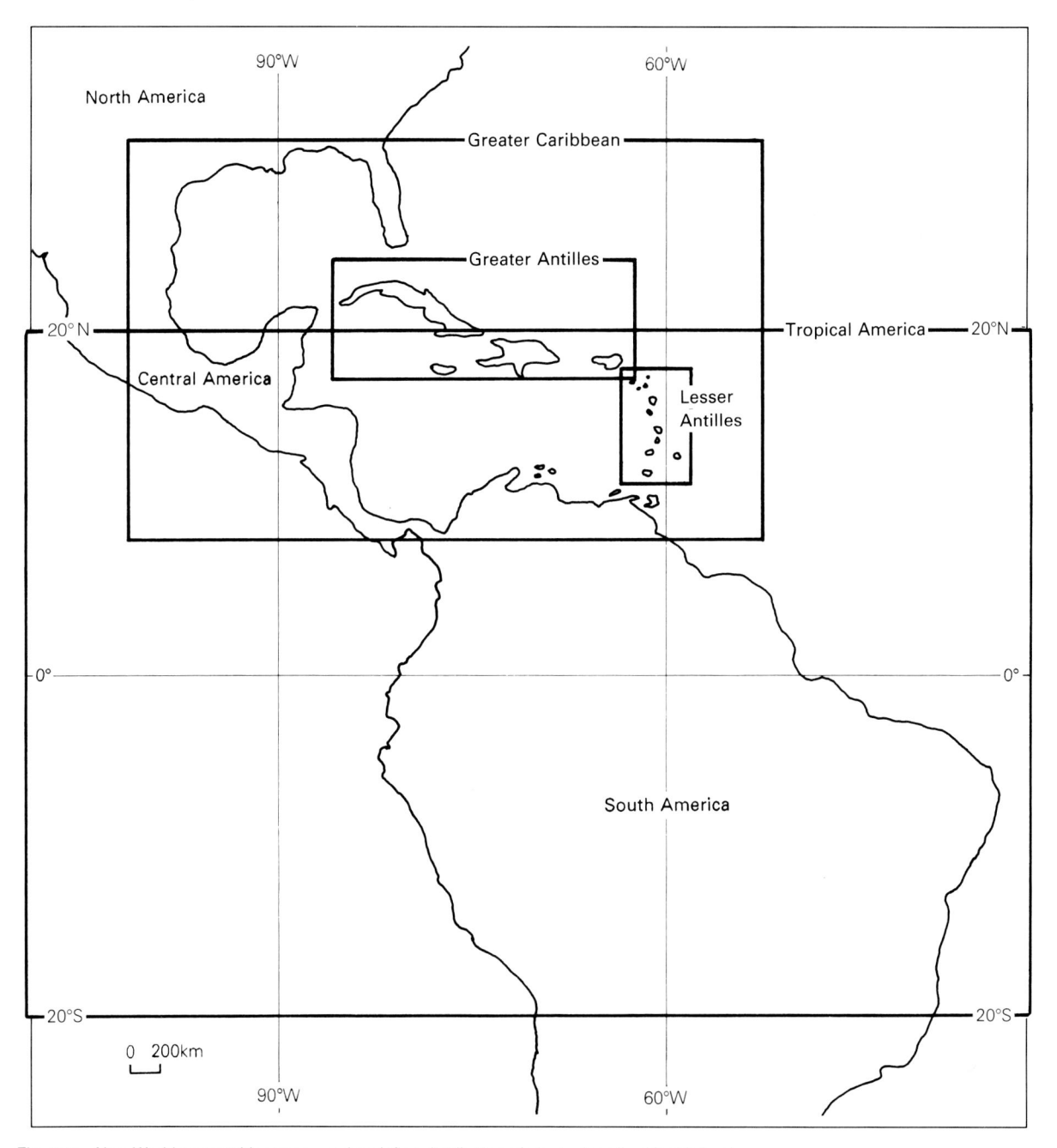

Figure 5 New World geographic zones used to define distribution of plants described in this book

Most books contain a key comprising a series of questions which, by a process of elimination directs you to the family containing your plant. Unfortunately, family designation and keys rely heavily on specialised aspects of flower structure which many people find hard to grasp. A more basic approach has therefore been used in this book.

How to identify monocotyledonous and dicotyledonous plants

Flowering plants are built on one of two basic body plans, constituting the two groups known as monocotyledonous and dicotyledonous plants. Monocotyledons generally have elongated leaves with parallel veins running lengthwise and flowers with parts in multiples of three (for example three petals). Most flowering plants are, however, dicotyledons with the main veins of the leaf branching outward from the midrib instead of running parallel to it and the flower parts in multiples of four or five.

How to identify monocotyledons

The number of families of monocotyledonous plants is small, and for these it is suggested that you simply turn to the early part of this book where these plants are described. Several of these families are commonly recognised, for example grasses, sedges, palms, lilies and orchids. Setting aside the grasses and sedges which are not included in this book, you will quickly learn to recognise these monocotyledonous families and should then easily track down the unknown plant within its family. Key features in recognising a few of these monocotyledonous families are shown in Figure 6.

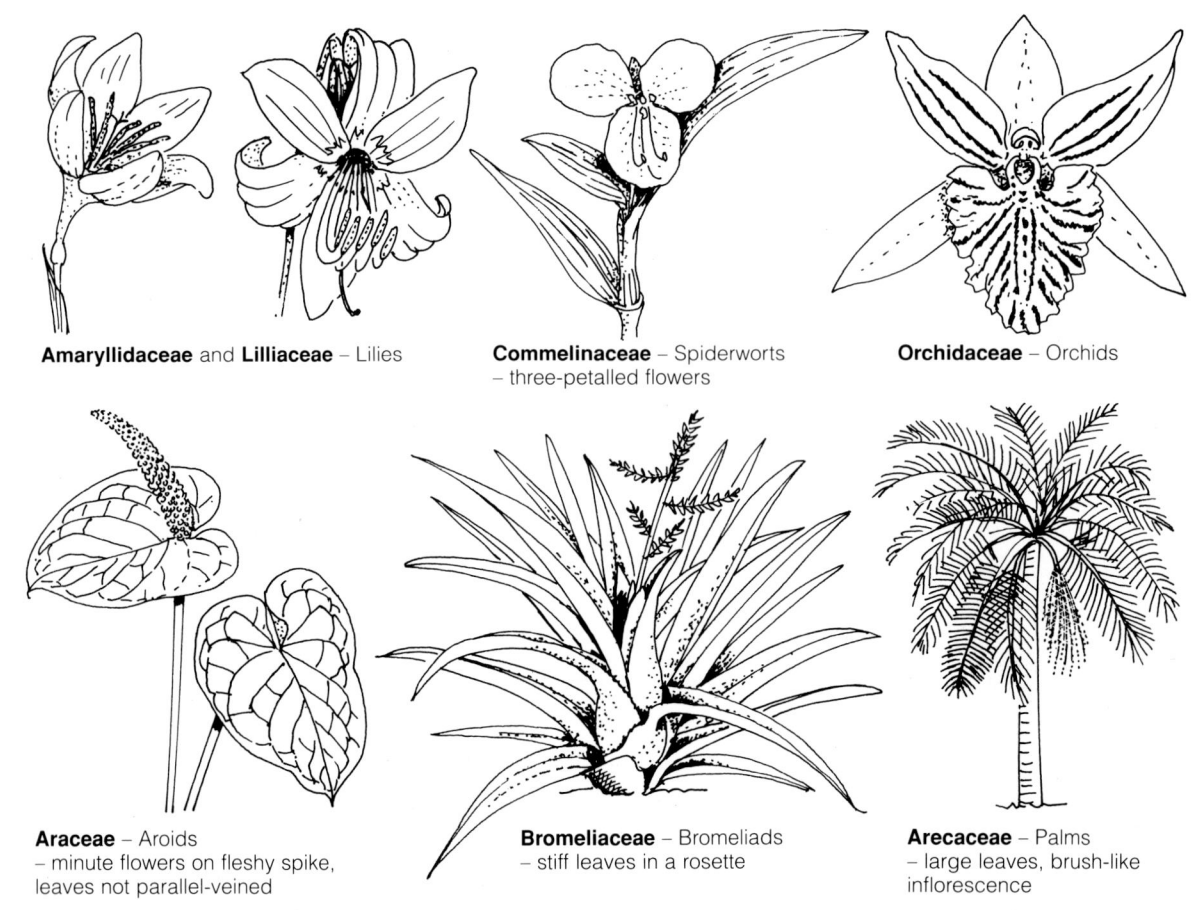

Amaryllidaceae and **Lilliaceae** – Lilies

Commelinaceae – Spiderworts – three-petalled flowers

Orchidaceae – Orchids

Araceae – Aroids
– minute flowers on fleshy spike, leaves not parallel-veined

Bromeliaceae – Bromeliads
– stiff leaves in a rosette

Arecaceae – Palms
– large leaves, brush-like inflorescence

Figure 6   Key features of some selected monocotyledonous families

How to identify dicotyledons

The majority of plants are dicotyledons – there is a multitude of families and the task of identification is more difficult. As a 'quick and dirty' approach to placing your plant in its respective family there are certain features you should look out for. Rather than looking upon dicotyledons as a formidable monolithic assemblage you can learn to identify certain **key** families. The logic of this is clear when you realise that almost half of the wild plants of the Eastern Caribbean belong to less than ten families! Remember the families in this book are arranged on the basis of relatedness. If you learn to see plants with a botanist's eyes then even when the plant fails to turn up in the family you have selected it probably belongs to the family listed before or after the one you have chosen.

Major groups and key families to recognise

The approach advocated is to decide whether your plant fits into any of the seven groupings listed below, starting with the first group and going on in sequence to the next category.

1. Legumes
2. Daisy family (Asteraceae)
3. Plants with a milky latex
4. Vines
5. Plants with pinnate leaves
6. Plants with opposite, simple leaves
7. Plants with alternate, simple leaves

1 Legumes

This is probably the largest group of plants in our flora. These plants can be considered as one family, though in this book they have been subdivided into three families.

- Mimosaceae   (page 42)
- Caesalpiniaceae   (page 40)
- Fabaceae   (page 44)

All these plants produce a pod (termed a legume) which splits longitudinally to liberate seeds. The leaves are usually compound (being divided into leaflets), with each family having a distinctive flower type. The Fabaceae have pea/bean-type flowers, the Caesalpinaceae have an open flower with

Fruit – a pod or legume

Caesalpiniaceae – Cassia family – five spreading petals

Mimosaceae – Mimosa family – tubular flowers massed to form a pompom

Fabaceae – Pea family – pea-like flowers

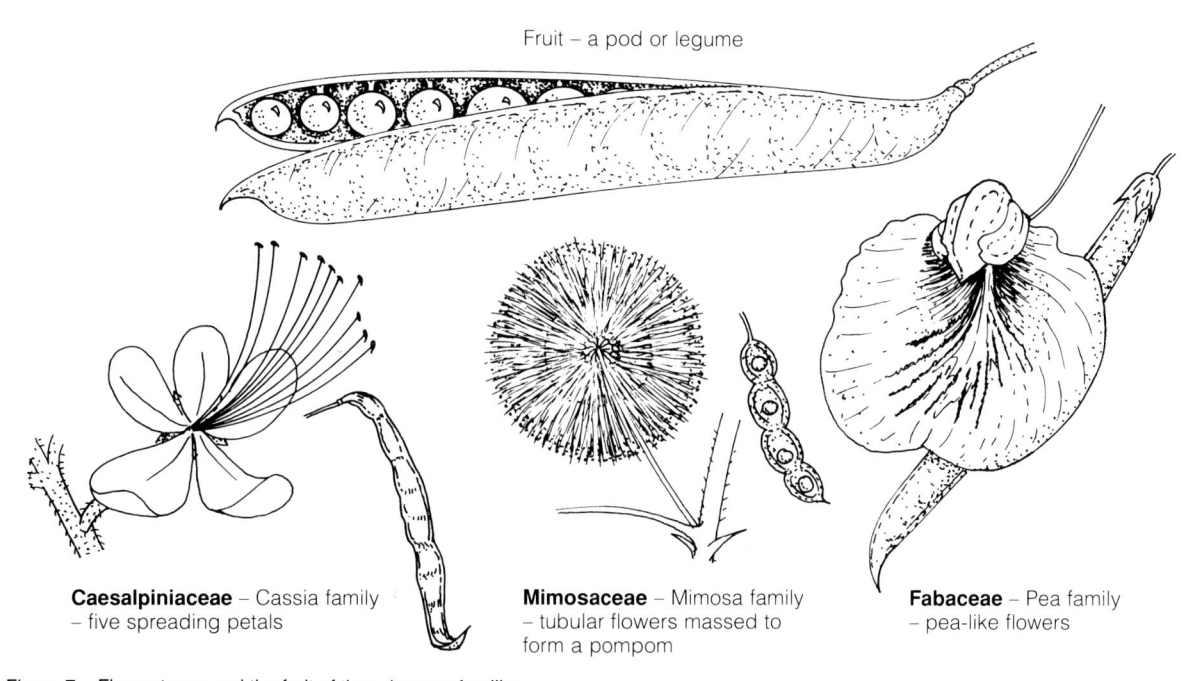

Figure 7   Flower types and the fruit of three legume families

spreading petals as typified by the well-known Pride of Barbados, while Mimosaceae flowers are tiny and tubular but are grouped together by their bases into pompom-like clusters (Figure 7).

2 Daisy family (Asteraceae)

What appear to be flowers in these plants are, in fact, inflorescences – heads comprising many reduced flowers (Figure 8). These flowers are usually given a special name, florets. In some members (for example, the sunflower, **Helianthus annuus**) the florets at the periphery are modified to look like petals and are termed ray florets. While there are several types of floret and different combinations of these given different types of heads, a simple system which recognises only two types of head is used in this book.

3 Plants with a milky latex

Virtually any plant exuding white sap on being bruised will be found among the following families.

- Euphorbiaceae★ (page 53)
- Apocynaceae   (page 74)
- Asclepiadaceae (page 74)
- Moraceae   (page 28)
- Sapotaceae   (page 72)

★The largest and most important member of the group

On the other hand, not all members of these families exude 'milk'!

4 Vines

The climbing habit has been adopted by plants in a wide range of families but there are certain plant families in which the vine habit predominates (Figure 9).

- Convolvulaceae (page 75)
- Cucurbitaceae   (page 97)
- Fabaceae   (page 44)
- Passifloraceae (page 66)

You will also encounter many woody vines or lianas. There is a sprinkling of these in many other families.

5 Plants with pinnate leaves

Several plant families show this distinctive leaf form in which leaflets are arranged on either side of the leaf axis (Figure 4).

- Legumes★   (see category 1 above)
- Sapindaceae★   (page 58)
- Burseraceae   (page 52)
- Rutaceae   (page 52)
- Zygophyllaceae   (page 51)

★The largest and most important members of this group

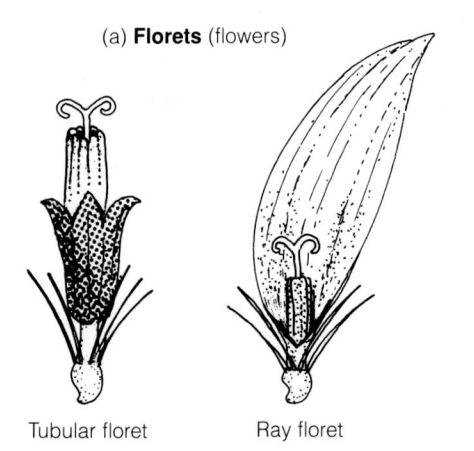

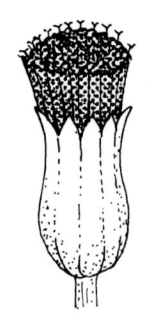

(a) **Florets** (flowers)

Tubular floret   Ray floret

(b) **Inflorescences** (heads)

Rayed head – central tubular florets and outer ray florets

Non-rayed head – lacks ray florets

Figure 8 Inflorescences and florets of the Asteraceae – Daisy family

Convolvulaceae – Sweet Potato family – trumpet-shaped flowers; no tendrils; twining stems

Passifloraceae – Passion Fruit family – flowers with crown of filaments; old tendrils coiled like springs

Cucurbitaceae – Cucurbit family – separate male and female flowers; old tendrils coiled like springs

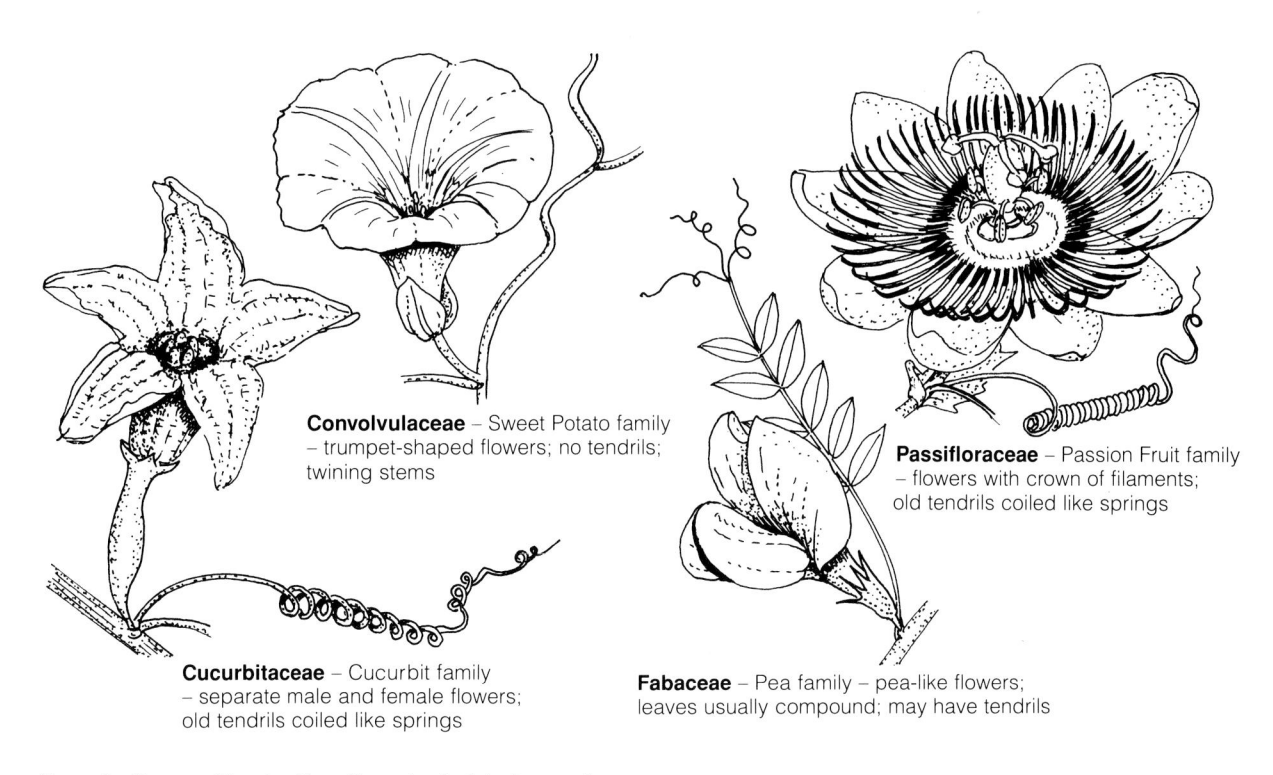

Fabaceae – Pea family – pea-like flowers; leaves usually compound; may have tendrils

Figure 9   Flowers of four families with predominately viny members

Lamiaceae – Mint family – lipped flowers; square-stemmed

Verbenaceae – Vervain family – almost symmetrical flowers; young stem square in cross-section

Myrtaceae – Guava family – free petals; many stamens

Acanthaceae – Acanth family – lipped flowers, often surrounded by bracts

Rubiaceae – Coffee family – tubular flowers; stipule(s) between each leaf pair

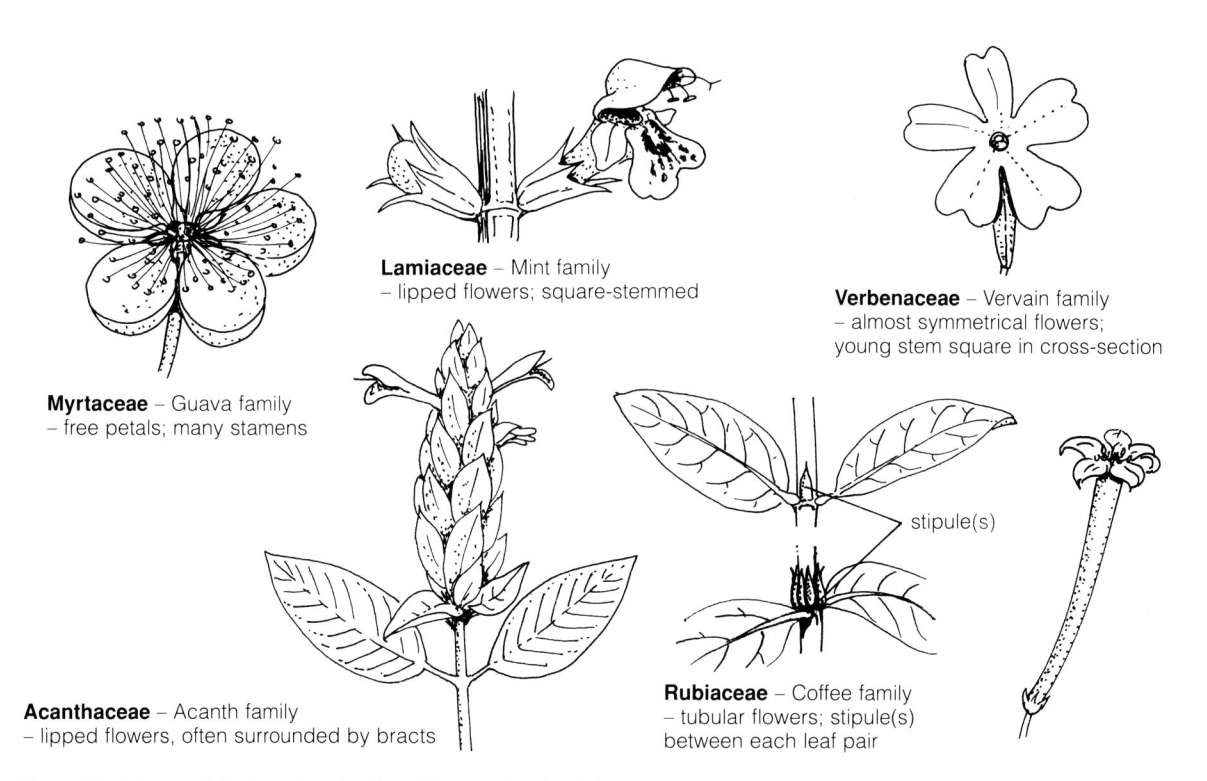

stipule(s)

Figure 10   Flowers of five important families with opposite, simple leaves

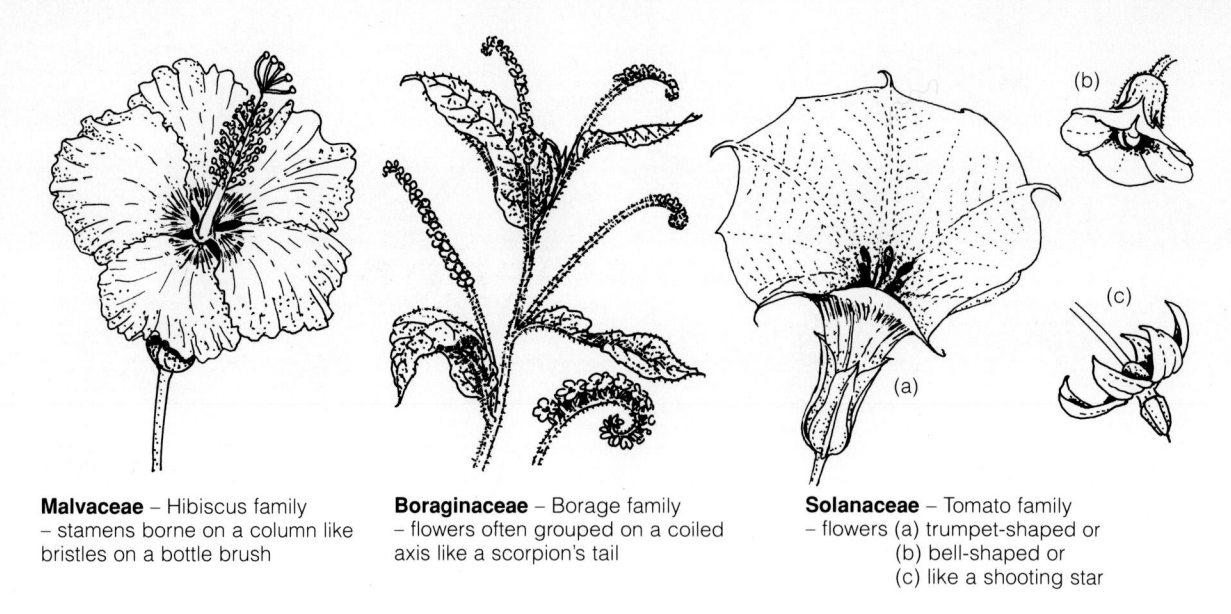

Malvaceae – Hibiscus family
– stamens borne on a column like bristles on a bottle brush

Boraginaceae – Borage family
– flowers often grouped on a coiled axis like a scorpion's tail

Solanaceae – Tomato family
– flowers (a) trumpet-shaped or
(b) bell-shaped or
(c) like a shooting star

Figure 11   Flowers of three important families with alternate, simple leaves

6 Plants with opposite, simple leaves

Five large families have their leaves arranged opposite each other, in pairs on the stem (Figure 10).

- Myrtaceae   (page 69)
- Lamiaceae   (page 85)
- Verbenaceae   (page 81)
- Acanthaceae   (page 90)
- Rubiaceae   (page 93)

7 Plants with alternate, simple leaves

This is the most common leaf arrangement and is in no way diagnostic. However, there are three large families with this trait, which you can learn to recognise from their flowers (Figure 11).

- Malvaceae   (page 62)
- Boraginaceae   (page 78)
- Solanaceae   (page 86)

Lastly, having found your wild plant, admire it, identify it, photograph it or otherwise artistically record its beauty, then leave it to continue to grow in its natural habitat for others to enjoy now and for years to come.

Monocotyledons

Cymodoceaceae –
Seagrass family

Halodule wrightii   Ascherson
shoal grass

Submerged marine plant with creeping rhizome, 1 mm thick, throwing up short, whitish, erect stems to 2 cm high, usually with two leaves at each node. Leaves fine, flat and linear, 5–10 cm long, to 1 mm wide. Male and female flowers borne on separate plants. Pollen threadlike with pollination taking place underwater. Flowers, simply two anthers in the case of the male, and a single pistil in the case of the female.

In sandy bottoms in shallow sea water, especially sheltered areas.

This and other sea grasses are important in providing food and spawning grounds for a wide range of marine life.

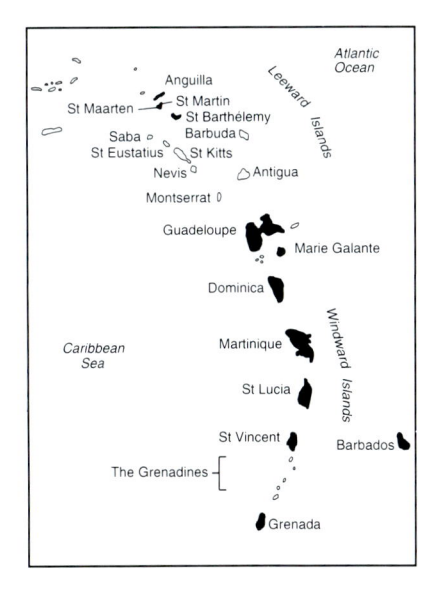

The Caribbean, Africa and Australia

Halodule wrightii (left)
Syringodium filiforme (centre)
Thalassia testudinum (right)

Syringodium filiforme   Kütz.
manatee grass

Submerged marine plant, with stout creeping rhizome, 2 mm thick, and short shoots of two or three leaves. Superficially like **Halodule** but larger and stouter. Leaf sheaths to 6 cm long, leaves cylindrical, 10–30 cm long, 8–20 mm wide. Male and female flowers on separate plants, pollination underwater by threadlike pollen. Male flower comprising simply two anthers, the female two pistils.

In shallow sandy bottoms.

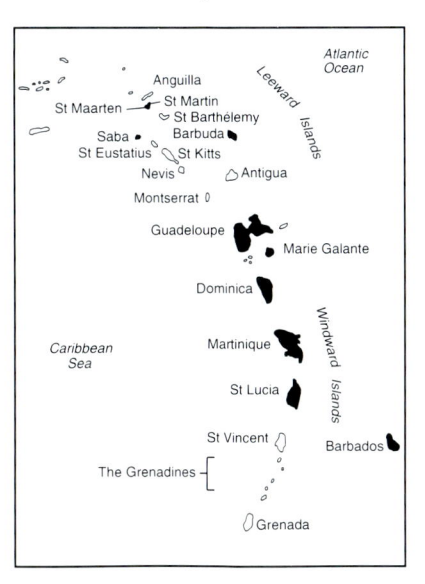

Subtropical and tropical America

Hydrocharitaceae –
Turtle grass family

Thalassia testudinum
Banks & Solander ex König

turtle grass

Submerged marine perennial with stout rhizome to 5 mm diameter, giving rise at intervals to tufts of leaves on very short stems. Leaves flat and strap-shaped, to 20 cm long and 12 mm wide, tip rounded, upper parts bright green, lower sheathed portion whitish. Separate male and female flowers, adapted for underwater pollination.

On sandy bottoms and in shallow areas of the coral reef.

An important food for green sea turtles, manatees and herbivorous reef fish. Turtle grass beds provide shelter for invertebrates and young fish and serve as a baffle, slowing water movement and stabilising the near-shore environment.[5],[44]

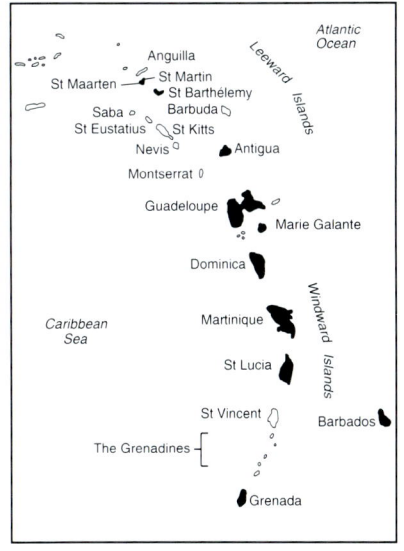

Waters of coastal Texas down to northern South America

Arecaceae (Palmae) – Palm family

Aiphanes minima (Gaertner) Burret
macaw palm; *gwigwi*; *chou pikan*; *glouglou (wouj)*

Single-stemmed to 10 m tall, trunk covered in slender, menacing black spines, each to 6 cm long. Leaves 10–20, pinnate, to 2 m long, with sharp spines on leaf axis and underside of leaf blade. Inflorescence a panicle, about 1.5 cm long, bearing a strap-like, often spiny bract. Flowers, creamish, either male or female. Fruit a globular, red berry, about 15 mm in diameter.

An understorey palm of forests at mid elevations.

A variable plant, once considered five distinct species.[10] The fruit is dried in the sun or boiled and the central kernel cracked open to expose the edible seed. This has a texture like coconut but with a distinctive nutty flavour. Not to be confused with another spiny palm, also called *glouglou* (**Acrocomia aculeata**) which has larger fruit, a stouter stem and pointed leaflets. Twelve palms are native to the Lesser Antilles.[30]

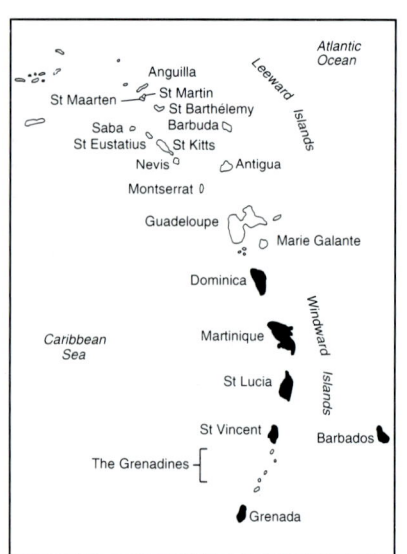

Eastern Caribbean endemic

Araceae – Aroid family

Anthurium willdenowii Kunth
polycrozier; wild anthurium

Stout-stemmed plant, spreading and trailing. Leaf blades more or less elliptic, 15–40 cm long, 4–12 cm wide, with a prominent central vein and furrowed petiole, 5–20 cm long. Inflorescence borne on a stalk to 40 cm long. Spathe green and strap-shaped, coiling back, to 12 cm long. Spadix cylindrical, often curved, to 20 cm long, the fruit becoming purple and fleshy with age.

Rooted on trees or boulders in forest areas at low elevations predominantly.

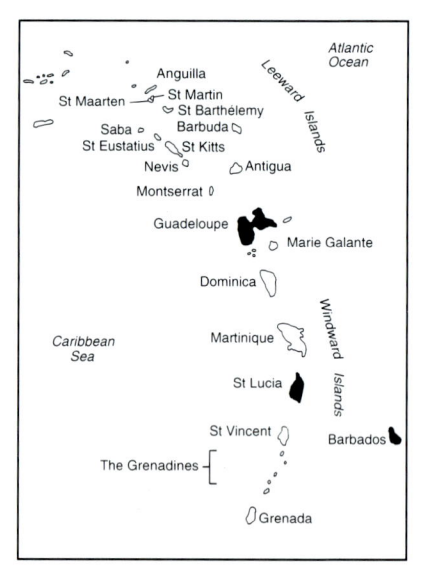

Endemic to the Lesser Antilles

Aiphanes minima

Anthurium willdenowii

Pistia stratiotes L.
water lettuce/lily; *(zèb a) chans*

Floating rosette plant, typically 20 cm in diameter. Leaves corrugated lengthwise and densely covered in microscopic hairs which form an 'unwettable' surface. Young plants bud off vegetatively while sexual reproduction is by miniature white **Anthurium**-like inflorescences in the leaf axils.

Naturalised in ponds and slow streams where it can become a serious weed. Can be used to absorb pollutants from waterways. ▶

Pistia stratiotes (large)
Lemma perpusilla (small)

Aechmea lingulata

Lemnaceae –
Duckweed family

Lemna perpusilla   Torrey

duck/pond weed; *vèdégwi*

Tiny floating plant comprising what appears to be little more than a floating leaf, 3–8 mm long, 2–6 mm wide, and tiny threadlike roots. Shoot not differentiated into leaf and stem, the floating leaf-like structure termed a thallus.

An aggressive weed of ponds and slow streams.

The duckweeds are the smallest flowering plants known. Young plants simply bud off vegetatively though minute flowers are produced and sexual reproduction occurs as well.

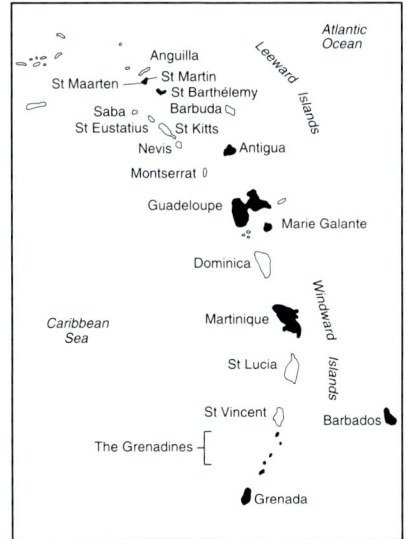

Worldwide

Bromeliaceae –
Bromeliad family

Aechmea lingulata   (L.) Baker

monkey banana; wild pine; *annanna mawon*

Rosette plant comprising a clump of strap-like, greyish leaves, to 1 m long, 4–7 cm wide, with tiny curvedstem prickles along the margins. Inflorescence, a loose, yellow-green panicle to 1 m high. Flowers about 1 cm long.

Common in wetter parts.

Rooted on trees (epiphytic) or in rock crevices in forests at low to mid elevations.

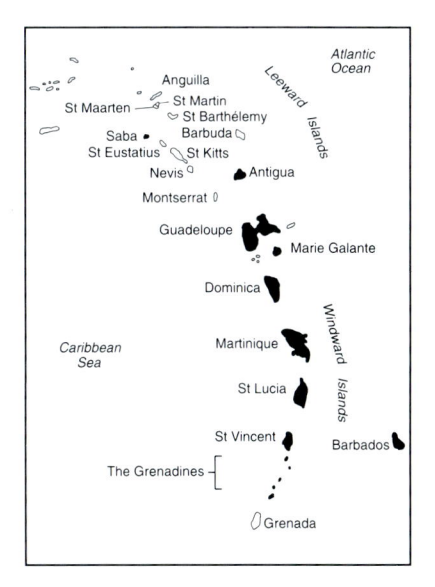

The Caribbean, Central and South America

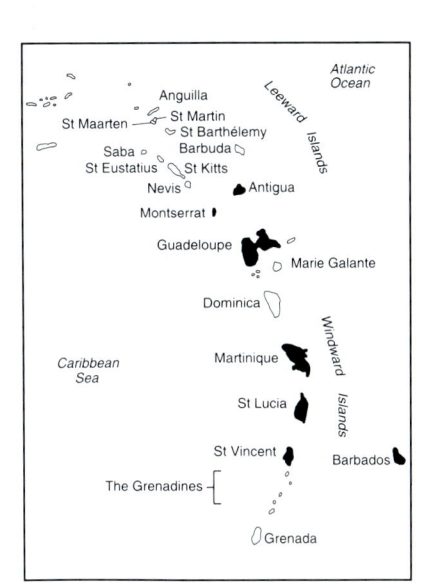

Throughout the Tropics

Bromelia plumieri   (Morren) L.B. Sm.

pingwing; monkey banana; wild pine; *karatas; pengwen*

Plants with long, narrow, fleshy leaves arching outwards in an open rosette. Leaves to 4 m long, 3 cm wide, linear, gutter-shaped, the margin bearing curved prickles. Flowers embedded in a flattish, domed head at the centre of the rosette and surrounded by small reddish leaves, appearing May–June. Corolla mauve, fleshy, to 10 cm long, but seeming shorter. Calyx with brown silky hairs. Fruit edible, cream-coloured, to 9 cm long, not unlike a miniature banana but filled with a watery, acid pulp with numerous small brown seeds, ripe October–November.

In sheltered rocky areas at low elevations, usually in shade.

Although the fruit is edible it can cause soreness of the throat or skin,[46] probably due to the presence of proteolytic enzymes.

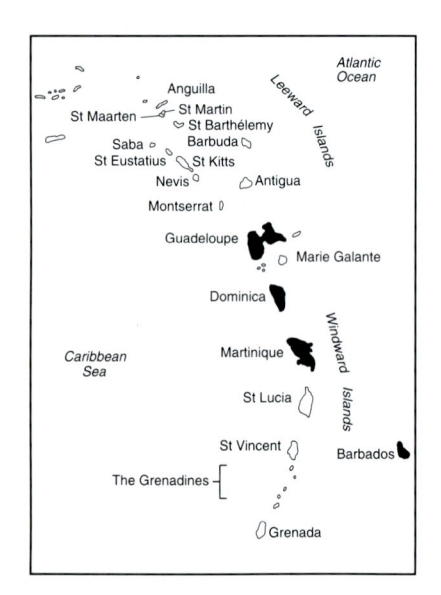

Bromelia plumieri

Commelina elegans

Pitcairnia angustifolia

Smilax oblongata

The Caribbean, Central and South America

Pitcairnia angustifolia   Ait.

annanna bata wouj

Plant with long, narrow, fleshy leaves arching outwards in an open rosette. Leaves to 1 m long, linear to lanceolate, scaly beneath, margin spiny. Inflorescence erect, to 1.5 m high, loosely branched, bearing conspicuous red flowers, each to 5 cm long. Fruit a spike-tipped capsule, about 1 cm long.

On cliff faces near the coast to rain forests at high elevation. ▶

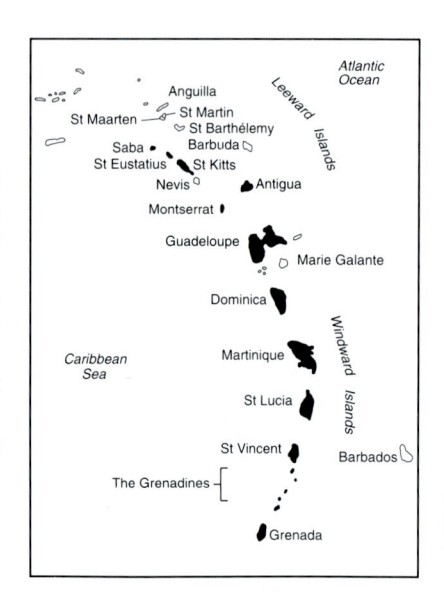

Endemic to the Greater and Lesser Antilles

Commelinaceae – Spiderwort family

Commelina elegans   Kunth

pond/water/cockroach grass; French/pig weed; *kiwaj; zèb gwa*

Spreading herb with erect shoots and fleshy stems. Leaves alternate, lanceolate to narrowly elliptic, 3–8 cm long, 10–25 mm wide, with virtually no petiole. Leaf base sheathing the stem and bearing no hairs. Flowers pale blue, emerging from a purse-like spathe, borne at the shoot tips and on low-lying leafless runners.

Weed of roadside ditches and damp places.

Used to stop bleeding and to treat fever[55] and pneumonia.[16] Two other **Commelina** species, very similar to this one also occur in the region.

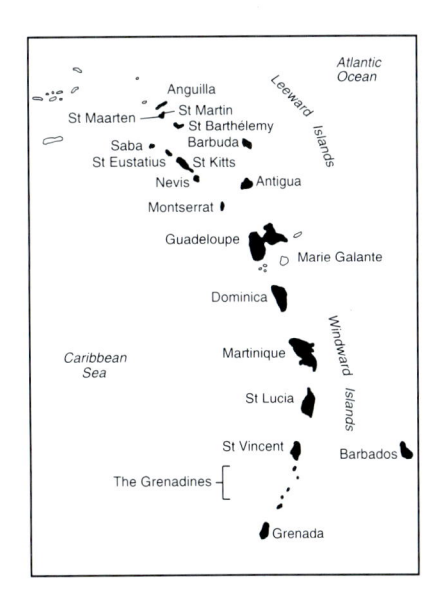

The Caribbean, Central and South America

Smilacaceae – Sarsaparilla family

Smilax oblongata   Sw.

goat/yam wiss; *lyann noyo; boyo chat/djab*

A woody vine bearing sharp, curved spines on the stem and leaf midrib. Leaves, heart-shaped to broadly ovate, leathery, the petiole bearing tendrils. Plants either male or female with flowers borne in a simple umbel, like spokes on a hub. Fruit a black berry, 1 cm in diameter.

In forests at low to mid elevations.

The stem stripped of spines is plaited to make baskets.[11] Root extracts of other **Smilax** spp., known as sarsaparilla, were once widely used as a tonic, a remedy for syphilis and a flavouring for soft drinks.[54] Two other **Smilax** spp. occur in the region, with a predominately northern distribution.

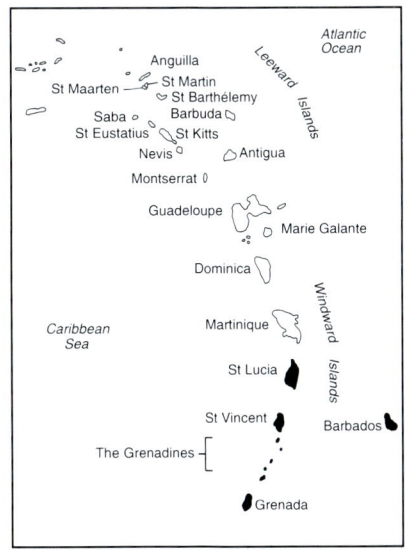

Endemic to the Lesser Antilles

Crinum bulbispermum

Amaryllidaceae – Amaryllis family

Crinum bulbispermum
(Burm.) Milne-Redh. & Schweick.

(river) lily

Herb forming dense clumps. Leaves, sword-shaped, to 1 m long, 4–8 cm wide, arising from an underground bulb. Flowering stalk green, flattened, to 70 cm long, with flowers nodding, radiating outwards from the end. Perianth funnel-shaped, segments white with a pale pink stripe down the middle, to 12 cm long. Flowering July–August.

Garden escape of dry coastal areas.

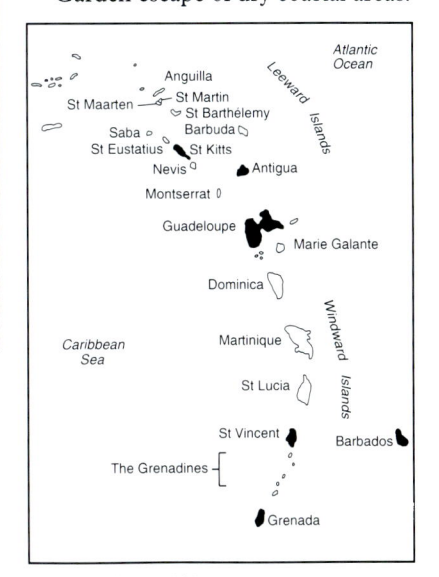

Native of South Africa

Hippeastrum puniceum

Hippeastrum puniceum   (Lam.) Ktze.

Easter lily; amaryllis; *lis wouj*

Bulbous herb with strap-like leaves, to 50 cm long, producing 2–4 flowers on the end of a long, erect stalk in March–April. Perianth orange-red, about 10 cm long, with a creamish throat.

Naturalised in pastures at mid elevations but also commonly cultivated.

The bulbs contain a toxin, lycorine, which induces vomiting and diarrhoea.[37]

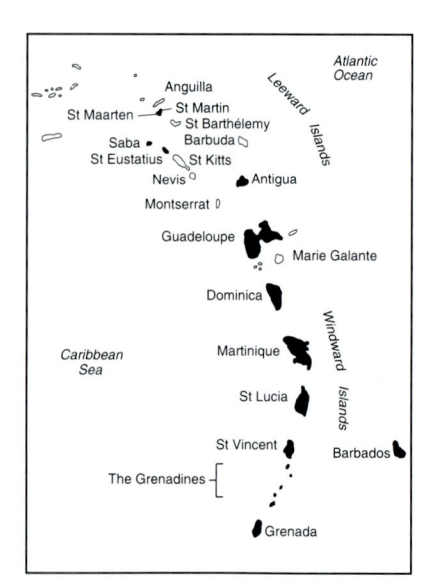

Tropical America

Hymenocallis caribaea

Hymenocallis caribaea
(L. emend. Ker Gawler) Herbert

spider/white lily; *lis blan*

Bulbous herb with leaves 30–60 cm long, broadest at mid-length. Flowering stalks to 60 cm tall, each bearing several flowers. Flowers white, with six petal-like segments, to 10 cm long. White webbing between the lower portions of the stamens forming a funnel-like staminal cup.

In full sunlight and shady habitats near the coast.

The bulb contains low levels of a toxin, lycorine.[37]   ▶

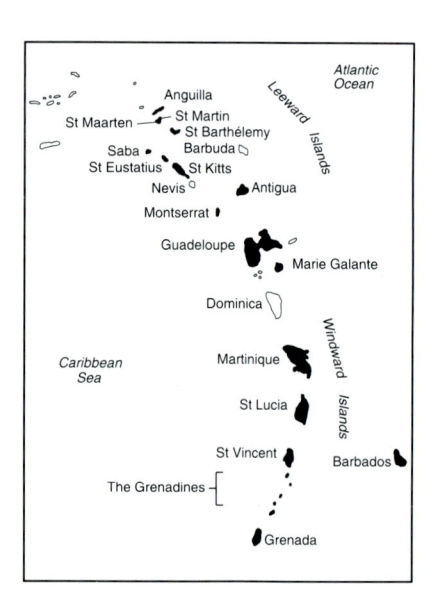

Jamaica and the Eastern Caribbean

20

Zephyranthes citrina

Zephyranthes citrina   Baker

yellow crocus; gutter lily; wind flower; wild onion; *ti lis jòn*

Herb with bulbs 2–3 cm across. Leaves linear, to 30 cm long. Flowering stalks similar in length to leaves and bearing single yellow flowers. Perianth funnel-like, six-lobed, about 3 cm long. Fruit a three-lobed capsule, 1 cm in diameter, containing black seeds.

In roadwise ditches.

Flowering apparently triggered by heavy rains. The bulb is poisonous, containing lycorine.[37] *Z. puertoricensis* is a common white-flowered relative.

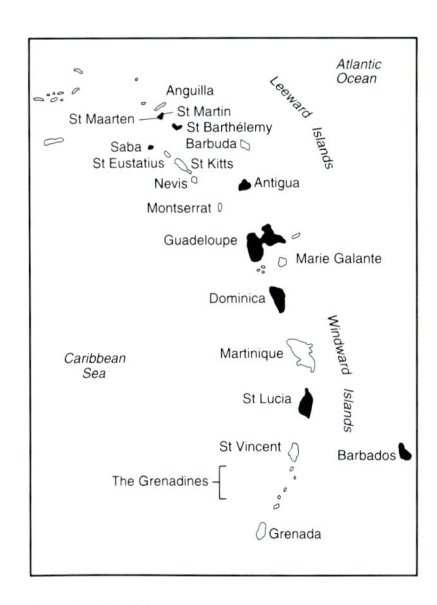

Greater Caribbean

Agavaceae –
Agave family

Agave barbadensis   Trel.

maypole

Plants with a rosette of dull green, narrowly-triangular leaves, to 2.5 cm long, the margins lined with fine prickles and each leaf ending in a sharp brown-black spine. Clusters of deep yellow flowers borne on side branches, in a pyramidal arrangement on a fleshy pole-like stalk, to 6 m high, appearing April–May. Fruit usually not produced, but bulbils, by which the plant reproduces vegetatively, typically form on the inflorescence.

Plant of coastal scrub vegetation.

Agave spp. are referred to as Century plants since it takes several years (but not a century!) before the tall pole-like inflorescence is produced. The inflorescence elongates at a remarkable rate and is used by fisherman as a float and for rafts. In the past it was also used when dry as a strop for sharpening cut-throat razors.[49] In rural areas, laundered clothes are spread over the plant to dry and youngsters often scrawl graffiti on the leaves. These plants are rich in steroids.[44]

There are five other superficially similar ***Agave*** spp., endemic to the Lesser Antilles and with quite distinct distributions: ***A. caribaeicola*** (Grenada to Martinique); ***A. dussiana*** (Martinique to St Bart's), ***A. karatto*** (La Desirade to Saba), ***A. schuermaniana*** (St Martin and Anguilla) and ***A. van grolae*** (St Eustatius, St Kitts and Nevis). Common names for these species include dagger, crata, *lapit, lang bèf* and *salspawèy*.

Agave barbadensis

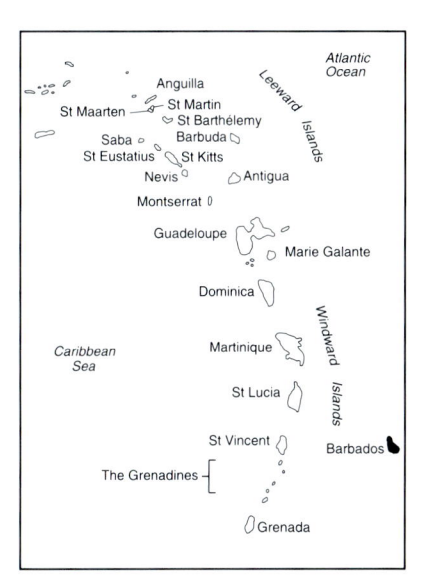

Barbados

Dioscoreaceae – Yam family

Dioscorea altissima Lam.

prickly yam vine; sarsparilla; barbed wire; *ziyanm bwa/kochon/mawon*

Woody vine with green stem, triangular in cross-section and bearing curved, flattened prickles along the margins. Leaves heart-shaped, up to 15 cm wide, with the characteristic palmate venation of a yam. Leaves not usually seen on the lower parts of the vine. Tubers, aerial, buff-coloured and irregularly-shaped, to 6 cm long, borne along the stem.

Liana of forests at mid elevations.

Several other species of yam introduced from West Africa and Asia are cultivated for their tubers.

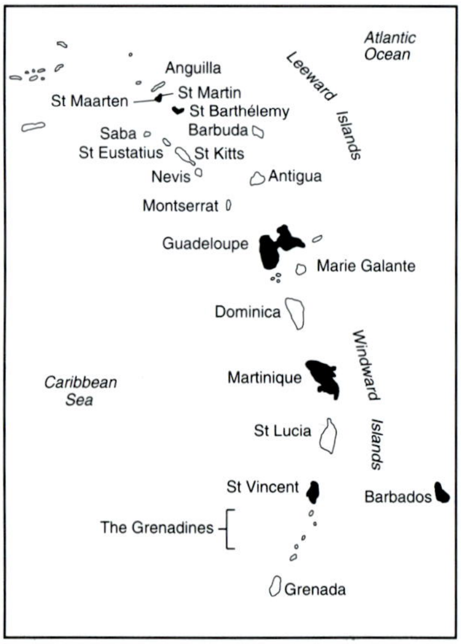

Lesser Antilles and Brazil

Iridaceae – Iris family

Trimezia martinicensis (Jacq.) Herbert

yellow/wild iris; *koko chat*; *lis jòn savann*; *lanvè jòn/mal*

Leaves, linear, to 30 cm long, 15 mm wide, arising from an underground storage organ. Flowers, bright yellow, single or few in number, emerging from a leaf-like spathe at the end of an erect flowering stalk. Outer three petal-like segments of the flower larger and bent outwards while the inner three smaller and reflexed inwards. Fruit an oblong, flat-topped and warty capsule, to 2 cm long.

Pastures and roadsides at mid elevations.

A tea made from the roots was once given to women in labour to facilitate childbirth.[31]

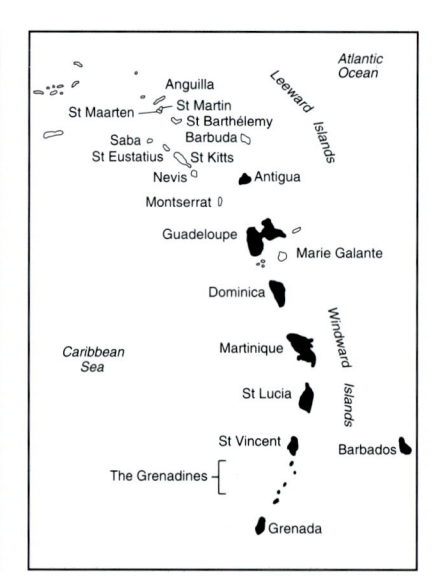

Tropical America

Dioscorea altissima

Trimezia martinicensis

Heliconiaceae – Heliconia family

Heliconia bihai (L.) L.

wild plantain; *balizyé (wouj)*

Plant comprising a clump of leaves, 1.5–4 m tall, arising from an underground rhizome. Leaves, banana-like, oblong blade to 2 m long and 20 cm wide, the petiole as long. Inflorescence erect, borne midway along the petiole, with scarlet, yellow-edged, boat-like bracts, to 13 cm long, each containing a whitish flower. Fruit blue.

Forest gaps, mid to high elevations. Root extract used medicinally in snake bites[31] and to promote urination.[9] Grown for cut flowers with a range of cultivars and hybrids in cultivation. The bloom is the emblem of one of Trinidad's oldest political parties. ▶

Heliconia bihai

Epidendrum ciliare

Orchidaceae – the Orchid family

Epidendrum ciliare L.

eyelash orchid

Stem, stout and bulbous in part, with thick, leathery, more or less elliptic leaves, 10–20 cm long. Flowers fragrant, white to creamish. Petals and sepals similar, of a narrow spreading form, to 8 cm long. Lip divided into three lobes, the lateral pair finely fringed, hence the common name. Flowering February–April.

On tree trunks and rocks in dry areas.

The orchid flora of the Lesser Antilles numbers some 129 species,[15] most of which are described in a profusely illustrated companion volume in this series.[36]

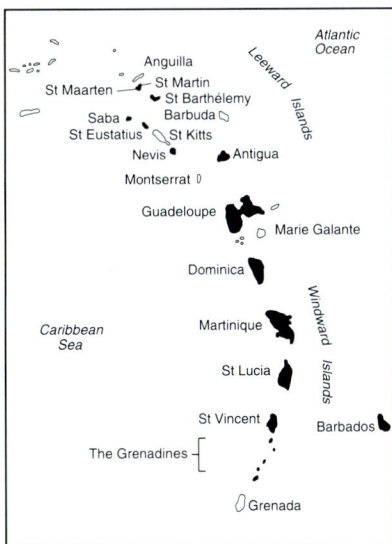

Tropical America

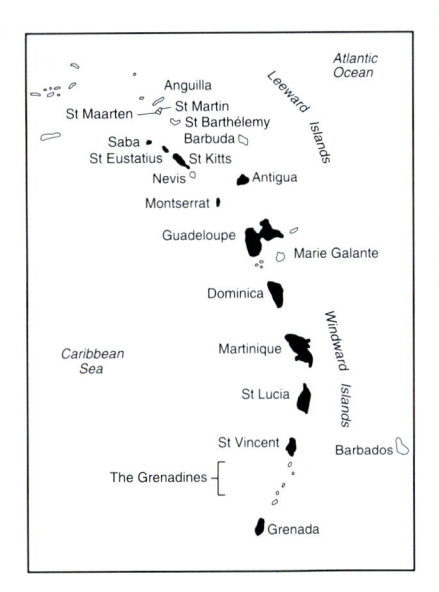

Greater and Lesser Antilles

Spiranthes lanceolata

Spiranthes lanceolata

(Aublet) Léon.

Terrestrial plant to 60 cm high with fleshy roots and 2–3 oblong to lanceolate leaves, absent during flowering in March–May. Flowering stalk to 50 cm high, bearing several scale-like leaves and striking, tubular orange flowers clustered at the top.

Roadsides and pastures in wetter areas.

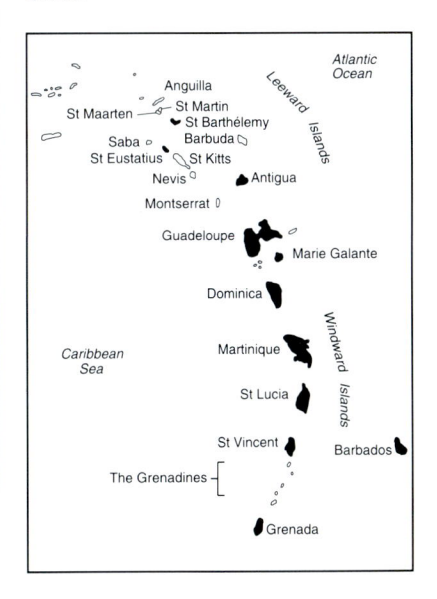

Tropical America

Dicotyledons

Lepianthes peltata

Peperomia pellucida

Piper dilatatum

Piperaceae – Pepper family

Lepianthes peltata (L.) Raf.

monkey hand; cowheel (bush); *mal dòmi/tèt*; *chapo glo*; *bwa annizèt*

Shrub to 2 m high. Leaves alternate, rounded to slightly heart-shaped, to 30 cm diameter. Petiole usually entering the leaf on the lower surface near the centre. Flowering spikes, slender, each to 10 cm long, several per stalk arising from the leaf axil.

In shady damp places.

The leaves are applied to the forehead to relieve headache.[28],[50]

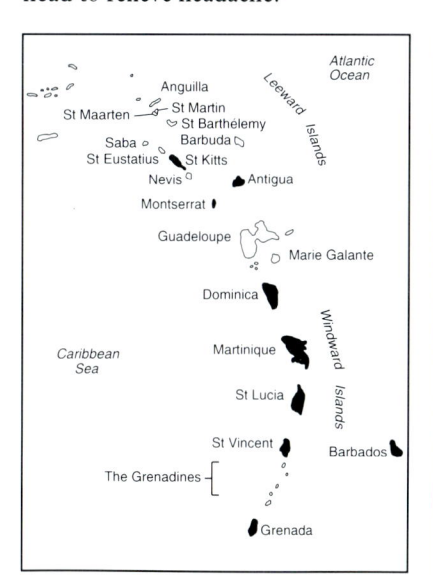

Peperomia pellucida (L.) Kunth

shine/shining/silver/information bush; water cress(ie); *koklaya*; *zèb (a) kouwès*

Erect, delicate, translucent herb to 30 cm tall. Leaves alternate, roughly heart-shaped, to 3 cm in diameter. Erect, slender flowering spikes to 5 cm long. Fruit round, to 1 mm across, conspicuously dark on the fertile spike.

A weed of damp, shady places.

Used throughout the Caribbean as a multipurpose tea,[9],[16],[25],[29] while the fresh leaf is eaten to soothe sore throats[35],[51] or applied as a poultice.[31] Juice from the leaf has been claimed to treat cataract.[4]

Many ***Peperomia*** species are cultivated as houseplants. A total of 18 species are native to the Eastern Caribbean.[30]

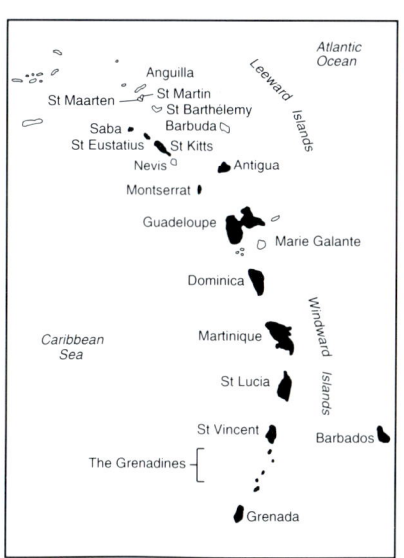

Piper dilatatum Rich.

candle/doctor/elder/joint/rock bush; crapaud bones; *malenmbé*; *mal èstomak*; *bwa chandèl/syèj*

Shrub to 3 m tall. Stem hairless or almost so, with jointed nodes. Leaves ovate to elliptic, 9–18 cm long, 5–12 cm wide, with pinnate venation. Flowering spikes, erect and file-like, to 12 cm long.

Moist, shady areas.

Peppercorns are the dried fruit of the related **P. nigrum**.

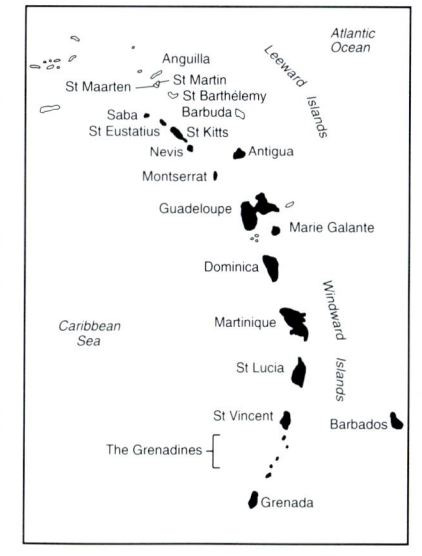

Tropical America

Throughout the Tropics

Central America, Greater and Lesser Antilles

Moraceae – Breadfruit family

Cecropia schreberiana Miq.

trumpet tree/bush; pop-a-gun; *bwa kannon*

Tree to 20 m tall with hollow stems of a jointed appearance due to prominent leaf scars. Leaves peltate, with 8–10 lobes radiating from a central disc, grey-green and rough-surfaced above, whitish below, to 30 cm in diameter. Male and female flowers in separate spikes, male spikes numerous per cluster, female spikes few per cluster.

A tree of disturbed forests and clearings.

The leaves when dry give the appearance of a clenched fist, dark brown above, grey-white below, and are used by flower arrangers. A tea made from the leaves is used to lower high blood pressure,[25] and treat headache,[16] diabetes,[6],[23] and urinary tract infections.[9]

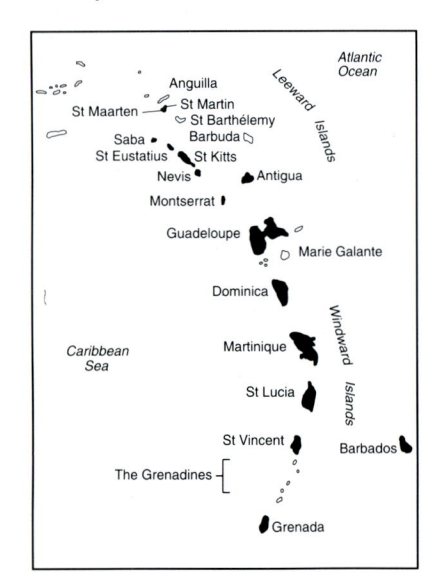

Maclura tinctoria (L.) D. Don ex Steudel

fustic; *bwa dowanj*; *mûrier pays*

Tree to 15 m tall with slender spines on young parts and a yellowish sap throughout. Trunk often with short, spiny spurs. Leaves, lanceolate to elliptic, 5–12 cm long, 2–5 cm wide, with coarsely-toothed margins and a characteristic drooping habit. Trees male or female (photograph is of female tree). Female flowers borne on fleshy green spheres to 1 cm in diameter while male flowers grouped as slender, hanging, catkin-like spikes to 15 cm long. Flowering June–July.

In dry woods but more commonly as a cultivated tree in plantation yards.

Yields a hard timber, primarily used in making the felloes of cartwheels. The wood also yields a yellowish dye once used in the production of khaki.[57] The fruit, resembling green raspberries, is edible and much liked by pigs.[46]

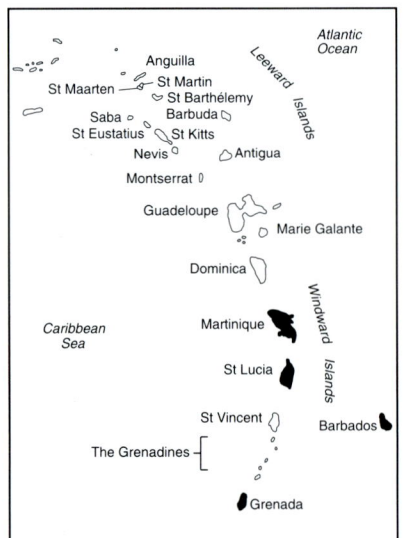

Cecropia schreberiana

Maclura tinctoria (♀)

Greater and Lesser Antilles

Tropical America

Boehmeria ramiflora

Laportea aestuans

Pilea nummulariifolia

Urticaceae – Nettle family

Boehmeria ramiflora Jacq.

zouti bwa

Sprawling shrub to 2 m tall with alternate leaves markedly different in size. Leaves alternate, lanceolate to ovate, 5–25 cm long, 2–8 cm wide, the base unequal-sided and the margin toothed. Petioles reddish. Flowers in tight clusters of one sex only, occurring at the nodes, both types on one plant.

In damp shady places.

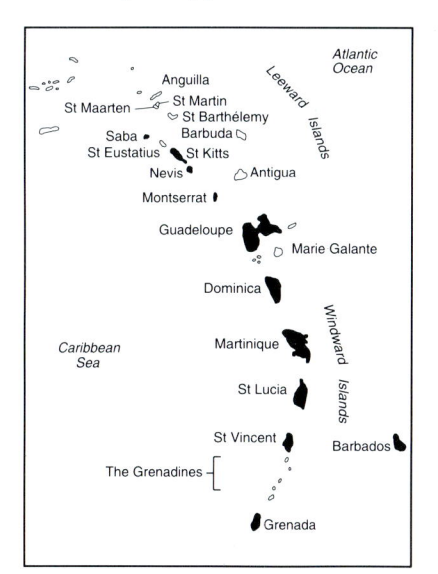

Tropical America

Laportea aestuans (L.) Chew

(stinging) nettle; *zouti (bwilan)*; *zèb bwilan*

Annual herb to 2 m high, stems and petioles reddish. Entire plant covered in bristly, stinging hairs. Leaves alternate, ovate, 7–20 cm long, 3–12 cm wide, prominently veined and with a toothed margin. Leaf surface with a crinkly or puckered appearance. Inflorescence a tight, flattish panicle of minute, pinkish male and female flowers.

Weed of waste ground especially in damp areas.

A tea made from this plant is taken to promote urination.[23],[50],[56]

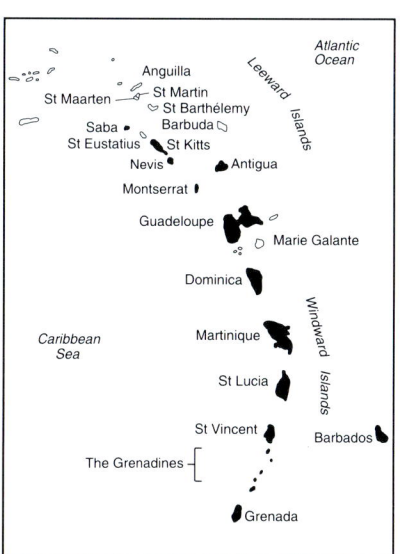

Tropical America

Pilea nummulariifolia (Sw.) Wedd.

creeping Charlie; Aaron's beard; water mint; *ti teny won*

Prostrate herb, rooting at the nodes. Entire plant covered in slender scattered hairs. Leaves opposite, more or less round, 1–2 cm in diameter, on equally long petioles. Leaf venation conspicuous and inlaid, margin scalloped. Flowers, tiny, in delicate branched inflorescences borne in the leaf axils.

A ground cover of damp, shady places.

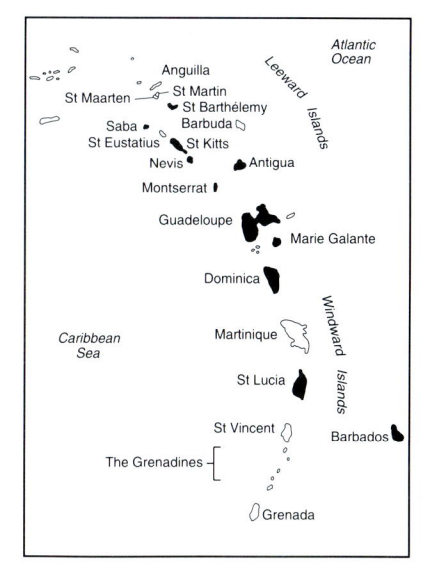

Lesser Antilles

Olacaceae

Schoepfia schreberi J. Gmelin

(ti) kafé bwa; bwi

Shrub or small tree to 6 m high. Leaves alternate, ovate to lanceolate, often yellowish and brittle, 4–8 cm long, 2–4 cm wide. Flowers, up to three in a cluster. Corolla tube yellowish, four- to five-lobed. Fruit, fleshy, oval, about 1 cm long, smooth and reddish at maturity.

In dry, rocky areas.

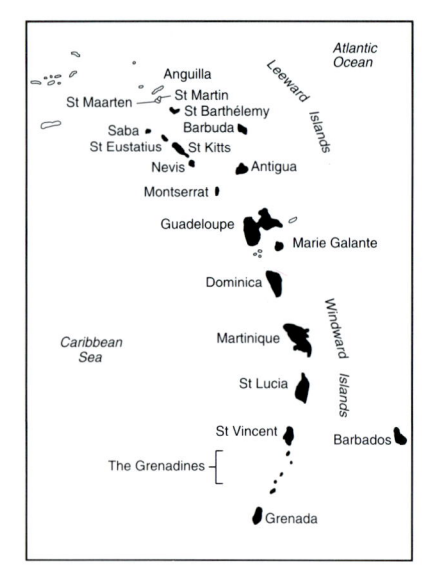

Greater Caribbean

Loranthaceae – Mistletoe family

Dendropemon caribaeus
Krug & Urban

mistletoe; man 'pon tree; *teny wouj*

Small shrub, the young stems smooth and four-angled. Leaves opposite, leathery, brownish, obovate, 2–4 cm long, 1–2 cm wide, each pair at right angles to the next. Racemes of tiny flowers borne in the leaf axils. Flowers six-petalled, star-shaped. Petals 2 mm long, cream inside, red outside. Fruit, a reddish oblong berry, to 8 mm long, exuding a cream-coloured latex when bruised.

Growing semi-parasitically on trees at mid elevations.

The mistletoes associated with Christmas celebrations in North America and Europe belong to the closely related family **Viscaceae**.

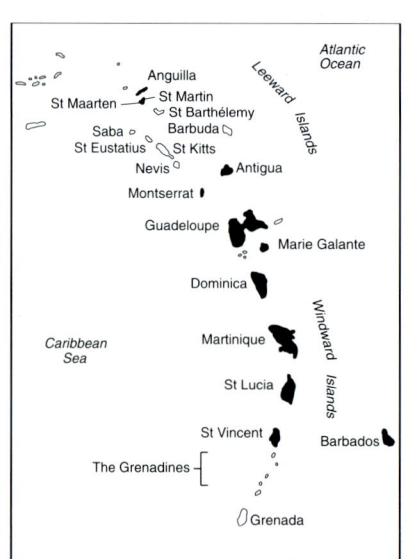

Puerto Rico, the Virgin Islands and the Lesser Antilles

Schoepfia schreberi

Dendropemon caribaeus

Aristolochiaceae – The Dutchman's pipe family

Aristolochia trilobata L.

six-sixty-six; *twèf*

Vine with alternate, three-lobed leaves, 5–15 cm in diameter. Flowers yellowish-green, unpleasant-smelling, borne singly in the leaf axils. Perianth a bent, inflated tube, about finger-length, the tip extending considerably more as a slender thread. Fruit, a cylindrical capsule, to 10 cm long, splitting along several lines.

A climbing plant of forested areas.

Used as an abortifacient[51], as an aid in childbirth, and against snake-bite.[9],[18],[28],[49],[50] Sudorific[18],[49] and once used to treat colds and fevers.[31]

▶

Aristolochia trilobata

Antigonon leptopus

Polygonaceae – Sea Grape family

Antigonon leptopus Hook. & Arn.

coralita; coralila; cemetery vine; *la belle mexicaine*; *zèb sémityè*

Herbaceous vine, climbing by means of tendrils arising from the inflorescence. Leaves heart-shaped, 6–12 cm long, with conspicuous sunken venation. Flowers bright pink or white.

Introduced as a garden plant but now a troublesome weed.

The tubers are apparently edible.[42] A tea for coughs and sore throats is made from the leaves and flowers.[5]

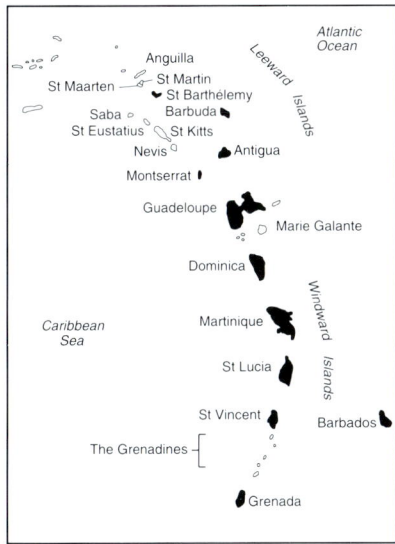

Native of Mexico

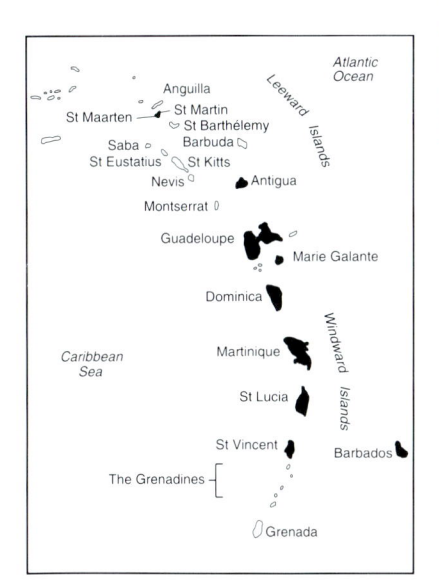

Central America, Greater and Lesser Antilles

Coccoloba pubescens

Coccoloba pubescens L.

leather-coat tree; ducana leaf; *wézinyé*; *gwan fèy*

Tree to 6 m high. Leaves alternate, strikingly large (breastplate-sized) and round to 60 cm across, though leaves from mature shoots often considerably smaller. Stem and undersurface of the leaves covered with brown hairs. Ochrea 1 cm long, also hairy, encircling the stem above each petiole. Trees bear either male or female flowers. Flowers, white and small, borne in terminal racemes.

Forested areas at low to mid elevations.

Provides good firewood and charcoal.[35] Extracts are used to treat diarrhoea, dysentery and bleeding.[9]

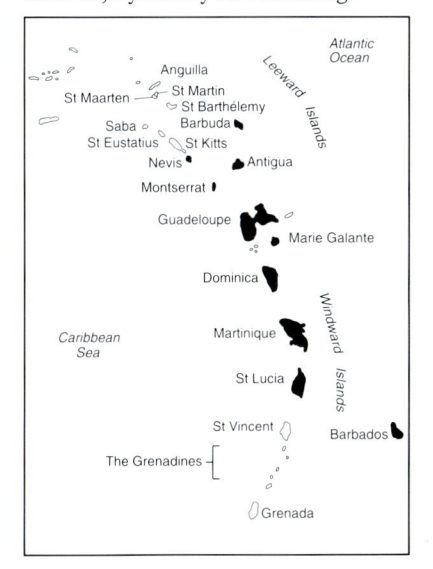

Hispaniola, Puerto Rico and the Lesser Antilles

Coccoloba uvifera (L.) L.

sea grape; *wézinyé lanmè*; *wézen*

Tree, 2–15 m tall. Leaves alternate, saucer-like, leathery, 8–20 cm in diameter, glossy and reddish when young, attached by stout petioles to the smooth stem. Ochreae 3–8 mm long, deciduous, leaving a scar. Trees functionally male or female. Inflorescence, 15–30 cm long, covered in small creamish flowers. Fruit reddish-purple when ripe, hanging in clusters like grapes, the fleshy portion derived from the swollen perianth which develops around the true fruit, a stony achene.

On seashores, but also inland where it can attain a considerable height.

In the French islands a red tea made from the bark or wood is used as a diarrhoea remedy as well as a gargle for throat infections.[45]

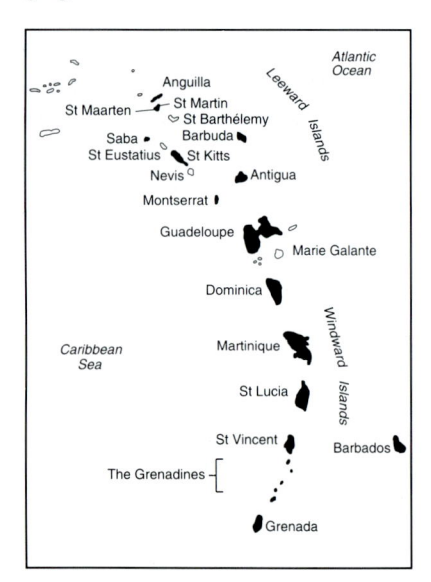

Coccoloba uvifera

Greater Caribbean

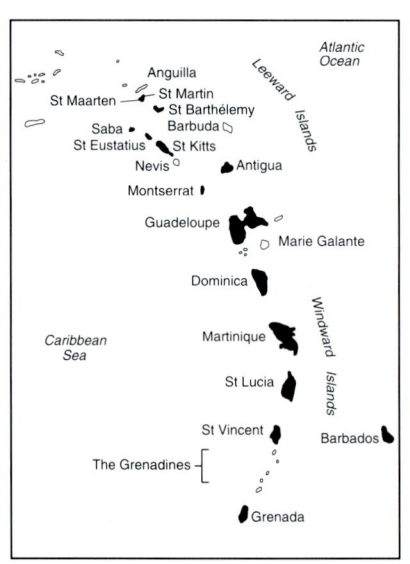

Widespread but probably native to Central America ▶

Chenopodiaceae – Beet family

Chenopodium ambrosioides

Chenopodium ambrosioides L.

worm bush/draft/grass/weed/wood; vermifuge; *simen kontwa*; *zèb à vè*

Annual aromatic herb to 1 m high, young parts slightly pubescent. Stem ribbed or grooved. Leaves alternate, narrowly elliptic, 2–9 cm long, 1–2 cm wide, the upper ones smaller and almost linear. Leaf margin shallowly toothed. Flowers, small and inconspicuous, in spikes in the upper leaf axils.

Weed of damp places, also cultivated.

World-renowned as an antihelminthic or 'worming' agent, although an overdose can cause death.[3] Also applied to the skin to treat fungal infections[45],[47] and even used as a minor component of toiletries.[14]

Alternanthera tenella

Amaranthus dubius

Blutaparon vermiculare

Amaranthaceae – Amaranth family

Alternanthera tenella Colla

rabbit weed; *zèb a albimin*

Spreading to semi-erect herb, young stem with short, hairy stubble. Stem reddish, swollen at the nodes. Leaves opposite, elliptic to 6 cm long, 2 cm wide, on a distinct petiole. Inflorescence axillary or terminal, globular, unstalked. Yellow anthers visible within the whitish-green perianth.

Weed of damp open habitats.

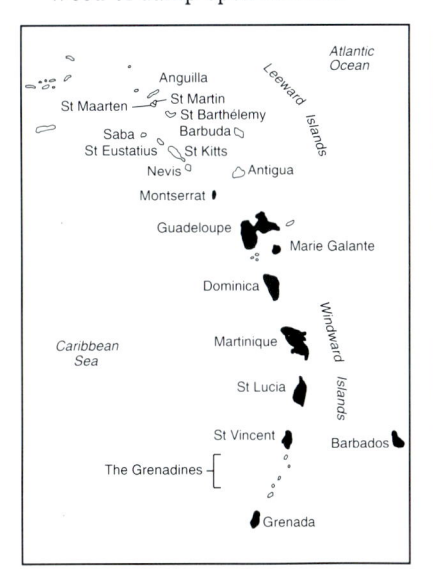

Tropical America

Amaranthus dubius C. Martius

(wild) spinach; bhaji; bower; *zépina (péyi)*

Erect, shrubby herb to 1 m tall, with stout, branched, often reddish stem. Leaves alternate, ovate to lanceolate, blunt-tipped, to 10 cm long, on yet longer petioles. Flowers in dense, narrow spikes to 20 cm long.

Roadside weed.

Leaves cooked as a spinach and also applied as a poultice on boils.[23],[45]

A. viridis and ***A. spinosus*** are easily mistaken for this plant although the latter is prickly.

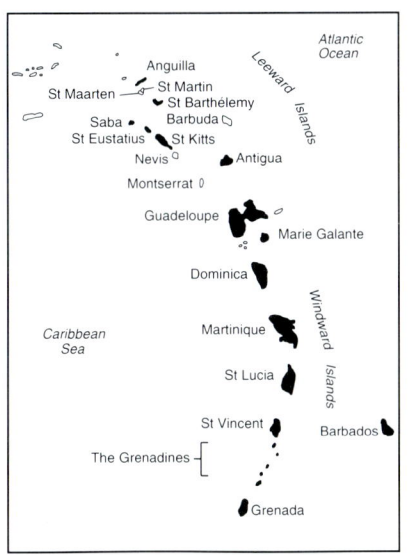

Tropical America

Blutaparon vermiculare (L.) Mears

Spreading, fleshy, perennial herb, rooting at nodes, often red-stemmed. Leaves oblong to linear, succulent, rounded in cross-section, without petioles, 1–4 cm long. Inflorescence a terminal globular to elongated white spike.

Sandy shores above the high tide mark, sea rocks and muddy banks of swamps.

The shoots can be cooked and eaten.[44]

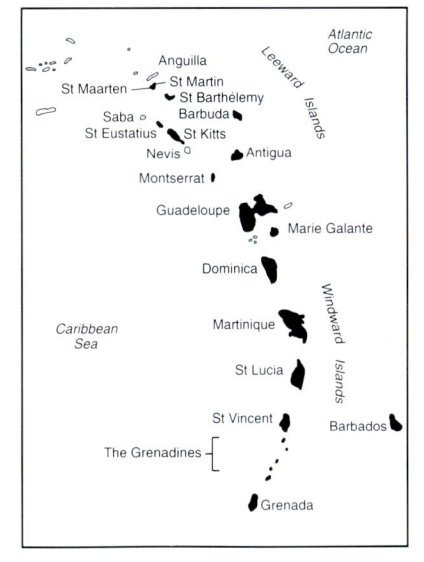

Tropical America

Nyctaginaceae –
Bougainvillea family

Boerhavia coccinea   Miller

hog butter/feed/food/weed; broadback; *patagon (wouj)*; *valéryan*

Prostrate or semi-erect herb to 60 cm high. Leaves opposite, spade-like, ovate or elliptic, to 3.5 cm long, margin wavy or uneven. Clusters of crimson flowers borne on an axillary stalk to 4 cm long. Fruit oval, 3 mm long, covered with sticky hairs which aid in fruit dispersal.

On wasteland, especially newly cleared areas.

A tea made from the leaves or root promotes sweating and is also used as a tonic.[9],[18]

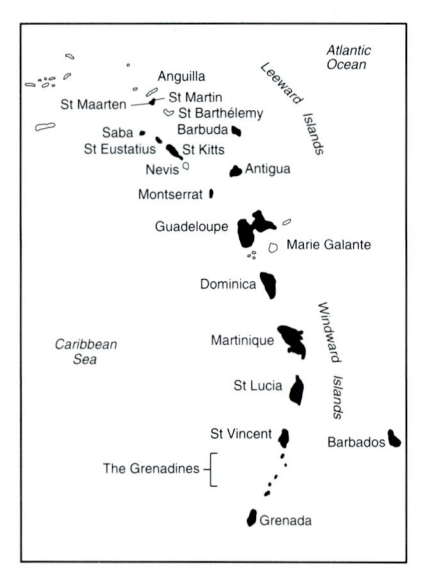

Boerhavia coccinea

Pisonia fragrans   Dum.-Cours.

black loblolly; jug plum; beefwood; *mapou (ti fèy)*

Tree to 15 m high with shiny, fleshy leaves. Leaves opposite, elliptic to obovate, 5–15 cm long, 3–6 cm wide. Trees male or female. Male flowers, whitish and funnel-shaped, stamens protruding, in tight panicles. Female flowers tubular and fragrant, in looser panicles. Fruit fleshy and oblong, to 15 mm long, purple-black when ripe.

Typically coastal or in dry forests.

Useless for firewood[29] but provides a tea reputedly effective against typhoid.[44]

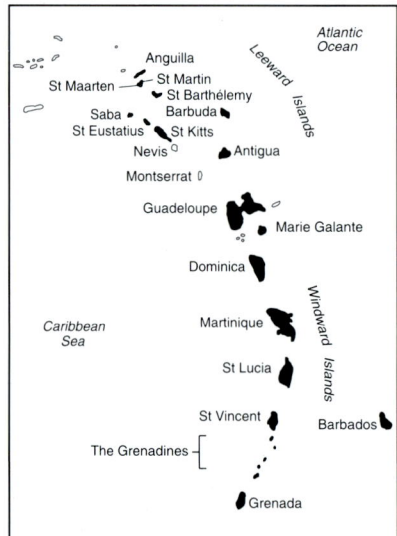

Pisonia fragrans

Petiveria alliaceae

Throughout the Tropics

Greater and Lesser Antilles and northern South America

34

Phytolaccaceae

Petiveria alliacea L.

conga/cudjoe/garlic/gully root; strong man bush; *danday; douvan(t) neg'; fèy douvant*

Erect, perennial herb, to 1 m high, the bruised root exuding a pungent, garlic-like odour. Leaves alternate, elliptic, 4–12 cm long, 2–6 cm wide, with minute stipules. Flowers whitish and star-like, at roughly 1 cm intervals, on a slender, arching spike. Fruit an oblong achene to 1 cm long, borne flat on the surface of the spike.

A weed of damp, shady places.

Can be used to ease labour during childbirth[45] and reputedly induces abortions.[6],[16],[23],[51] The leaf extract induces sweating[9] and is used to treat fever[28],[45] and colds.[56] The pungence of the root can be exploited as an insect repellant.[9],[45] Once used to treat epilepsy and hysteria.[31]

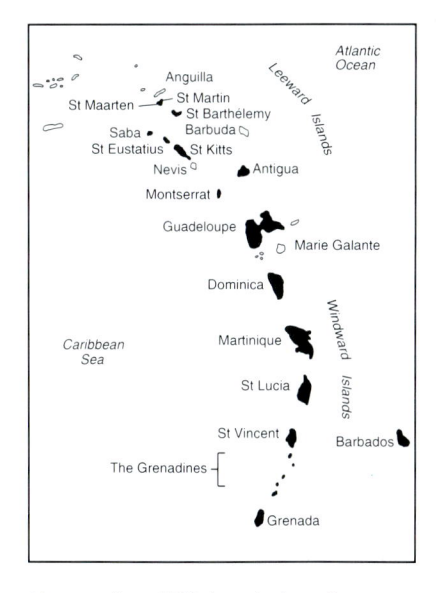

From southern USA down to Argentina

Rivina humilis L.

bloodberry; cat's blood; dog berry/blood; jumbie basil/pepper; *dimwazèl; zèb/lyann blan*

Erect, perennial herb to 1 m tall. Leaves alternate, ovate, to 12 cm long and 6 cm wide. Flowers white and cup-shaped of four perianth parts, loosely grouped in racemes, each to 8 cm long. Fruit a globular, bright red berry to 4 mm diameter.

A weed of shady habitats.

The plant is cultivated for a red, betalain-type dye, obtained from the berries. This provides amusement for children when rubbed on the skin as it bears a remarkable resemblance to blood.

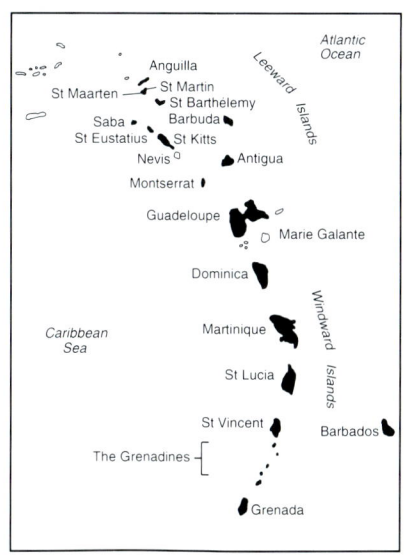

Rivina humilis

Southern USA and tropical America

Trichostigma octandrum (L.) H. Walter

hoop/small wiss; white hoop; *miwèt; lyann (a) bawik*

A woody, smooth-stemmed vine, clambering over trees and shrubs. Branches often hanging down with the tips curving up. Leaves alternate, elliptic to lanceolate, to 15 cm long. Flowers creamish, to 5 mm across, numerous, in racemes to 15 cm long. Fruit a globular, purplish-black berry to 4 mm diameter, the perianth still present but now reddish-purple.

In coastal areas and woods at low elevations.

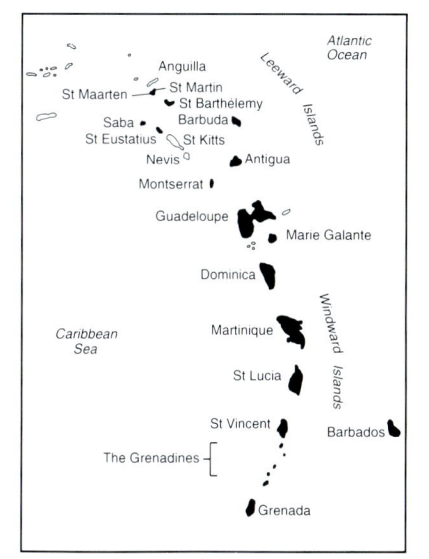

Trichostigma octandrum

Southern USA and tropical America

Aizoaceae –
Mesembryanthemum family

Sesuvium portulacastrum (L.) L.

seaside samphire; *poupyé bò-lanmè*

Succulent, spreading perennial. Leaves opposite, fleshy, often reddish, cigar-shaped, to 4 cm long, the bases clasping the stem. Flowers star-shaped, pink or, rarely, white, borne singly. Stamens numerous.

On cliffs, boulders and grassy verges near the sea.

The leaves provide a salty addition to salads and were once eaten as a scurvy treatment. Supposedly soothing when applied to lesions caused by venomous fish.[44]

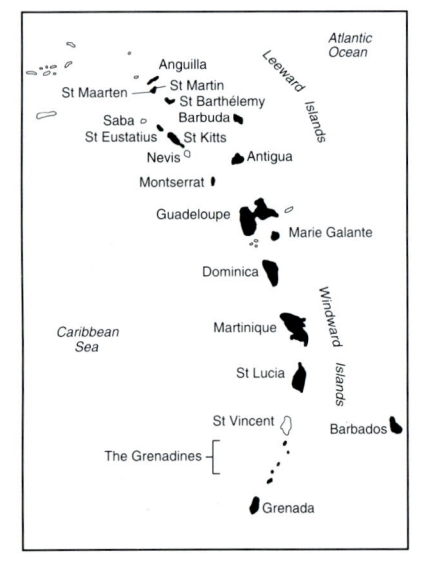

Sesuvium portulacastrum

Trianthema portulacastrum L.

horse purslane; turtle weed; *poupyé kouwan*

Shiny, fleshy, spreading herb. Leaves opposite, those of a pair quite different in size, elliptic, ovate or rounded, to 4 cm long. Flowers pink and cup-shaped, half-buried in the leaf axils. Fruit a capsule, 4–5 mm long.

Coastal, in full sun.

Should be treated as **poisonous** due to its high levels of oxalates.[3] Regarded in Ghana as an abortifacient.[1]

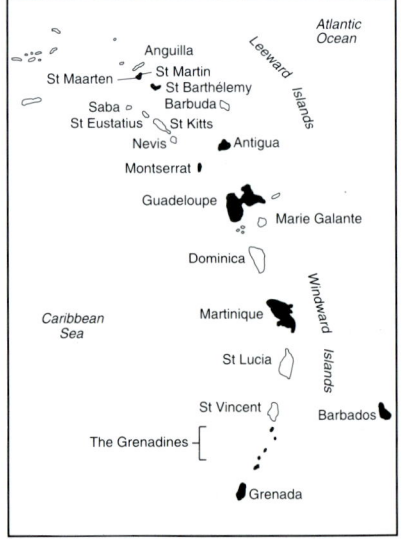

Tropics and subtropics worldwide

Southern USA and tropical America

Trianthema portulacastrum

Portulacaceae –
Purslane family

Portulaca oleracea L.

pussley; purslane; hog bhaji/meat; *poupyé*; *koupyé*

Fleshy, annual herb extremely variable in form. Under dry, seashore conditions, flat and spreading, with leaves alternate, elliptic, 4–7 mm long to 2 mm wide, without petiole. Under moist, shady conditions, erect to 40 cm high, green and shiny with leaves alternate, obovate, blunt-tipped, to 3 cm long. Stipules in the form of microscopic hairs at each node. Flowers, yellow and cup-shaped, with five notched petals, open only during the morning.

A common seashore plant and garden weed.

Culinary herb of antiquity[54] and used in salads and callaloo in some islands,[18],[45] although it can contain toxic levels of oxalates.[3],[44] The fresh leaf is applied as a poultice to sprains and swellings in the Caribbean[23],[28],[45],[50] and Ghana.[1] Application of the crushed leaves also apparently soothes prickly heat.[44] ▶

Portulaca oleracea

Argemone mexicana

Nymphaea ampla

Nymphaceae – Water lily family

Nymphaea ampla   (Salisb.) DC.

white water lily; *gwan folet*; *chapo dlo*; *nénuphar*

Large aquatic with long petioles and rounded, wavy-toothed, floating leaves to 30 cm across. Flowers to 15 cm across, raised above the water, opening in the day, lasting two–three days. Petals numerous, white, oblong to 8 cm long. Stamens and carpels numerous, yellow, crimson at base.

Commonly cultivated; also naturalised in ponds and swamps.

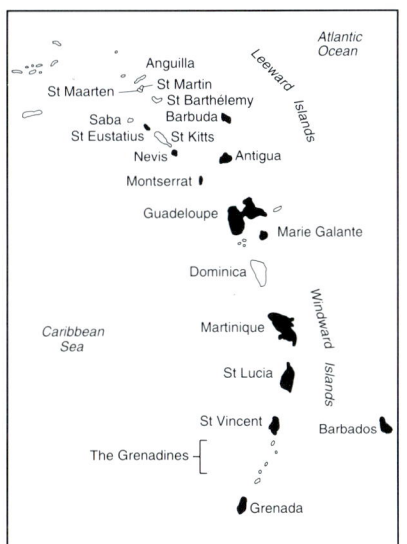

Papaveraceae – Poppy family

Argemone mexicana   L.

Mexican poppy; yellow (holly)hock; thistle; sissel; dry juice; pickle ash; *chadwon (mawbwé)*; *zèb dwagon*

Herb to 1 m tall with yellow sap and armed with spines. Leaves alternate, grey-green with veins distinctly paler, pinnately lobed, to 20 cm long and 8 cm wide, margin spiny, lower surface spiny on veins. Flowers yellow and cup-shaped, to 4 cm across, with leaf-like bracts at the base. Stamens numerous. Stigmas dull red. Fruit a spiny, ovoid capsule to 4 cm long, splitting into 4–6 segments.

A weed of open, disturbed habitats. The plant is used in bush teas in Barbados and Ghana[1] to promote urination, while the caustic sap is used to treat ringworm[56] and remove warts.[24],[25],[50] The emetic and purgative properties of the seeds have long been known.[31] The plant contains alkaloids with possible narcotic properties and should be treated as **poisonous**.[14] Youngsters use the seeds as bait in bird traps.

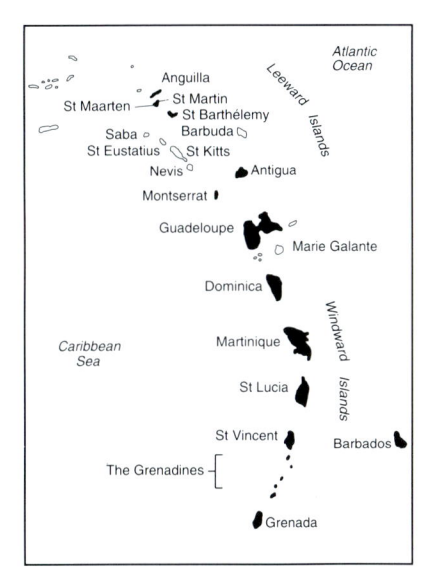

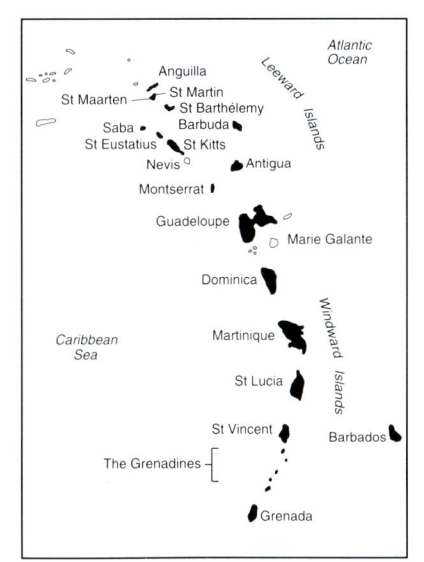

Tropics and subtropics worldwide

Southern Texas down through Central America and the Caribbean to Brazil

Tropical America

Brassicaceae (Cruciferae) – Cabbage family

Lepidium virginicum L.

wild cress; wild pepper grass; poor man's pepper; *kwèson savann*

Annual branching herb to 60 cm high. Lower leaves alternate, to 10 cm long, obovate or pinnately lobed with leaf segments winging the long petiole, margin coarsely toothed. Upper leaves, more or less linear, to 4 cm long, margin notched and spurred. Flowers, white, cross-shaped, 6 mm across. Fruit, round and flattened, to 3 mm in diameter.

A weed of waste places.

The leaves have a pleasant peppery taste and can substitute for cress in salads.[8],[28]

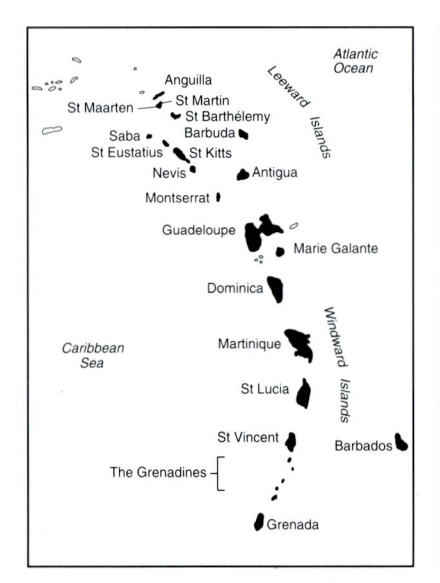

Native of North America, introduced and naturalised

Capparaceae – Caper family

Capparis cynophallophora L.

black willow; *bwa koulèv/nwè/pouant*

Small tree to 10 m tall, trunk blackish, stems with a brown, scaly covering. Leaves alternate, elliptic or oblong, to 15 cm long, dark glossy green above, greyish and scaly below. Juvenile leaves linear, to 20 cm long. Flowers fragrant, in corymbs at the shoot tips or nearby leaf axils. Sepals four, bent backwards, about 10 mm long. Petals four, white to mauve, to 15 mm long. Stamens numerous, filaments turning purple with age, to 3 cm long. Ovary 5 mm long on a gynophore to 3 cm long. Fruit cylindrical but knobbly, to 3 cm long, tapered at both ends, splitting to reveal a bright scarlet interior.

A tree of dry and coastal areas but also planted as a hedge.

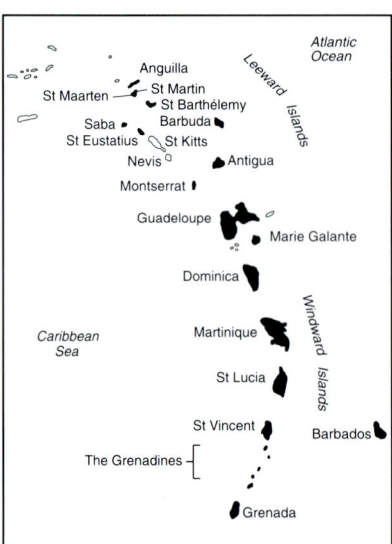

Greater Caribbean

Lepidium virginicum

Capparis cynophallophora

Capparis flexuosa (L.) L.

dog wood; man-of-war bush; bat tree; broken skull; bottle brush; *pwa mabouya*; *mabouj*; *bwa koulèv*

A scrambling shrub or small tree. Leaves alternate, elliptic to oblong, 4–10 cm long, 2–5 cm wide, leathery. Flowers white, few to several, large, fragrant, at or near the shoot tips. Stamens white and numerous, to 7 cm long, giving the appearance of a dishevelled shaving brush. Fruit 10–20 cm long. Seeds white and wet-looking, embedded in scarlet pulp.

Mainly in dry coastal woods.

The tree flowers infrequently in flushes during the rainy season, the flowers opening at dusk. The split stems are used for basketry in Barbados.[11] The seeds are supposedly **poisonous**.[49] ▶

Capparis flexuosa

Bryophyllum pinnatum

Cleome gynandra L.

stinking miss; stink bush; sambo; spider whisp; purple fifi; masambay; *mouzanbé/kaya blan*

Erect herb to 90 cm high. Stem usually with glandular hairs. Leaves alternate, compound of three–five elliptic leaflets, each 2–5 cm long. Flowers in terminal racemes each in the axil of a three-parted bract. Petals white, spoon-shaped, to 2 cm long, pointing upwards. Gynophore purple, sticking out horizontally from the flower, the stamens, with purple filaments, emerging from this at mid length. Fruit a cylindrical capsule, 4–6 cm long.

Wayside weed.

In Ghana it is used as a spinach and also as a fish poison.[1]

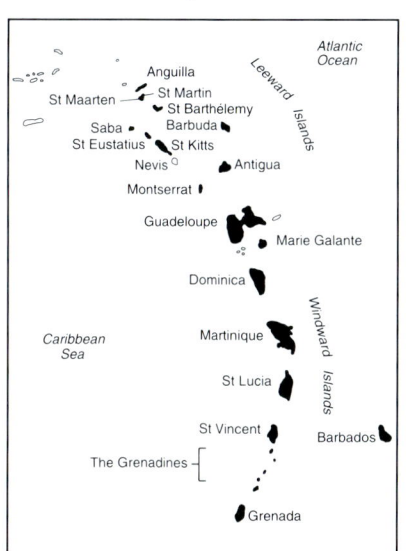

Cleome gynandra

Crassulaceae –
Kallanchoë family

Bryophyllum pinnatum (Lam.) Oken

wonder-of-the-world; salt fish; leaf-of-life; baby/colic/love bush; *lamowi*; *fèy chofi*; *plòk*; *géwitout*; *zèb malotèt*

Erect, succulent herb, tinged with red when growing in full sunlight. Leaves opposite and fleshy, clustered as in a rosette, lower leaves elliptic to 20 cm long, upper leaves often seemingly pinnate. Leaf margin scalloped, often with plantlets in the notches. Flowers, hanging down, in a terminal panicle to 1 m high. Calyx a broad, four-toothed tube to 3.5 cm long, yellowish-green to reddish, the corolla tube just visible within this.

Typically in dry areas.

The leaf extract is taken to promote urination while whole leaves are applied to swellings and sprains both in the Caribbean[6],[23],[45],[47],[50],[56] and Ghana.[1] Leaves applied to the brow are claimed to relieve headaches.[45],[47]

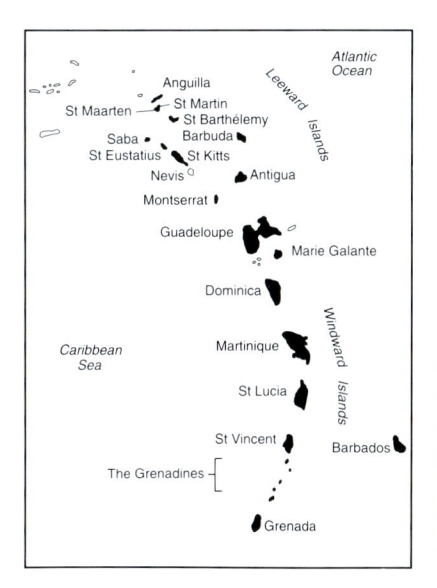

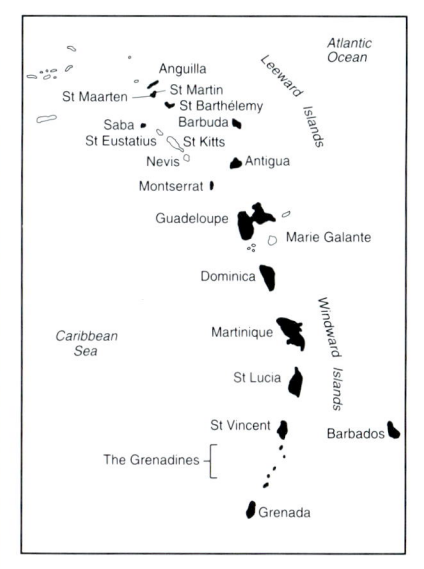

Greater Caribbean

Native of Africa, naturalised

Native of Madagascar

Chrysobalanaceae –
Fat pork family

Chrysobalanus icaco L.

fat pork; coco plum; *zikak*

Scrambling shrub, without hairs. Leaves alternate, leathery, broadly elliptic to obovate, 4–8 cm long. Stipules small, readily shed. Flowers creamish and small, few per raceme. Fruit, globular to ovoid, to 4 cm long, skin purple-red with a dull waxy appearance, the pulp white, edible but astringent.

Dry, coastal areas.

The plant is rich in tannins and a bark extract is used in the French islands against diarrhoea and dysentery.[45] The wood was also used for torches by the Caribs.[28]

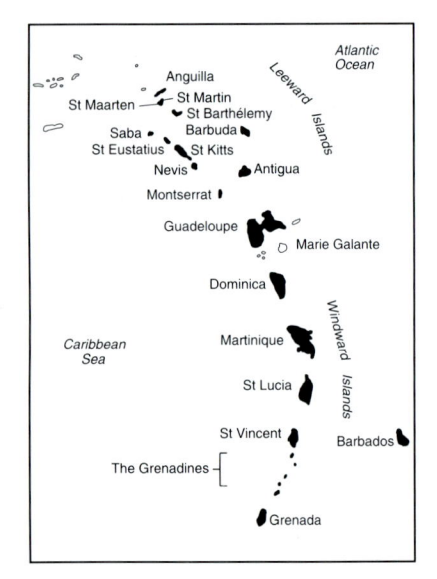

Chrysobalanus icaco

Caesalpinia bonduc

Caesalpiniaceae –
Cassia family

Caesalpinia bonduc (L.) Roxb.

(horse) nicker/nickel; warri seed; horse eye; jumbie soursop; manicou feed; *kannik; kach-kach; zyé a chat*

Scrambling shrub to 6 m high, the entire plant covered in short curved prickles, young parts with a golden brown pubescence. Leaves alternate, even-pinnate or bipinnate. Leaflets ovate to elliptic, spike-tipped, 2–5 cm long. Flowers yellowish, on slender erect spikes. Pod brown and woody at maturity, roughly ovoid, about 6 cm long, 4 cm wide, covered in prickles. Seeds grey, rounded to oval, 2 cm long.

In coastal thickets.

A common childhood prank is to rub the seed on the road or concrete causing it to become quite hot and then to touch this onto the skin of an unsuspecting individual. In Ghana the seeds are the most popular form of counter for the game oware,[1] likewise in Barbados and Antigua where the game is known as warri. The seeds are **poisonous** due to high levels of tannins[37] but can safely be used as a coffee substitute once roasted.[6][44] In the eighteenth century Caribbean this shrub served the role of modern-day barbed wire, being planted in front of coastal entrenchments.[33] ▶

Chamaecrista glandulosa

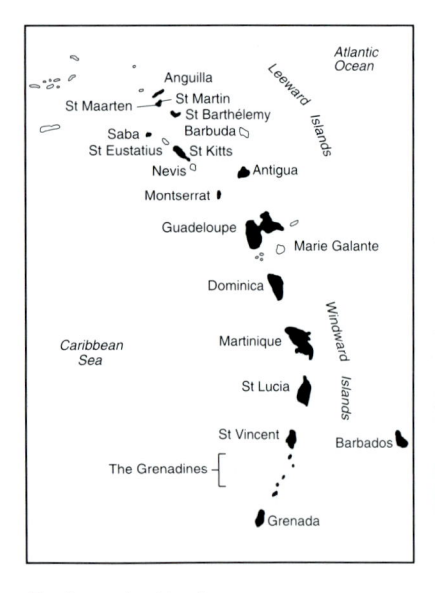

Greater Caribbean

Tropics and subtropics

Chamaecrista glandulosa

(L.) Greene var. ***swartzii***
(Wikstr.) Irwin & Barneby

wild/river tamarind; wild peas/senna; broom cassia; dutchman's butter; *ti tanmawen*; *bal(y)é savann*; *gwo bal(y)é*; *zingting*; *dyotin*

Shrub to 1.5 m high, young stems and leaf rachis often brown. Leaves alternate, even-pinnate, with 10–18 pairs of narrowly oblong leaflets, each 10–15 mm long. Leaflet tip rounded but spike-tipped. Gland, purple-red, mushroom-shaped, on the petiole. Stipules, lanceolate to 2 mm long. Flowers yellow, to 3 cm across, normally borne singly in the upper leaf axils. Sepals, yellowish, narrowly lanceolate to 14 mm long. Petals unequal, yellow with orange markings at the base, cupping the single carpel and ten stamens, three of which longer and red-purple. Fruit a reddish-brown, flat pod with 3 mm long rectangular seeds.

Wayside weed in dry areas.

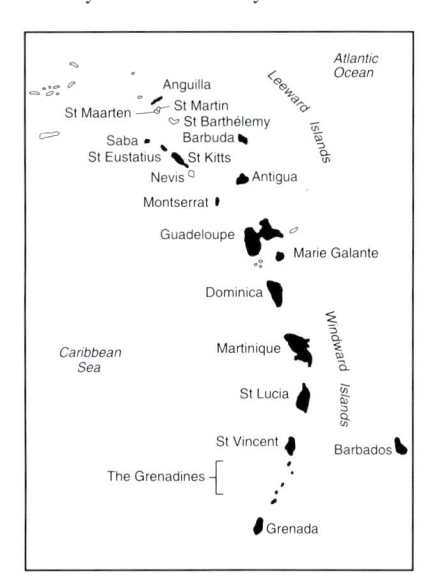

Puerto Rico and the Lesser Antilles

Haematoxylon campechianum

Haematoxylon campechianum L.

logwood; *kampèch*

Tree to 8 m high with a greyish, gnarly trunk and stout spines to 1.5 cm long. Leaves alternate, even-pinnate or bipinnate, of 4–8 obovate leaflets, each 1–3 cm long, notched at the tip. Flowers yellow and fragrant in dense bottle-brush racemes, arising from the axils. Fruit flat, wafer-like, elliptic, to 5 cm long.

In coastal and dry forests.

Once cultivated as a dye wood, source of the stain haematoxylin, but also a fine timber. Makes high quality charcoal.[35] The crushed leaves are considered to have haemostatic and fever-reducing properties.[45] A good honey plant.[42]

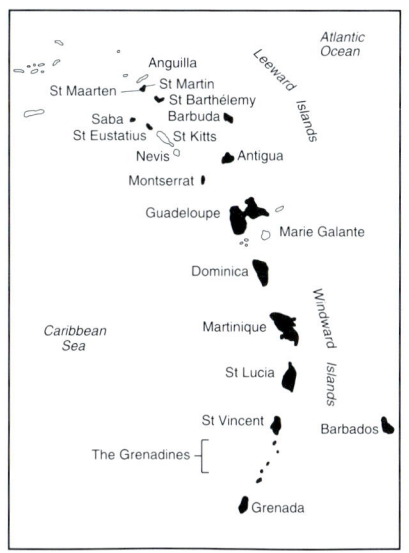

Native of Central America, introduced and naturalised

Senna bicapsularis

Senna bicapsularis

(L.) Roxb. var. ***bicapsularis***

Christmas/dog/money bush; blydog; monkey tamarind; rata sugar; pissabed; *soumaké*; *kaka béké/bétjé*

Spreading shrub to 3 m high. Leaves alternate, even-pinnate, comprising 3–5 pairs of leaflets, obovate, each 1–4 cm long, 1–2 cm wide, with a club-shaped gland between the lowest pair. Flowers yellow, 2 cm across, in few-flowered racemes. Fruit cigar-shaped, to 15 cm long.

Wayside shrub.

The brown pulp around the seeds smells like tamarind and is apparently edible. A leaf extract has long been used to treat skin disorders.[16],[31]

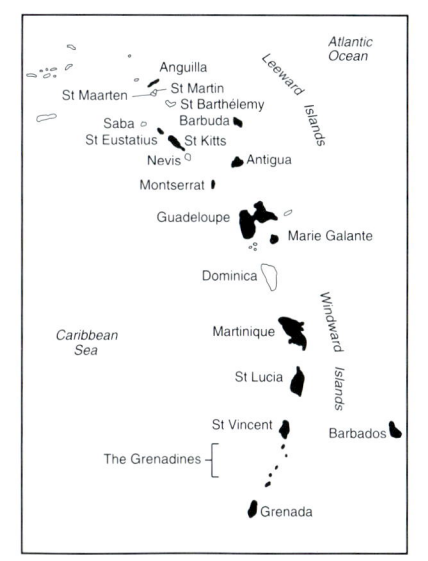

Florida and the West Indies

Mimosaceae –
Mimosa family

Acacia tortuosa   (L.) Willd.

sweet briar; cossie; cassie; (dutch) casha; *ponpon jòn*; *zakasya*

Shrub or small tree to 6 m high, with paired, straight stipular spines to 4 cm long. Leaves alternate, even-bipinnate, of 2–8 pairs of pinnae, each comprising 10–20 pairs of linear to oblong leaflets, each 4–7 mm long. Leaves bearing an oblong gland on the petiole and small circular glands on the axis towards the leaf tip. Flowers bright yellow and fragrant, in spherical heads. Pod 8–15 cm long, 8 mm thick, constricted between the seeds which occur in one row.

In dry, open habitats.

The related **A. farnesiana** is easily confused with this but instead has two rows of seeds in the pod.

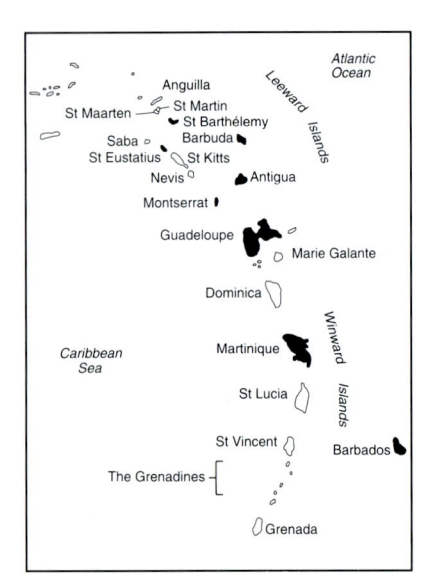

Acacia tortuosa

Inga laurina

Albizia lebbeck

Leucaena leucocephela

Greater Caribbean

Albizia lebbeck   (L.) Benth.

woman's/mother-in-law tongue; shak-shak; shushel; thibbet; *bwa nwè*; *vyé fiy*; *kaka béké*

Tree to 10 m high. Leaves alternate, bipinnate, of 2–4 pairs of pinnae, each comprising 4–9 pairs of oblong, unequal-sided leaflets, each to 5 cm long, 2 cm wide. Flowers creamish, in broom-like heads. Pods flat and oblong, to 30 cm long and 4 cm wide, papery and straw-coloured, the imprint of the seeds apparent. Pods present year-round, even when leaves are shed in the dry season.

A tree of dry, open habitats.

Produces a fine furniture wood, East Indian walnut, once exported from India to Europe.[5] ▶

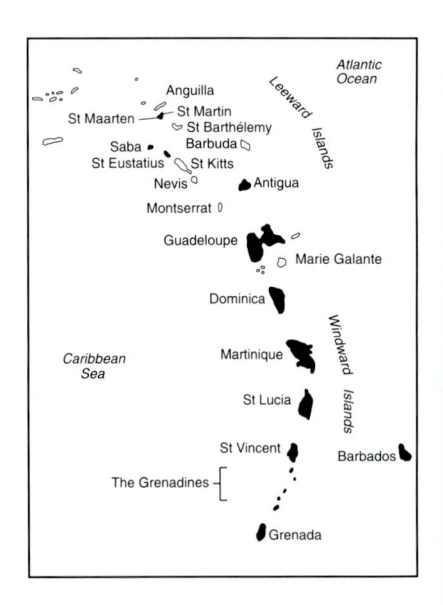

Native of tropical Asia, naturalised

Mimosa pudica

Inga laurina (Sw.) Willd.

Spanish oak; red wood; *pwa dou*

Tree to 15 m high with deep green foliage. Leaves alternate, even-pinnate of two pairs of elliptic leaflets with drip tip, each 5–12 cm long, 2–5 cm wide. Leaf axis with cup-shaped gland between each pair of leaflets. Flowers white, in axillary, bottle-brush spikes, to 15 cm long. Pod oblong, to 15 cm long and 3 cm wide.

In forests at mid to high elevations.

This and its many related species have fruit with a sweet white pulp, evoking the common name 'ice cream bean' elsewhere. It is a favourite with children.

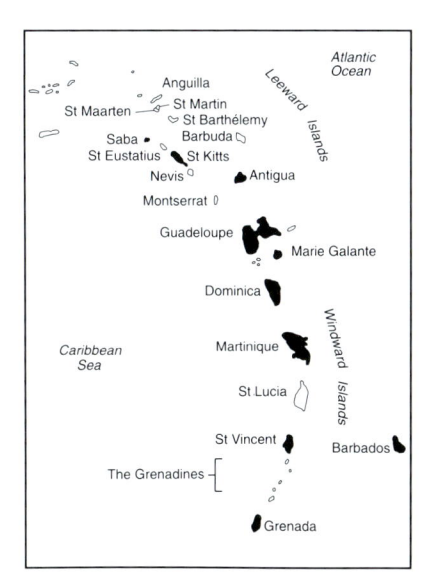

Greater and Lesser Antilles and Trinidad

Leucaena leucocephela (Lam.) De Wit

wild/river tamarind; miamossi; brush William; goat meat; tan-tan; zing-zing; pwi-pwi; *tamawen bata*; *makata (bous)*, *monval*

Shrub or small tree to 6 m high, young stems appearing powdery-surfaced. Leaves, alternate, even-bipinnate, of 3–8 pairs of pinnae, each comprising 10–14 pairs of narrowly oblong, pointed leaflets, each to 15 mm long. Inflorescence axillary. Flowers creamy-white, in ball-like heads, to 2 cm across. Pods red-brown, oblong and flattened, tapering at both ends, to 15 cm long, 3 cm wide.

A tree of open habitats.

Introduced as a quick-growing tree with protein-rich foliage, but the presence of mimosine causes hair loss in animals with a mane. Makes good charcoal.[5] In Barbados fishermen use it for making the frames of fish pots (traps).

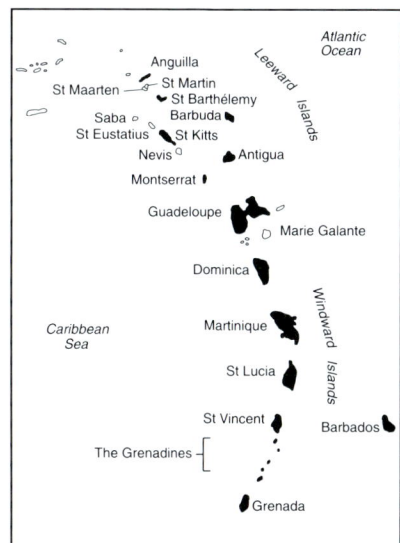

Tropical America

Mimosa pudica L.

mimosa; shame bush/lady/weed; (shame-)lady-shame; shut-your-house-man-a-come; pissabed; shameful; sensitive plant; *Mawi hont*; *mèzè/ti Mawi*; *Mawi Jann*; *hontèz*

Woody herb, generally low-lying and spreading, often hairy, with curved prickles on the stem. Leaves sensitive to touch, leaflets and pinnae 'collapsing' immediately on contact. Leaves alternate, comprising four pinnae, each of 10–30 pairs of linear, 1 cm-long leaflets. Flowers pink to mauve, in ball-like or slightly elongated heads, 15 mm across. Pod narrowly oblong, to 2 cm long, often with bristles.

In full sunlight in waste places.

The touch stimulus is transmitted as an electrical impulse within the plant, the movements being achieved by rapid redistribution of water at the 'joints' at the bases of the leaves, pinnae and leaflets.

The root has long been used as an antidote to poisoning,[31] possibly as it is a purgative and emetic.[1],[9],[28],[45] The whole plant is used to make a tea for numerous disorders.[35],[45],[51]

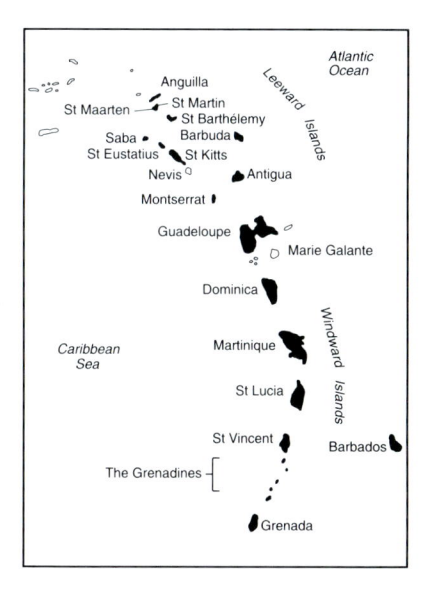

Tropical America

Neptunia plena

Pithecellobium unguis-cati

Alysicarpus vaginalis

Neptunia plena   (L.) Bentham

shame bush/lady; water thistle; *ponpon jòn*

A low, speading, branched herb. Leaves sensitive to touch. Stipules ovate, to 6 mm long. Leaves alternate, even-bipinnate of 2–4 pairs of pinnae, each of 10–40 pairs of linear leaflets, each to 1 cm long and with the lower part whitish. Inflorescence borne singly, ball-like, yellow, 2 cm across, comprising central bisexual flowers surrounded by petal-bearing, sterile flowers. Fruit a pod, oblong and flattened, to 5 cm long and 1 cm wide, with a beak tip.

In damp, sunny habitats.

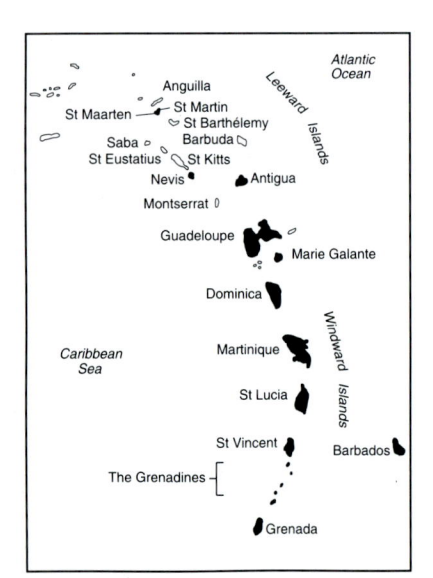

Pithecellobium unguis-cati   (L.) Bentham

bread and cheese; beef steak; crab wood; money bush; *bwa kwab*; *gwif chat*

Shrub or small tree to 6 m high, with stipular spines to 2 cm long. Leaves alternate, of two pinnae, each of two lopsided, obovate or elliptic leaflets, to 5 cm long. Flowers creamish, often reddish at the base, clustered into ball-like heads, 2 cm across. Pod curved, reddish-brown, splitting to reveal several shiny black seeds, each half-buried in a fleshy, white or red edible aril.

In dry forests; also used as a hedge.

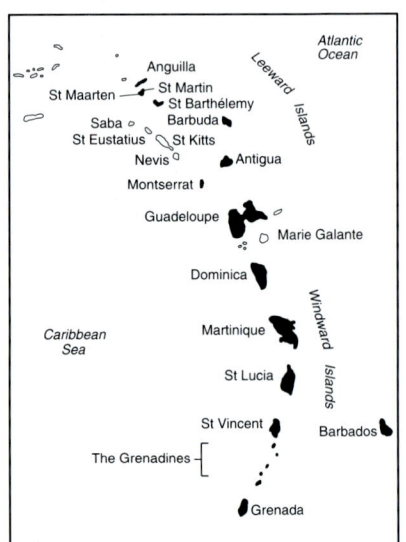

Fabaceae – Pea family

Alysicarpus vaginalis   (L.) DC.

Low, spreading herb. Stipules chaff-like, partly sheathing the stem, lanceolate to 7 mm long. Leaves alternate, simple, rounded to boat-shaped, to 3 cm long. Flowers reddish-purple, in tight clusters on an erect stalk. Fruit dark brown, tubular, hooped, to 2 cm long, often held erect.

A weed, common in lawns. Recognised as a highly nutritious animal fodder.[42]

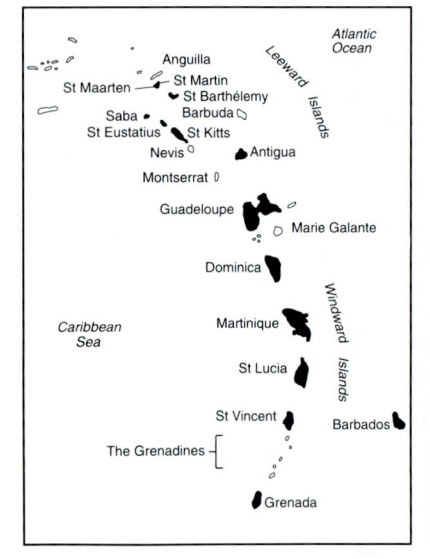

Tropical America

Florida, through the Caribbean to Venezuela

Native of tropical Asia

Canavalia rosea

Centrosema virginianum

Clitoria ternatea

Canavalia rosea (Sw.) DC.

sea(side)/horse bean; *(pwa) vonvon*; *pwa bò-lanmè*

Smooth-stemmed, creeping vine. Leaves alternate, of three rounded to oblong leaflets, to 10 cm long, on a stout petiole. Flowers in axillary racemes. Corolla pink-violet with white markings; standard about 2 cm long. Pod flattened and bean-like, to 15 cm long, 3 cm wide.

A seashore vine, although sometimes found in waste places inland.

The seeds are **poisonous**[9] unless roasted[44] and the dried pod has dangerous hallucinogenic properties.[44]

Centrosema virginianum (L.) Bentham

bluebell; wild pea; winer; fifi; *ti pwa*; *pwa-pwa*; *pwa savann*

Fine-stemmed, twining herb. Leaves alternate, of three lanceolate to ovate leaflets, to 5 cm long. Flowers one to a few per axillary stalk. Standard large and broad, to 3 cm across, purple with white markings or vice versa. Pod almost black, curling into a spiral on splitting, about 10 cm long and 4 mm wide, tapering to a 1 cm long, narrow tip, ribbed near the margin.

Weed of roadside verges and waste places.

Clitoria ternatea L.

blue fifi/vine; *pwa savann*

Twining vine, the young parts downy. Leaves alternate, odd-pinnate, of 5–7 elliptic leaflets, to 4 cm long, 2 cm wide. Flowers borne singly, November–March, with two rounded bracts at the base. Standard prominent, hanging down, to 4 cm long, royal-blue with a white throat tinged with yellow. Pod buff-coloured, to 12 cm long, with a sharp 1 cm long tip.

Wayside weed.

A double form of this is cultivated.

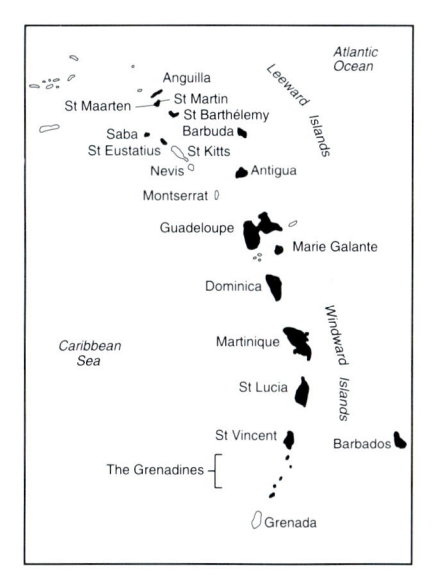

Tropics and subtropics

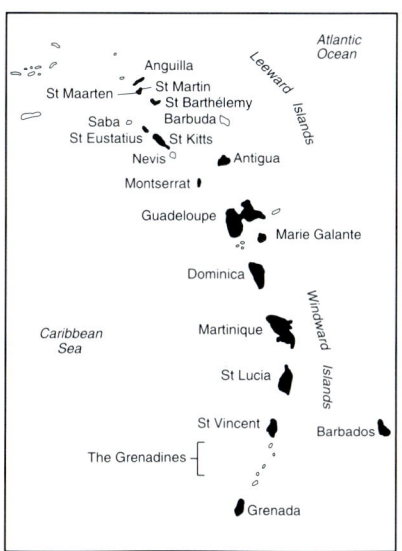

Tropical and subtropical America

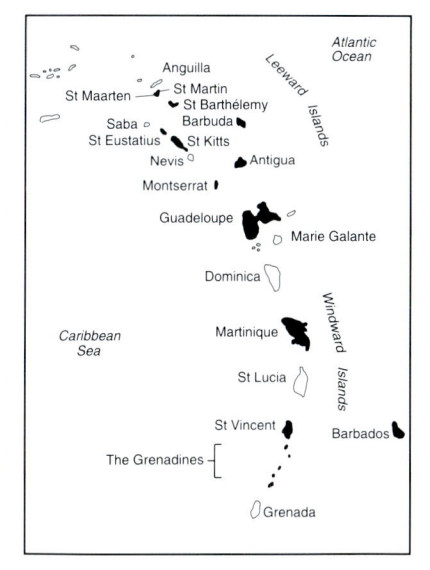

Native of Old World Tropics

Crotalaria retusa L.

wild/yellow sweet pea; (yellow) shak shak; jumbie earring; *pwa zonbi*; *sonnèt*

Annual herb to 1 m tall, the stems finely pubescent. Stipules threadlike, to 3 mm long, or absent. Leaves alternate, simple, narrowly obovate, to 10 cm long, 2 cm wide. Flowers many per erect terminal raceme. Corolla yellow; standard reddish-brown on the reverse side, to 2 cm high. Pod black, tubular, oblong, to 4 cm long.

Weed of pastures.

Contains pyrrolizidine alkaloids which can cause liver failure if eaten.[37] An eighteenth century introduction via the St Vincent Botanic Garden.[30] The inflated, blimp-like pods are a distinctive feature of this genus, twelve species of which are found in the region.[30]

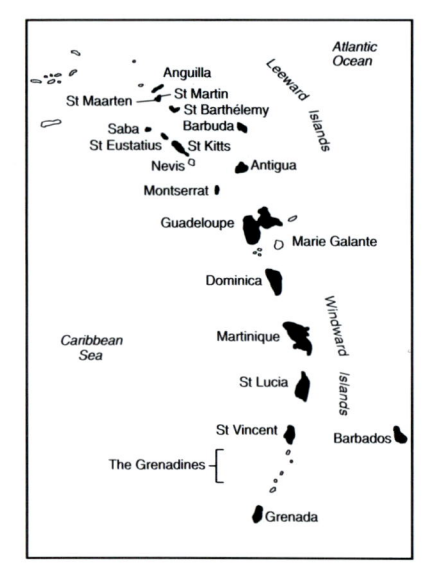

Crotalaria retusa

Native of Asia

Dalbergia ecastaphyllum (L.) Taubert

hoop wood; bottle cod; *lyann (a) bawik*; *lyann mang*

Small tree or shrub with trailing branches. Stipules strap-like and pointed, silky-haired, 1 cm long. Leaves alternate, ovate to elliptic, 6–10 cm long. Flowers creamish, about 5 mm long, in dense axillary panicles, slightly longer than the petioles. Pod a roundish, flattened disc, to 3 cm long.

In coastal thickets

The branches were once used for barrel hoops.[24],[49] The bark and root contain a fish toxin.[44]

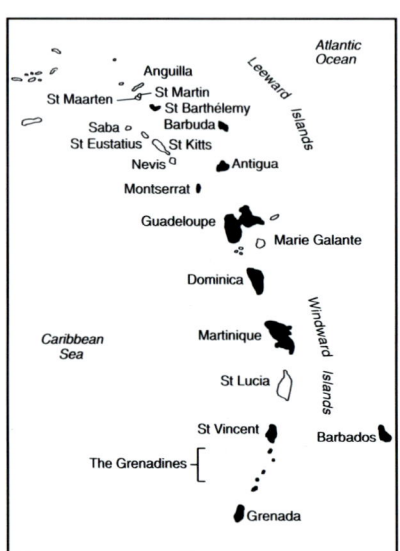

Dalbergia ecastaphyllum

Greater Caribbean and West Africa

Desmodium incanum DC.

sweetheart; man-to-man; bread; bud grass; *kòlan*; *kòd a vyélon*

Semi-erect to shrubby herb, usually to 30 cm high, stem often with tiny hairs. Stipules lanceolate, paired, to 1 cm long. Leaves alternate, of three elliptic to lanceolate leaflets, 2–6 cm long, often with white markings along the midrib. Flowers in loose axillary and terminal racemes. Corolla pink, bluish or almost white, about 6 mm long. Pod, to 4 cm long, 3–8 jointed, notched along lower edge only, covered in tiny hooked hairs which cause pod segments to adhere to clothing.

A common weed.

The distinctive pod, which breaks into segments, is characteristic of the genus **Desmodium**, ten species of which are found in the region.[30] ▶

Desmodium incanum

Erythrina variegata L.

Judas/lent/devil tree; immortel; *(bwa) mòwtèl*

Tree to 15 m tall. Bark with light green, vertical striations. Twigs and trunk with short black spines. Leaves alternate, of three leaflets, broadly ovate to delta-shaped, 6–15 cm long, 3–16 cm wide. Leaves shed February–April when flowering occurs. Flowers scarlet, in dense racemes, horizontally arrayed. Standard to 7 cm long, stamens well displayed. Pod, about 20 cm long, brown and knobbly. Seeds, 2 cm long, the colour and shape of a kidney bean.

Cultivated, but also naturalised along river banks at low elevations.

There are two other commonly cultivated forms of this tree, one with yellow-white leaf variegation, another with white flowers.

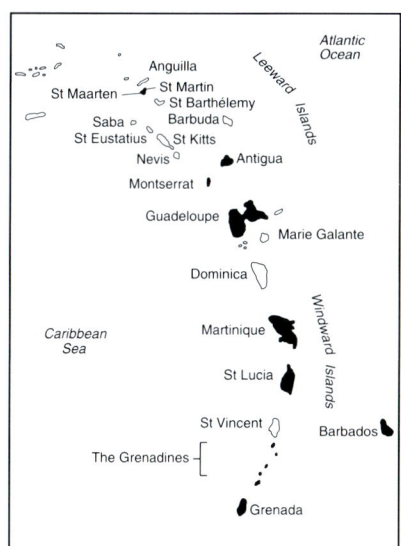

Erythrina variegata

Flemingia strobilifera

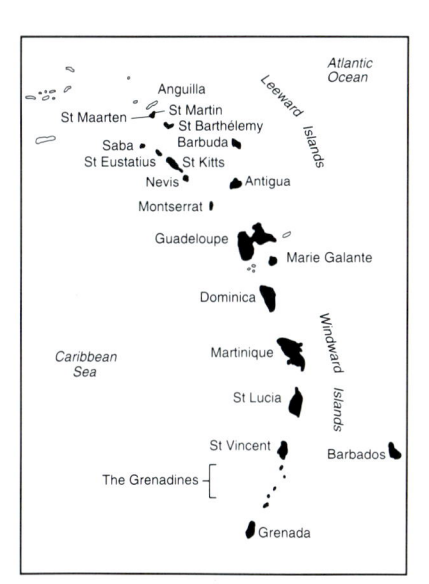

Tropics worldwide

Flemingia strobilifera (L.) Aiton. f.

wild hops; luck bush; *zèb sèk*

Shrub to 2 m tall, young stems and petioles pubescent. Leaves alternate, elliptic, to 20 cm long and 10 cm wide, with conspicuous pinnate venation. Inflorescences, 15 cm long racemes towards the shoot tips, dominated by papery, brown, 2 cm long bracts. Flowers creamish, within the bracts, standard about 6 mm long. Pod 1 cm long.

Along roadsides and in abandoned fields.

The inflorescences, with their conspicuous bracts, are used in dried floral arrangements.

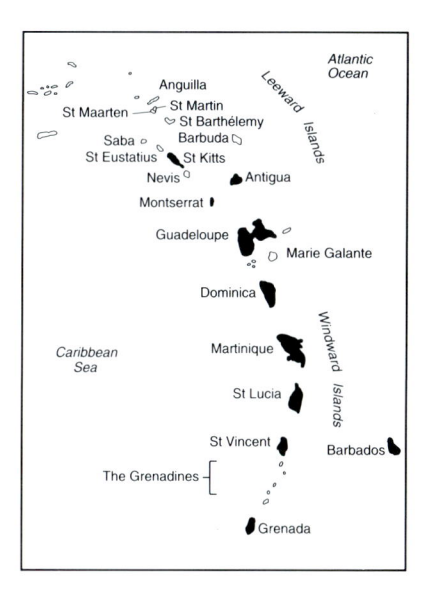

Native of tropical Asia

Native of Asia

Indigofera suffruticosa   Miller

indigo; *endigo bata*

Shrub, 1–2 m tall, stem with a whitish pubescence. Leaves alternate, odd-pinnate, of 9–15 leaflets, narrowly elliptic to obovate, minutely spike-tipped. Inflorescence a spike-like axillary raceme, erect, shorter than the leaves. Corolla pink. Pod sausage-like, sickle-shaped, 1–1.5 cm long.

In waste places.

A source of indigo dye, now superceded by synthetic aniline dyes. The plant steeped in water yields a colourless solution, the deep blue colour only developing after the dyed cloth is exposed to the air.[52] Abandoned earlier elsewhere, indigo remained a crop in Mustique and Bequia up to the 1850s.[29]

Indigofera suffruticosa

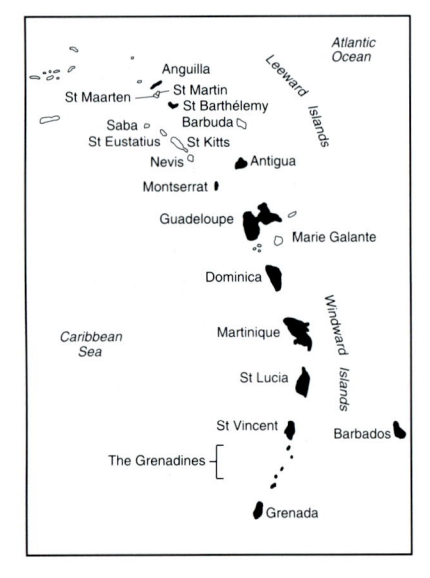

Lablab purpureus

Lablab purpureus   (L.) Sweet

bonavist; *(pwa) boukousou*

Trailing, twining vine. Leaves alternate, of three leaflets, triangular to ovate, often unequal-sided, 6–10 cm long. Flowers in erect, axillary inflorescences. Corolla usually white, standard 15 mm long. Pod flattened, broadly oblong, bean-like, 4–8 cm long, the periphery with warty bumps (as if welded together!).

Cultivated for food, but also a weed.

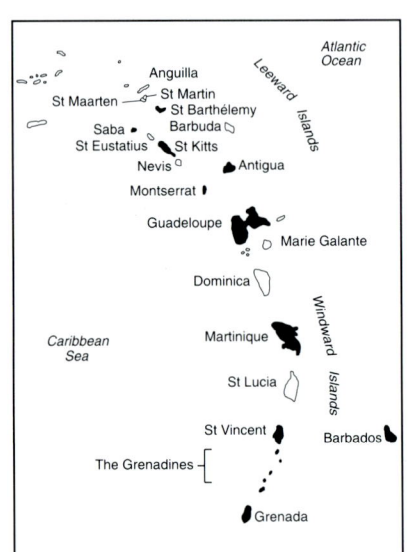

Macroptilium lathyroides   (L.) Urban

wild dolly/pea; *pwa pijon/pwazon/wouj/zonbi*

Erect or trailing herb, to 60 cm high. Stem with scattered silky hairs. Leaves alternate, of three leaflets, elliptic to lanceolate, 3–6 cm long. Flowers on erect axillary stalks. Corolla deep crimson, sometimes almost black. Standard about 1.5 cm long. Pod a slender tube, about 10 cm long, 3 mm wide.

A weed of waste places.

Its creole names suggest it is **poisonous**.

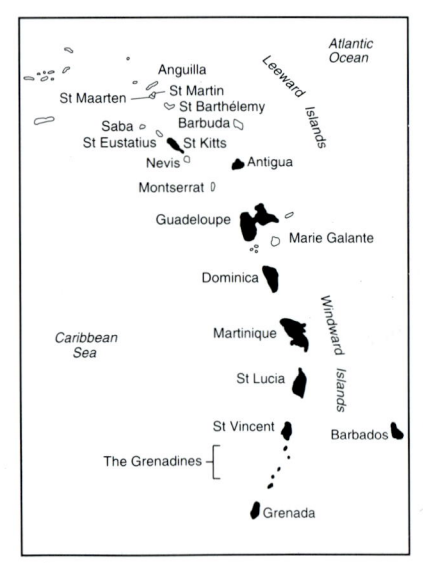

Tropical America

Native of Africa

Greater Caribbean

Macroptilium lathyroides

Mucuna pruriens

Rhynchosia minima

Mucuna pruriens (L.) DC.

cowitch; *pwa gwat(é)*

Twining vine. Leaves alternate, of three leaflets, the terminal one trowel-shaped, the laterals lopsidedly ovate, each 7–14 cm long. Flowers purple, hanging like a cluster of grapes. Fruit an oblong pod, 4–10 cm long, with a brown felt-like appearance due to stinging hairs.

A weed in areas of abandoned agriculture.

The hairs on the pods cause severe skin irritation but, boiled in syrup and ingested, are an effective old remedy for dispelling worms.[9],[31] The seed is believed to absorb venom from scorpion wounds.[25]

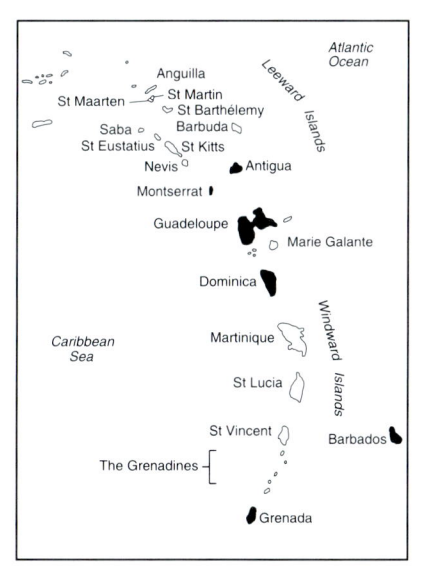

Greater Caribbean

Rhynchosia minima (L.) DC.

burn-tongue/burn-mouth vine; horse/donkey rub-down; *pwa hazyé/zwèzo*

Slender twining vine, stem with short, microscopic hairs. Leaves alternate, of three leaflets, ovate to diamond-shaped, 1–3 cm long, smooth to velvety below. Flowers yellow, in erect, axillary racemes to 12 cm long. Pod dark brown, oblong to somewhat club-shaped, slightly curved, 1–2 cm long.

Weed of waste places.

Fatal if eaten by rabbits. In St Kitts this is the bush of choice for treating colds, fever and flu.[56]

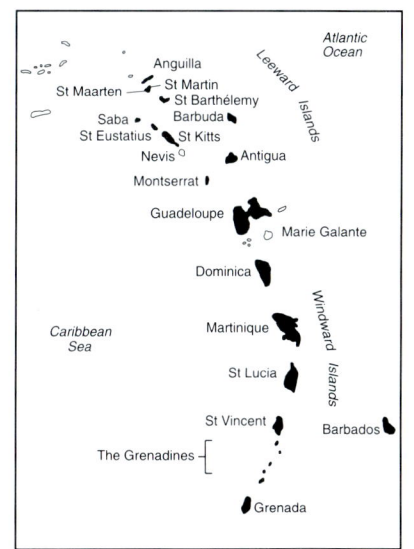

Tropics worldwide

Stylosanthes hamata

Vigna luteola

Vigna vexillata

Stylosanthes hamata   (L.) Taubert

Garfield bush; mother sigil; sweet weed; *ti twèf*; *twèf jòn*

Spreading, somewhat woody herb. Leaves alternate, of three leaflets, each lanceolate to elliptic, white-veined below, 1–2 cm long, 2–5 mm wide. Flowers in short spikes with leaf-like bracts. Corolla yellow; standard yellow with reddish markings. Pod of two segments, each about 2 mm wide and slightly longer, beak equalling these in length.

Weed of lawns and waste places.
Used to make a 'cooling tea'.

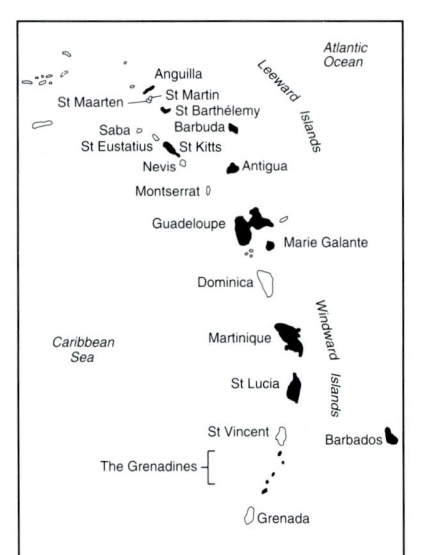

Vigna luteola   (Jacq.) Bentham

pwa jòn/zonbi

Trailing herb, usually smooth-stemmed. Stipules ovate–lanceolate, 4 mm long, with two lobes at the base. Leaves alternate, of three ovate leaflets, to 7 cm long and 4 cm wide. Petiole angled, longer than the leaflets, bulbous at its junction with the stem. Flowers single to a few, on erect axillary stalks. Corolla yellow; standard 2 cm across. Pod slightly curved, 4–8 cm long, 4 mm wide, dark brown, slightly constricted between the seeds and with scattered hairs.

Waste places, especially sunny, damp areas.

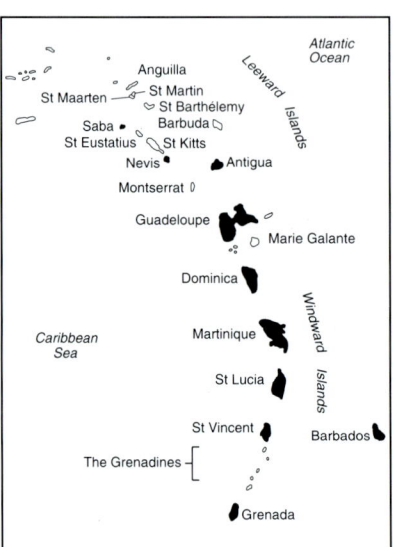

Oxalis debilis var. *corymbosa*

Kallstroemia pubescens

Greater Caribbean

Tropical America

Vigna vexillata   (L.) A. Rich.

pwa pwazon/zonbi

Trailing vine. Stem with scattered hairs, rough to the touch. Stipules lanceolate, 4 mm long, base with a slight notch and lifting off the stem. Leaves alternate, of three leaflets, lanceolate to narrow, 5–10 cm long, upper surface of young leaves with scattered, low-lying hairs. Flowers at the end of an erect, minutely-barbed stalk, to 20 cm long. Corolla pale lilac turning yellowish with age; standard 2–3 cm across; keel upturned and twisted sideways, projecting from between the pale mauve laterals. Pod straight to slightly curved, cylindrical, 5–10 cm long, 4 mm wide, covered with short, brown, bristly hairs.

Roadside verges and waste areas.

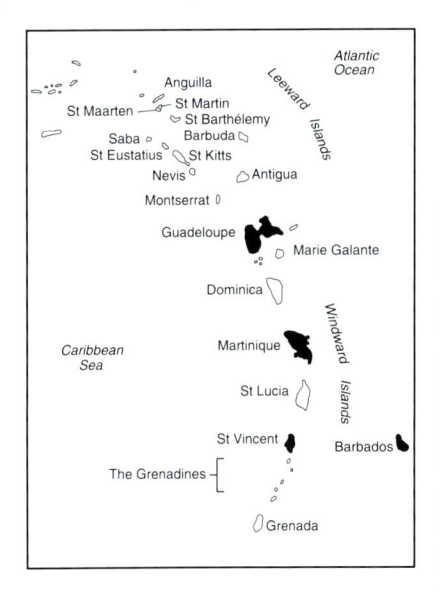

Native of tropical America

Oxalidaceae –
Oxalis family

Oxalis debilis   Kunth
var. ***corymbosa***   (DC.) Lourteig

shamrock; malgoj; *zèb vochlè*; gwan twèf

Stemless herb. Leaves and flowering stalks arising from a scaly bulb. Leaves of three, broadly heart-shaped, leaflets, joined centrally by the point of the heart to a petiole, 10–20 cm long. Flowers pink, 1.5 cm across, clustered on the end of a long stalk. Fruit a cylindrical capsule, to 2 cm long.

In shade in wet areas.

The leaves are chewed or taken in a tea as a sore throat remedy.[28]

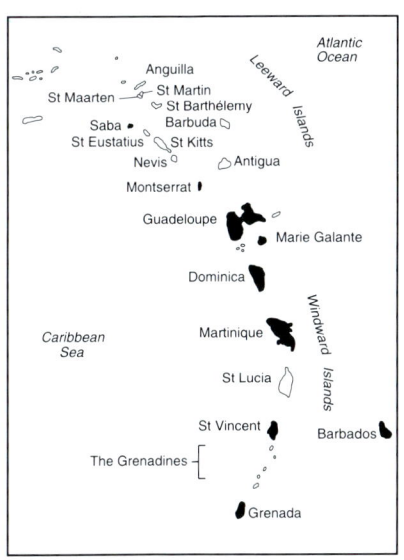

Greater Caribbean

Zygophyllaceae –
Lignum vitae family

Kallstroemia pubescens   (Don) Dandy

police macca; *kwèson kouwan*; koupyé/poupyé bata

Creeping herb with fine hairs on the stem. Leaves opposite (sometimes without matching opposite leaf), even-pinnate, of three pairs of leaflets, each elliptic, the terminal pair lop-sided, to 3 cm long. Flowers occurring singly on an axillary stalk. Corolla cream-coloured, forming a shallow bowl, about 1 cm across. Fruit ten-lobed, pyramid-like, 8 mm long.

A weed of open habitats.

The ornamental tree, lignum vitae, ***Guaiacum officinale***, is a member of this family and though native to the Caribbean is nowadays mainly found in cultivation.

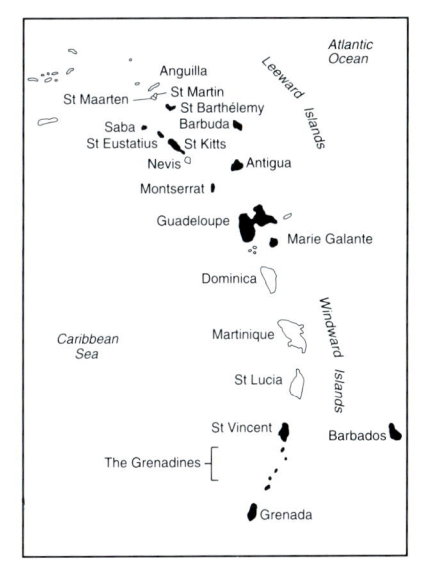

Greater Caribbean

Rutaceae – Citrus family

Zanthoxylum caribaeum Lam.

white harklis; *lépini (blan/wouj)*

Shrub or small tree to 15 m high, the trunk and branches with stout spines, the whole plant aromatic. Leaves alternate, odd-pinnate, of 7–13 leaflets, each elliptic, 3–9 cm long, gland-dotted all over, margin scalloped. Flowers greenish-white, unisexual, 5 mm across, with five petals and five sepals, in terminal panicles. Fruit dry, kidney-shaped, 5 mm long, splitting on one side to reveal a shiny black seed.

In dry forests.

Bark and twigs chewed as a toothache remedy.[41] Provides good timber, walking sticks[35] and tool handles.[49]

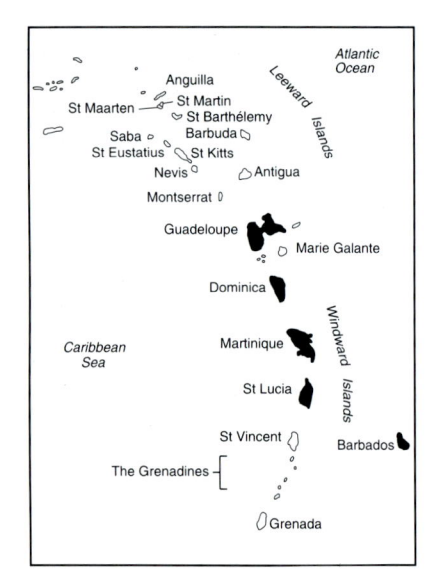

Greater Caribbean

Burseraceae – Frankincense family

Bursera simaruba (L.) Sarg.

birch gum; naked indian; turpentine/tourist/gum tree; *go(n)myé wouj/modi*

Deciduous tree, to 15 m high, producing resin. Bark copper-coloured, peeling in papery layers. Leaves alternate, odd-pinnate, of 3–9 leaflets, each ovate to elliptic, pinkish when young, 4–10 cm long, with a drip tip. Leaves shed January–March. Flowers small, in axillary panicles, usually unisexual, with trees typically male or female. Fruit reddish-purple, shaped like an American football, about 1 cm long.

Common in coastal and dry forests.

The aromatic resins myrrh and frankincense, used in perfumery, are obtained from trees in this family, native to Arabia and East Africa.[26] The resin from this plant can be used to make a varnish[57] or can be applied to sprains.[34],[45] Branches are used as living fence posts.[34] In Florida the tree is called gumbo limbo and is planted as an ornamental on account of its lustrous bark.[8]

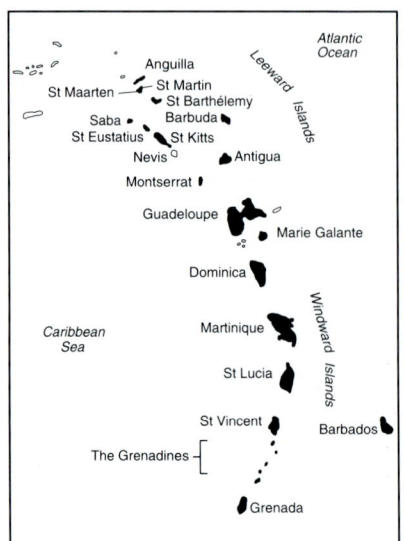

Tropical America

Zanthoxylum caribaeum

Bursera simaruba

Stigmaphyllon ovatum

Malpighiaceae – West Indian cherry family

Stigmaphyllon ovatum
(Cav.) Niedenzu

Low shrub to 1 m tall. Leaves opposite, ovate to lanceolate, 8–12 cm long. Flowers pale yellow, 3 cm across, in umbels or singly. Fruit breaking into three winged nutlets, the nutlet and wing portions each to 8 mm long.

In coastal wetlands.

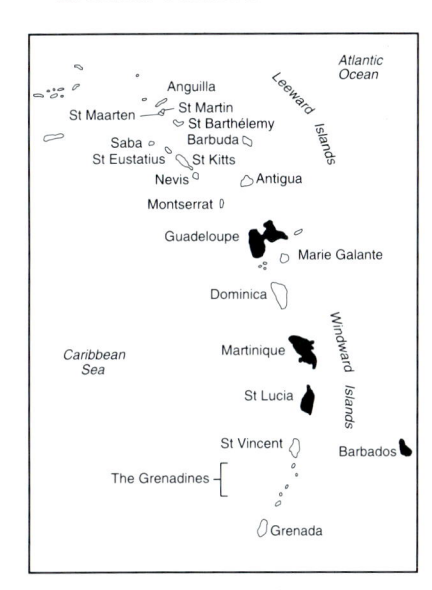

Greater Caribbean and Brazil

Securidaca diversifolia

Polygalaceae

Securidaca diversifolia (L.) S.F. Blake

Easter vine; *lyann Pak/bwanda/wòz*

Woody vine, stem often 4 cm in diameter or more in mature, high-climbing specimens. Bruised root of young plant smelling of wintergreen. Leaves alternate, elliptic to ovate, 2–8 cm long. Flowers somewhat pea-like, pink-purple, in loose panicles appearing March–April. Fruit dry and winged, 4–6 cm long, superficially like a mahogany seed.

In forest canopies at low to mid elevations.

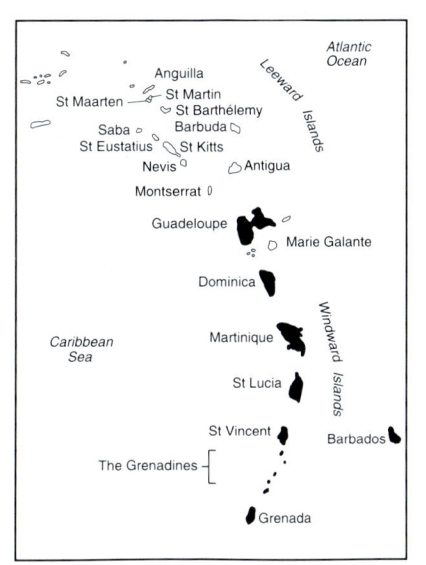

West Indies, Central and South America

Acalypha poiretii

Euphorbiaceae – Poinsettia family

Acalypha poiretii Sprengel

wild okra; cure-for-all

Erect herb, to 50 cm high. Stem with long, stiff hairs. Leaves alternate, ovate, 2–8 cm long, margin toothed. Petiole usually shorter than the leaf. Inflorescence an axillary oblong spike, to 3 cm long, comprising both male and female flowers with toothed bracts.

Weed of damp places.

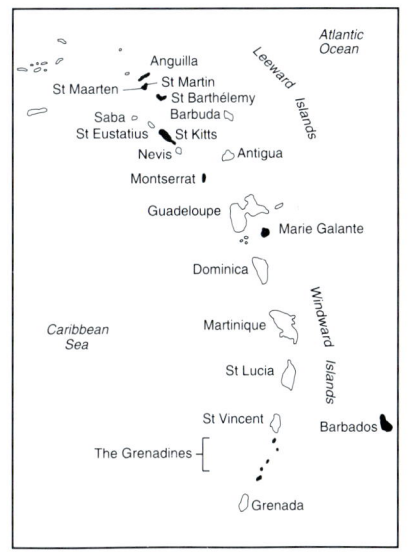

Old World native

Argythamnia polygama (♂)

Argythamnia polygama
(Jacq.) Kuntze

bwa lajan

Shrub to 1 m high. Leaves alternate, lanceolate to elliptic, 3–10 cm long, shortly petioled, margin finely toothed. Plants male (as in the photograph) or female. Male flowers massed at the shoot tips in tight, chaffy, axillary clusters; petals white, less than 6 mm long. Female flowers conspicuous, long-stalked, 1–2 per axil; petals white, 1 cm long. Fruit a three-lobed, hairy capsule, to 8 mm across.

A shrub of dry woods.

Chamaesyce hirta (L.) Millsp.

milk weed/grass; asthma plant; milky-milky; milky bush; checkweed; *malonmé vwè*; *zèb malonmé*

Annual, semi-erect herb, to 30 cm high, often branched at the base. Stem stout, downy and with long, scattered hairs. All parts exuding a white latex on bruising. Leaves opposite, narrowly elliptic to lanceolate, unequal-sided, to 4 cm long, 1.5 cm wide, margin sharply toothed for the most part, both surfaces with scattered hairs, sometimes with reddish blotches near the midrib. Cyathia short-stalked, green with minute purple glands, in tight clusters, to 8 mm across. Fruit a three-lobed capsule, covered in microscopic hairs, often reddish.

A weed of waste places.

The latex contains an irritant but is used to treat warts[45],[54] and tumours.[44] A tea prepared from the plant is used as a treatment for asthma[1],[25],[28],[45],[54] and also to reduce fever and promote urination.[28],[45] Its use in the Grenadines to stop diarrhoea is reflected in the name checkweed.[29]

Croton flavens L.

yellow balsam; rock/seaside sage; tobbo/broom broom; bitter shrub; *ti bôm*; *koupayou (bata)*

Shrub to 1 m high, pleasantly aromatic, the stems with a golden-brown scruffiness. All parts exuding a clear, yellow latex when bruised. Leaves alternate, long-petioled, ovate, to 8 cm long, appearing greyish, especially beneath, due to microscopic star-shaped hairs, turning bright orange before shed. Male and female flowers in separate, spike-like, terminal inflorescences. Male flowers fragrant, petals slender, bent back, alternating with the ovate sepals, both white, stamens many. Female flowers without petals. Fruit a capsule, almost globular, three-lobed, brown and rough-textured, 5 mm long.

In dry rocky places near the sea.

The golden sap has long been considered a good balm for sores and cuts[5],[9],[31],[33],[35] and a drop or two of this on some sugar was also taken as a remedy for colds and chest complaints.[23],[31]

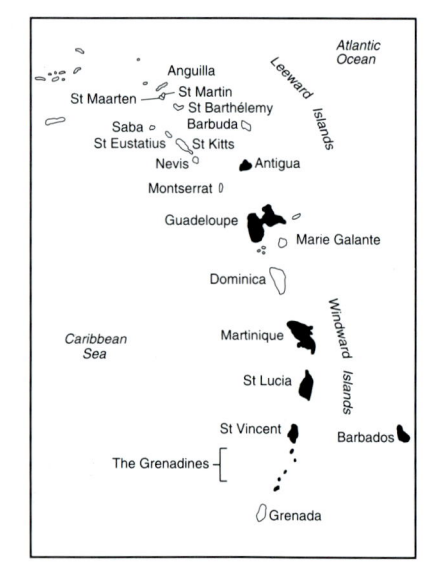

Northern South America and the Lesser Antilles

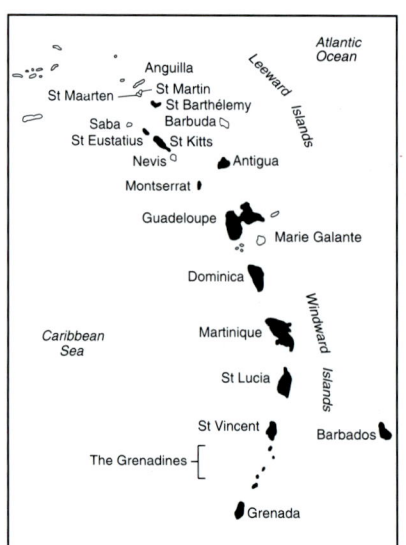

Throughout the Tropics

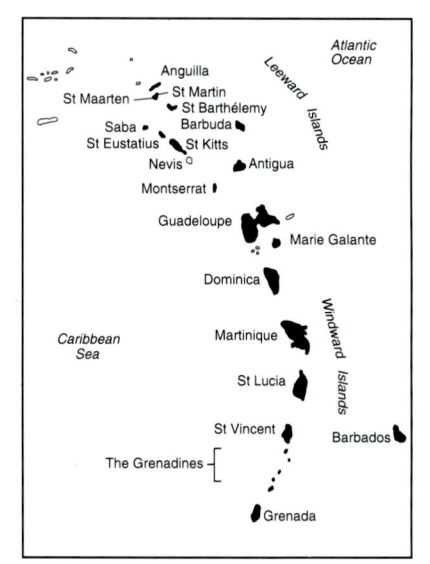

Greater and Lesser Antilles and Venezuela

Chamaesyce hirta

Croton lobatus

Euphorbia cyathophora

Croton flavens

Croton lobatus L.

croton; lilac bush; *mouzanbé blan*; *gonbo fwansèz*

Erect branched herb to 60 cm tall, the stem often with dense, long hairs. Leaves alternate, deeply three-to five-lobed, lobes elliptic to lanceolate, each to 4 cm long, with scattered silky hairs, margin toothed. Petiole, to 4 cm long. Inflorescence spike-like, axillary or terminal, to 10 cm long. Male flowers uppermost, short-stalked, small white petals. Female flowers towards the base, unstalked, petals absent. Fruit an ovoid capsule, three-lobed, 5 mm long, scattered hairs.

Wayside weed.

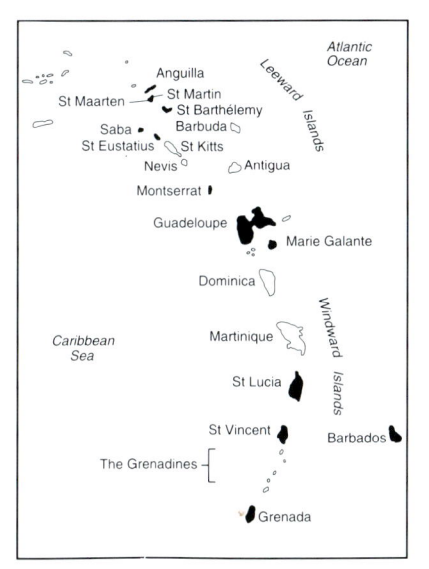

Tropical America

Euphorbia cyathophora Murray

wild poinsettia; milky-milky

Annual or perennial herb to 60 cm high, exuding a white latex when bruised. Leaves alternate, very variable, linear, fiddle-shaped, or elliptic with toothed margin, to 10 cm long. Uppermost leaves and bracts with pink or red blotches. Cyathia in a terminal cluster, surrounded by the coloured bracts. Fruit a three-lobed, globular capsule, 5 mm long.

A weed of pastures at mid elevations.

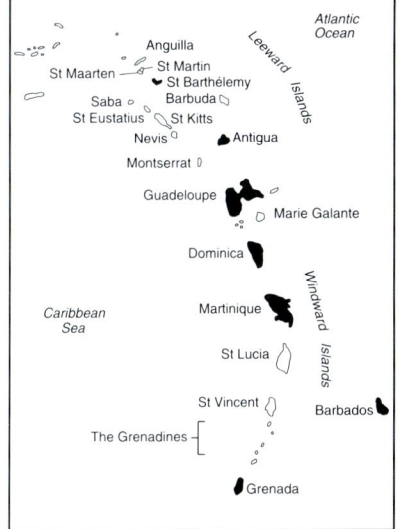

Tropical America

Hippomane mancinella L.

manchineel; beach/poison apple; *mannjini*; *mansniyé*; *médsinyé (modi)*

Tree to 10 m high, all parts containing a white caustic sap. Leaves alternate, shiny bright green, ovate to elliptic, 4–10 cm long. Male and female flowers in stout spikes, to 15 cm long. Fruit yellow-green, globular to slightly flattened, about 3 cm in diameter.

A seashore tree but often found in dry, rocky inland areas.

The sap on the skin can lead to blistering; in the eyes to blindness. The fruit is **poisonous** and if ingested in quantity can cause death, depending on the sensitivity of the individual and the potency of the tree. The reaction is apparently caused by the diterpenes hippomanin A and B.[37] Its beautiful wood was once used to make furniture.[46]

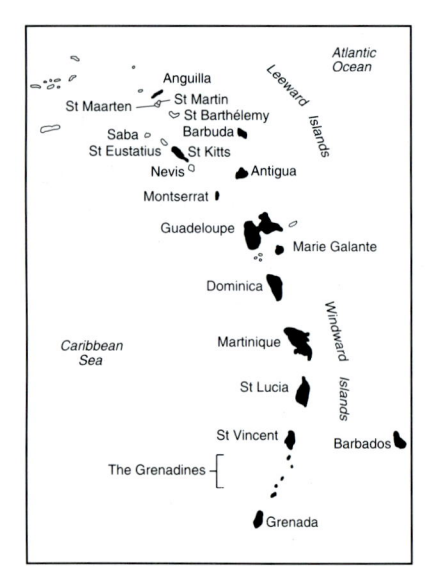

Greater Caribbean, introduced to West Africa

Jatropha gossypiifolia L.

bellyache bush; barricado; baby eye; wild physic nut; *médsinyé bata/wouj*; *bwa/gwèn zowtolan*

Erect shrubby plant to 1 m high, with yellowish sap. Young parts often covered in sticky glandular hairs. Leaves alternate, to 15 cm diameter, distinctly three- to five-lobed, long-petioled, the margins with tiny glandular teeth. Young leaves reddish. Inflorescence, long-stalked, a tight terminal cyme. Male flowers with deep red petals. Fruit an oblong capsule, three-furrowed, hairy, 1.5 cm long.

In dry, sunny habitats.

The seeds are a dangerous purgative.[9],[14],[31]

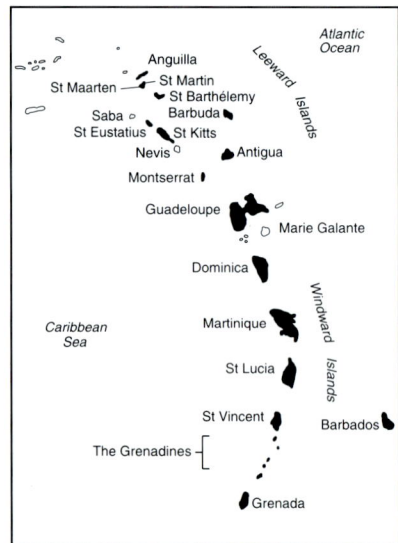

Tropical America

Hippomane mancinella

Jatropha gossypiifolia

Pedilanthus tithymaloides (L.) Poit.

lady's slipper; slipper plant; milk bush; *zèb a kò*; *pantouf*; *gwo zowèy*

Erect shrub, branching from the ground, to 1 m high, with white latex throughout. Stem and leaves fleshy, the leaves angled upwards. Leaves alternate, elliptic to obovate, to 8 cm long, 4 cm wide. Several red, slipper-like involucres clustered at shoot ends. Emerging from the tip of each 'slipper', a single female flower, reduced to a pistil, and several male flowers, each reduced to a stamen. Fruit a capsule, 8 mm long, three-lobed, beaked at the tip and on a fleshy stalk.

In rocky areas, often near the sea.

The latex is **poisonous**.[37] Numerous forms of this plant, differing in leaf shape and variegation, are cultivated. ▶

Pedilanthus tithymaloides

Phyllanthus amarus

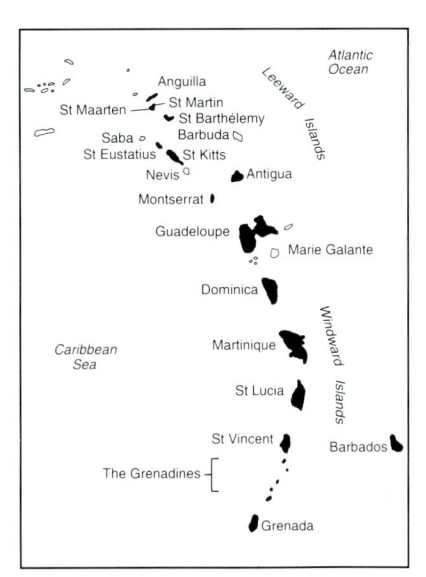

Phyllanthus amarus
Schum. & Thonn.

seed-under-leaf; bitter tamarind; children weed; *gwenn amba fèy (blan)*

Erect annual herb to 50 cm high, the whole plant pale green. Stipules minute, triangular and translucent. What appear to be alternate, pinnate leaves are branches with 10–30 oblong leaves, each about 1 cm long. Flowers occurring singly in leaf axils, arranged below the leaves. Fruit globular, 2 mm across, on a short stalk. Seeds with microscopic longitudinal ridges.

Weed of disturbed ground. Considered an abortifacient.[6],[23],[35],[51] A leaf tea of this and related species is taken to reduce fever.[29],[55] The tiny fruit is poisonous to rabbits.[35]

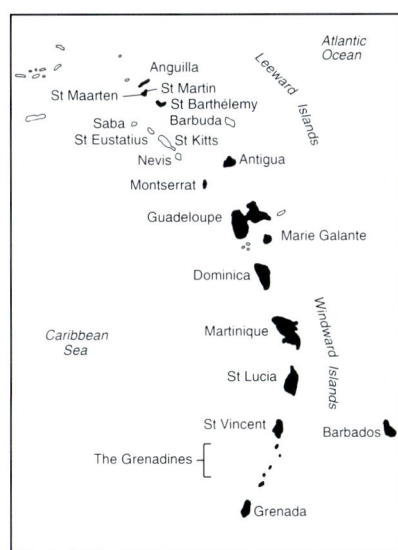

Phyllanthus epiphyllanthus

Phyllanthus epiphyllanthus   L.

monkey spoon; herringbone; billbush; mutton porridge; *fawin cho/zombi; lang a chat*

Shrub to 2 m high. True leaves scale-like. Leaf-like structures, termed phylloclades, paddle-like, to 15 cm long, with tiny flower clusters in the notches along the margins. Perianth of both male and female flowers red, the stamens of male flowers fused into a column. Fruit a capsule, three-furrowed, globular, 4 mm in diameter.

On rocky ground, near the sea and in wooded areas. Used medicinally in Antigua, especially for colds.

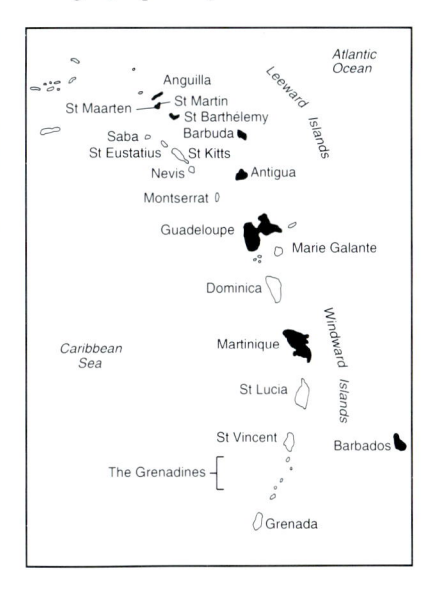

Tropical America

Throughout the Tropics

Florida, the Bahamas, the Greater and Lesser Antilles

57

Tragia volubilis

Tragia volubilis L.

vine nettle; (woman) stinging nettle; fireman; *lyann/zèb bwilan*; *zouti*

Twining, slightly woody vine, covered throughout in fine, stinging hairs. Leaves alternate, ovate to lanceolate, 3–6 cm long, margin toothed. Inflorescence a slender axillary raceme, to 7 cm long, of separate, inconspicuous male and female flowers. Fruit a capsule, roundish, flattened, hairy, 7 mm across.

Weed of thickets and waste places.

An effective treatment in the Grenadines for promoting urination.[29]

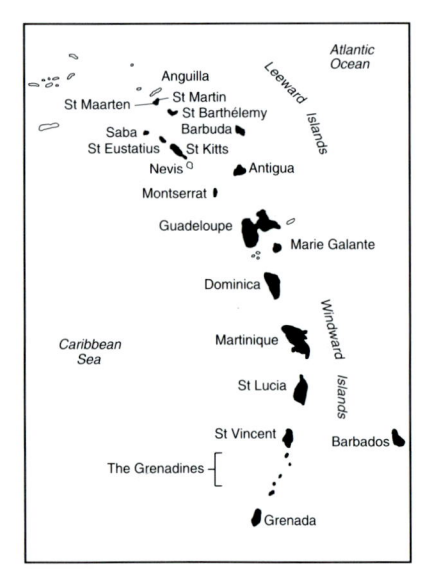

Tropical America

Sapindaceae – Ackee family

Cardiospermum microcarpum Kunth

heart seed; balloon vine; wild parsley; *lyann pèsi*; *pèsi bata*

Slender climbing vine with ribbed stem, square in cross-section and bearing minute scattered hairs. Leaves alternate, twice odd-pinnate, each leaflet conspicuously lobed, about 3 cm long. Inflorescence axillary, comprising a stalk about 5 cm long, bearing at the end two coiled tendrils and a few stalked flowers. Flowers with four white petals, 5 mm across. Fruit an inflated, three-lobed, bag-like capsule containing spherical seeds, 4 mm in diameter, black with a white heart.

A weed of agricultural fields and roadside verges.

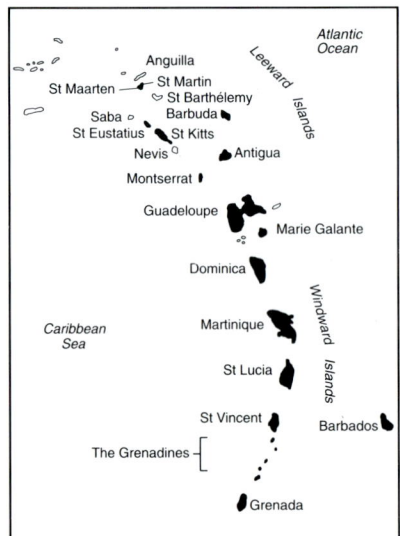

Throughout the Tropics

Cardiospermum microcarpum

Cupania americana

Cupania americana L.

candlewood/pearwood tree; *zyé a kwab*

Tree to 20 m high, young parts brown-felty. Leaves alternate, odd or even pinnate, leaflets 4–8, opposite or alternate, each obovate to 20 cm long, with conspicuous pinnate venation, tip blunt to notched, margin smooth or shallowly toothed. Flowers whitish, unisexual or bisexual, in terminal panicles, appearing March– May. Fruit a felt-covered, golden-brown, three-lobed capsule to 2 cm across, with shiny black seeds.

In woods at mid elevations.

A tea made from the leaves or fruit is taken for stomach problems.[9] ▶

Paullinia cururu

Paullinia cururu L.

sucking bottle; bread and cheese; *lyann a si*; *lyann mang*; *pèsi nwè*

Climbing vine, stem and leaves often reddish-purple. Leaves alternate, of three elliptic to ovate leaflets, each 5–12 cm long, margin coarsely toothed. Petiole winged. Stipules strap-shaped, to 5 mm long. Inflorescence, axillary, spike-like, to 15 cm long, with small white flowers and coiled tendrils. Fruit red, pear-shaped, to 2 cm long, splitting to reveal black seeds half-buried in a white, fleshy aril.

A climber in woods and waste places at low to mid elevations.

The stems are used in basket-making.

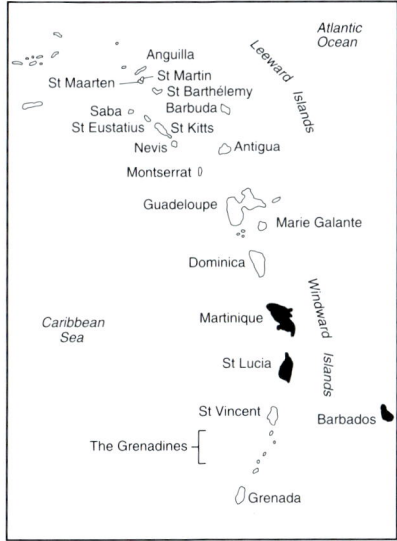

Tropical America

Impatiens balsamina

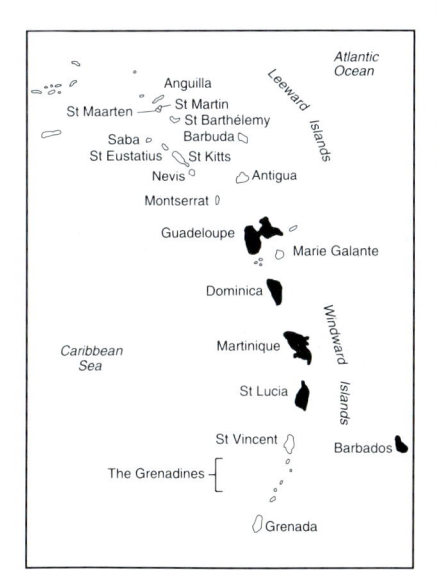

Greater and Lesser Antilles and northern South America

Balsaminaceae – Balsam family

Impatiens balsamina L.

(garden) balsam; impatience

Erect annual herb to 50 cm high. Stems succulent and smooth. Leaves alternate, narrowly elliptic to lanceolate, 6–14 cm long, margin toothed. Petiole bearing tiny, paired, oval to round glands. Flowers of various colours, 3 cm long, usually occurring singly in the upper axils. Sepals three, the lowermost petal-like, boat-shaped and with a long spur. Petals five, partly fused, the uppermost hood-like, the four laterals broad and spreading. Fruit an oval capsule, about 1 cm long, furry, long-stalked and splitting explosively.

In roadside ditches and waste places, a garden escape.

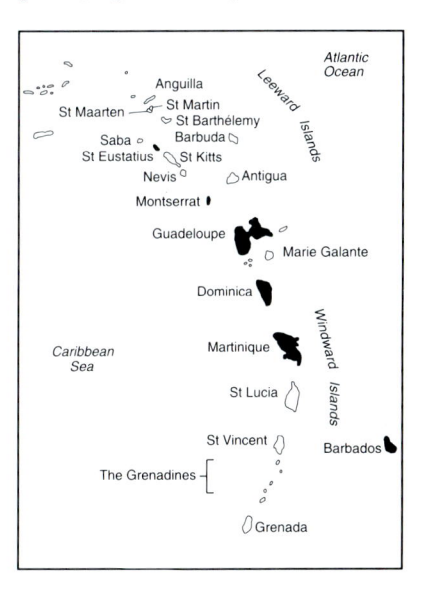

Native of Asia

Rhamnaceae – Dunk family

Colubrina arborescens (Miller) Sarg.

mauby; blackbead tree; snakewood; *mabi*

Small tree to 6 m high, the young shoots with a mat of short, dense, rust-coloured hairs. Leaves alternate, ovate to elliptic, 8–15 cm long, with a drip tip, paler below. Inflorescence a tight cluster in the axils, as long as the petioles. Flowers greenish, inconspicuous. Fruit a dry capsule, like a squashed ball, to 8 mm across, splitting into three to reveal shiny black seeds, 3 mm long.

In coastal and dry woods.

The bark can be used to make the bitter beverage, mauby,[51] but this drink is usually made from the related **C. elliptica**.

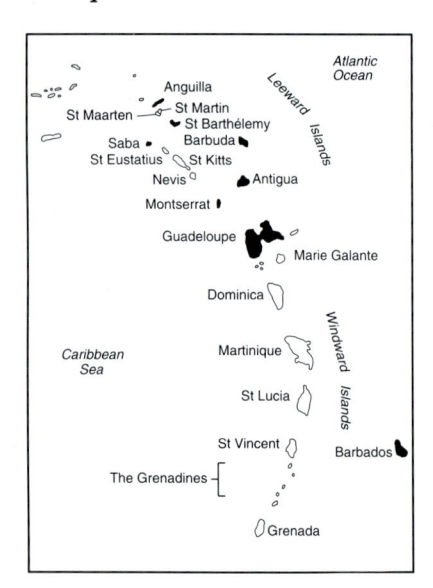

Greater Caribbean

Gouania lupuloides (L.) Urban

chaw/chew stick; white root; *lyann savon*

Climbing woody vine, with coiled tendrils at the base of the inflorescence. Leaves alternate, ovate, 5–8 cm long, often with a drip tip, margin shallowly toothed. Inflorescence axillary and spike-like, to 15 cm long, with small, fragrant white flowers. Fruit three-winged, 15 mm in diameter.

In woods and forests at low to mid elevations.

A woody twig is chewed at one end to create a brush and this, along with the foamy, bitter dentifrice generated, is rubbed over the teeth. A tea from the leaves was once considered a treatment for gonorrhea and an aphrodisiac.[23] A tea made from the bark is apparently good for indigestion.[9]

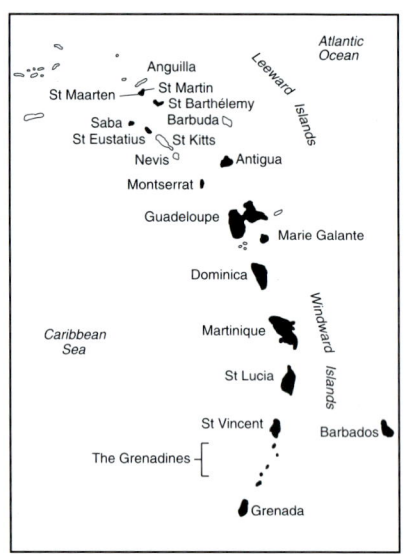

Greater Caribbean

Colubrina arborescens

Gouania lupuloides

Cissus verticillata

Vitaceae –
Grape vine family

Cissus verticillata
(L.) Nicolson & Jarvis

scratch wiss; skipping rope; pudding bush/wiss; *lyann mòl*; *lyann a dlo*; *kòd gwaté*; *(l)yàn(n) sèpan*

Climbing, somewhat succulent vine, stem often reddish. Leaves alternate, simple, shiny, ovate to heart-shaped but not sharp-tipped, to 8 cm in diameter, margin notched and spurred. Tendrils, axillary, tightly coiled. Inflorescence, a flat-topped, umbel-like cyme, borne opposite the leaf. Flowers pink to red-purple. Calyx cup-like. Petals four, triangular, each 2 mm long, bent back and readily shed. Stamens four, on the edges of a yellow disc through which the style protrudes. Fruit a black berry, globular to slightly ovoid, 8 mm long.

In forest canopies and by the roadside at low to mid elevations.

The leaves are applied as a poultice to sores and boils[6],[23],[31],[47] while the buds are used in a tea for stomach disorders.[49]

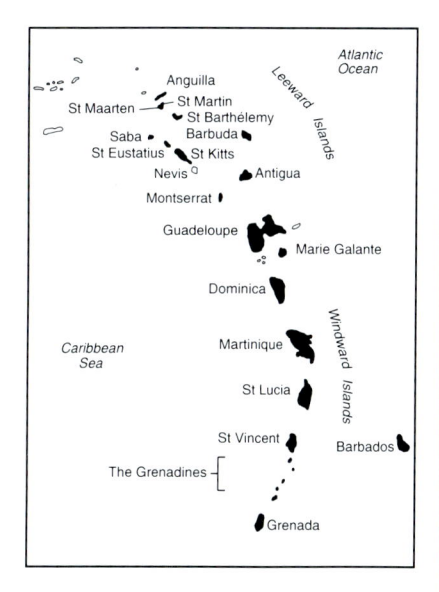

Greater Caribbean

Corchorus siliquosus

Tiliaceae –
Jute family

Corchorus siliquosus L.
broom(weed); widdi widdi bush; *ti bal(y)é*; *bal(y)é savann*

Woody shrub to 1 m high. Stem purplish. Stipules linear to lanceolate, to 6 mm long. Leaves alternate, ovate to lanceolate, to 15 mm long, margin toothed. Flowers yellow, about 5 mm across, single, or few to a cluster, in the axils. Capsule slim, cylindrical, 4–7 cm long, blunt-tipped, four small teeth at crown, almost hairless.

In pastures.

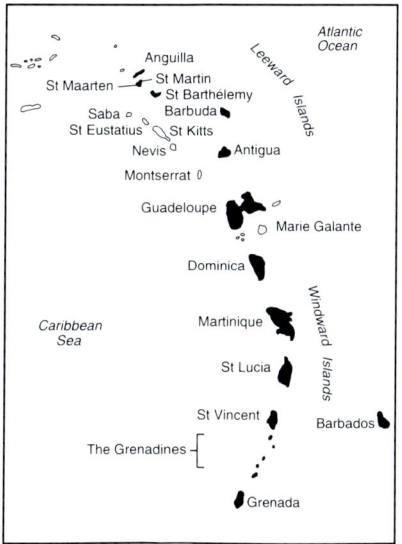

Greater Caribbean

Triumfetta semitriloba

Triumfetta semitriloba Jacq.
(wild) mahoe; black bush; *tèt a nèg*

Low, downy-stemmed shrub, to 1 m high. Stipules lanceolate and bristle-tipped, to 8 mm long. Leaves alternate, broadly ovate and often 3–5 lobed, to 12 cm in diameter, margin toothed, both surfaces velvety to touch. Flowers yellow, 8 mm across, clustered in the axils or opposite the upper, reduced leaves. Fruit a dry, spiny, globular capsule, to 5 mm in diameter.

A weed of damp places.

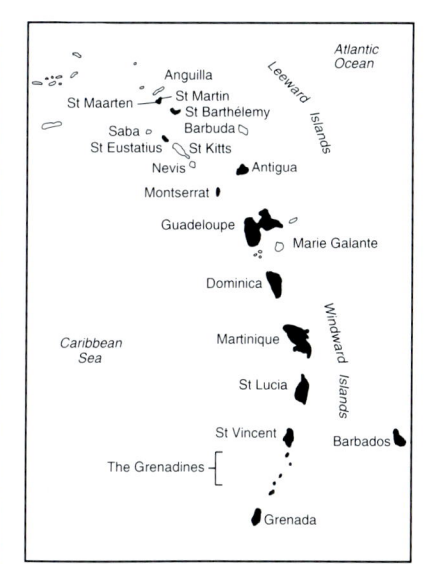

Tropical America and parts of Africa

Abutilon hirtum

Malachra alceifolia

Malvastrum americanum

Malvaceae – Hibiscus family

Abutilon hirtum (Lam.) Sweet

gwo mòv; *mòv savann*; *Mawi lopital*

Shrubby herb, 1–2 m high, with sticky glandular hairs. Leaves alternate, velvety beneath, heart-shaped, 3–12 cm long, petiole as long, margin toothed. Flowers yellow, often red-centred, occurring singly in leaf axils, 3 cm across. Fruit wheel-like, 2.5 cm across, of 20 or more kidney-shaped segments, radially arranged, each three-seeded.

Roadside weed.

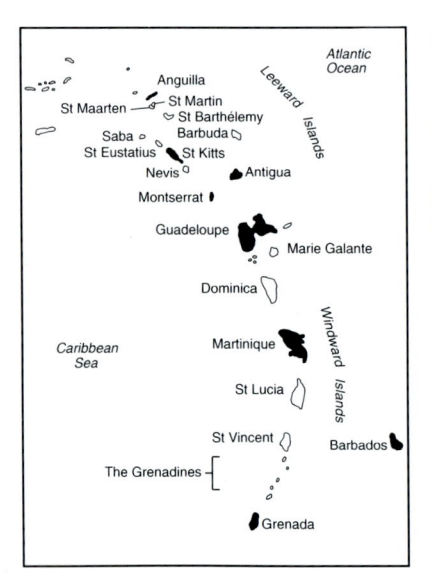

Malachra alceifolia Jacq.

wild okra; *gonbo bata/savann/zonbi*

Woody herb to 1 m high, often slender and unbranched, the stem densely covered in long, stiff, bristle-like hairs. Leaves alternate, rounded to ovate, rarely lobed, 3–10 cm long, margin toothed. Flowers yellow, 1–2 cm across, emerging from leafy bracts, several per axillary cluster. Fruit hemispherical, 4 mm across, of five segments, each one-seeded, enclosed by the dried leafy bracts.

Wayside weed.

A tea from the plant is reputedly a cold, cough[51] and thrush[16] remedy.

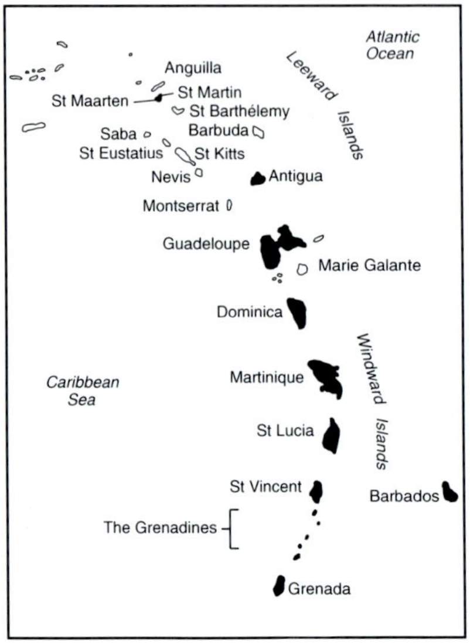

Malvastrum americanum (L.) Torrey

mòv savann; *Mawi lopital*

Perennial, shrubby herb to 1.5 m high, stem with tiny matted hairs. Leaves alternate, broadly ovate, 2–6 cm long, margin toothed. Flowers yellow, unstalked, about 1 cm across, in dense, chaffy spikes, the terminal ones at least 3 cm long. Flowers opening in the afternoon. Sepals hairy, persisting and enclosing the fruit. Fruit round, 5 mm across, comprising a ring of up to 15 horseshoe-shaped segments.

Roadside weed.

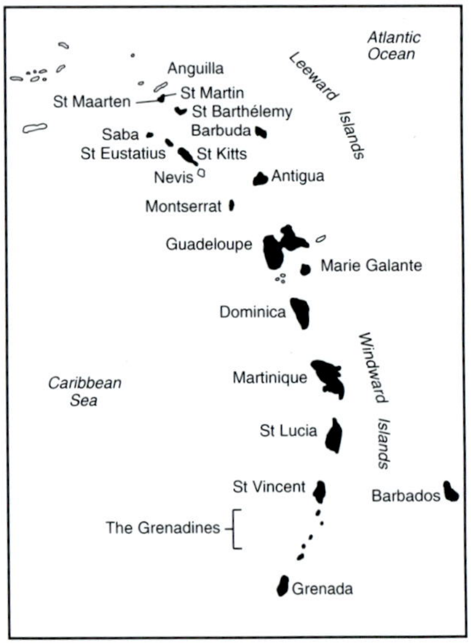

Old World native

Greater Caribbean

Tropics and subtropics

Sida acuta

Thespesia populnea

Sida acuta   Burm. f.

broom(weed); sweet broom; wire weed; *balyé midi/onzè/savann*

Bushy herb to 1 m tall, stem usually hairless. Stipules linear, 7 mm long. Leaves alternate, lanceolate to elliptic, 2–6 cm long, margin toothed above the base. Flowers yellow, 1 cm across, occurring singly or a few to each axillary cluster. Fruit round and flattened, to 5 mm across, of 8–10 spike-topped segments.

Wayside weed.

The pounded stem and root serve as a poultice for sprains.[28]

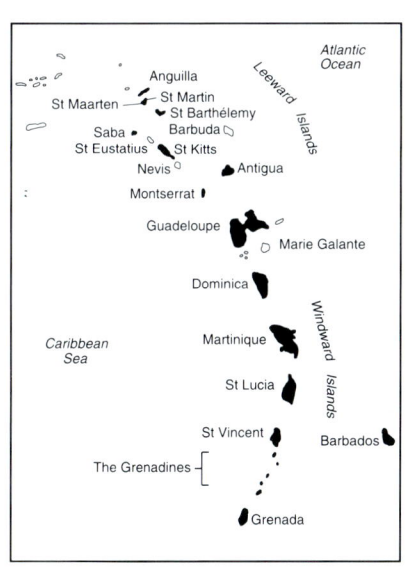

Throughout the Tropics

Thespesia populnea
(L.) Sol. ex Corr. Serr.

anodyne; (seaside) mahoe; hibiscus/snuff/tulip tree; binairy; John Bull tree; catalpa; *maho (bò-)lanmè*

Small tree to 10 m high. Leaves alternate, heart-shaped, 5–12 cm long, petiole as long. Flowers occurring singly in the axils. Calyx cup-like, to 8 mm deep, ringed by three bracts. Petals yellow, deep red at the base, turning pinkish with age, to 6 cm long. Fruit woody, like a squashed ball, about 3 cm in diameter.

Seashore and sandy beachlands.

Used as a living fence post in the Grenadines.[29] Provides a hard, termite-resistant wood[43],[44] used for boat-building[25],[49],[57] and even gunstocks.[42] Rope can be made from the bark[40] while the unripe fruit yields a yellow dye.[28] The flowers are edible.[40],[44] The leaves are applied to sores[35] and haemorrhoids[43] or made into a tea for high blood pressure.[45]

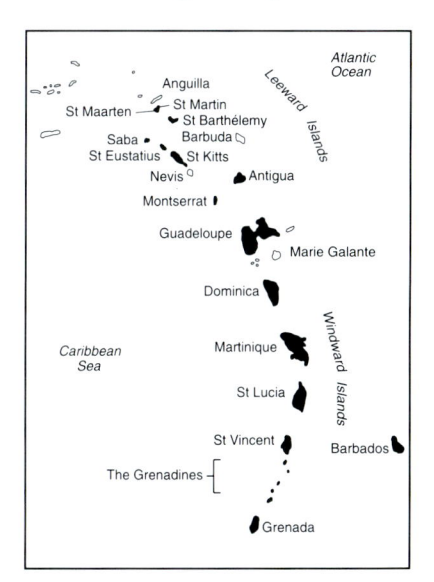

Throughout the Tropics

Urena lobata

Melochia nodiflora

Melochia tomentosa

Urena lobata L.

ballard bush; burr/indian mallow; *kouzen maho/wouj; gwan/pikan kouzen*

Shrub to 1.5 m high, reddish-stemmed and branched. Leaves alternate, irregularly lobed to ovate, 2–10 cm long, greyish beneath, margin irregularly toothed. Flowers pink, to 2 cm across, short-stalked and axillary. Fruit, to 1 cm across, a squashed globe of five segments, covered in hooked spines.

A weed of damp places.

An excellent source of fibre for sacking.[57] A tea from the leaves or flowers is drunk for stomach ache, colds and other ailments. [4],[9],[28],[51]

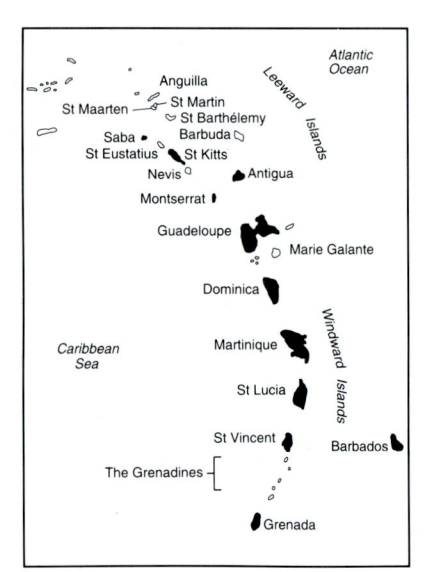

Sterculiaceae – Cocoa family

Melochia nodiflora Sw.

red dialthaea; broom; *mòv*

Bushy shrub to 1.5 m high, the young parts with fine hairs. Leaves alternate, ovate, 3–10 cm long, margin sharply toothed except the base. Inflorescence a reddish, ball-like cluster at the node. Flowers pink, virtually unstalked, appearing around December. Fruit almost globular, to 2 cm long, separating into five segments.

Roadside weed.

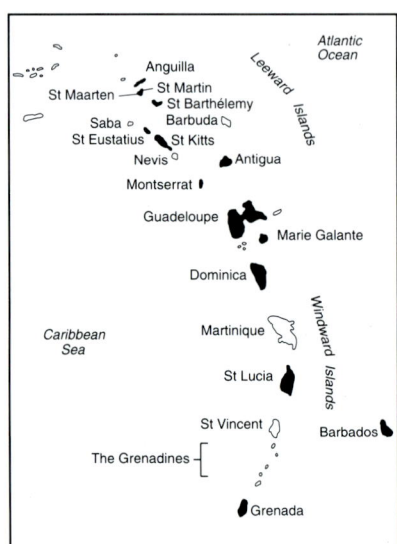

Melochia tomentosa L.

balsam; black torch/widow; sailor's broom; *bwa chanpinyon*

Shrub to 2 m high, greyish in colour due to fine woolly hairs. Leaves alternate, ovate to lanceolate, 2–7 cm long, with prominent pinnate venation, margin toothed. Stipules narrow to bristle-like, to 7 mm long. Flowers pink-purple, to 1 cm across, in axillary and terminal clusters, appearing December–April. Fruit a capsule, diamond-shaped in outline, to 9 mm long.

Roadside weed.

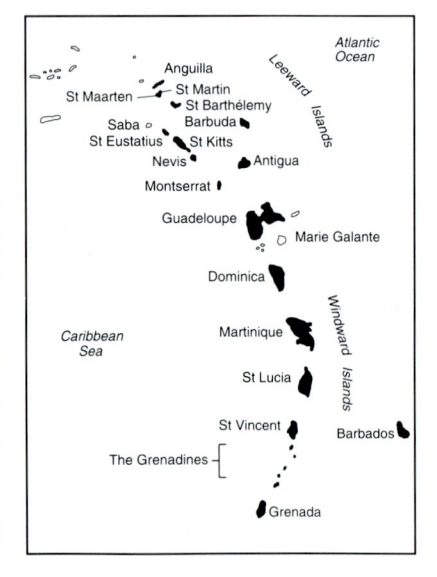

Virtually throughout the Tropics

Greater Caribbean

Greater Caribbean

Waltheria indica L.

buff/leather coat; marsh mallow; boater bush; *gimòv; mòv gwi*

Shrubby herb to 1 m high, the whole plant covered in short soft hairs. Stipules, lanceolate, to 8 mm long. Leaves alternate, oblong to trowel-shaped, 3–8 cm long, margin finely toothed. Flowers yellow, to 5 mm across, in ball-like clusters, arising from or sitting in the axils. Fruit a capsule, 2 mm long.

Wayside weed.

A red tea made from the shoots of this plant is considered 'cooling' as well as good for colds,[23],[28] infections,[4] thrush[16] and anaemia.[29] In Ghana the root is used as a chewing stick and the plant is considered an abortifacient.[1]

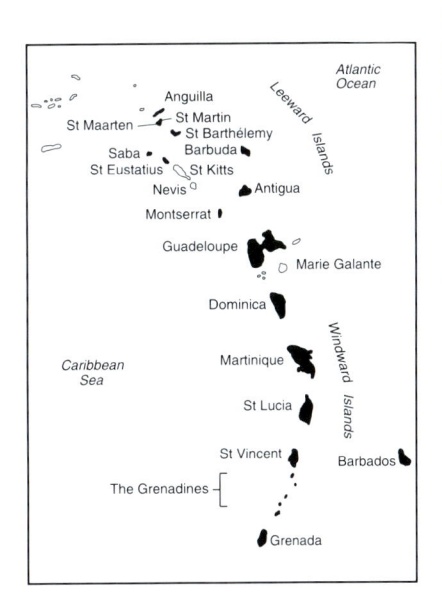

Waltheria indica

Clusia plukenetii

Tropical America, naturalised elsewhere

Clusiaceae (Guttiferae) –
Mammey apple family

Clusia plukenetii Urban

(gully) balsam; *awali*

Tree to 10 m high, with white latex and long hanging roots. Leaves opposite, dark green and fleshy, obovate, 7–14 cm long, round-tipped, stout-petioled. Plants either male or female. Inflorescence loosely branched. Flowers to 5 cm across, with 6–9 white or pink petals. Stamens numerous in male flowers and lacking anthers in female flowers. Fruit a spherical capsule, red and shiny, to 3 cm in diameter.

On rocky cliff sides and talus slopes and even as an epiphyte.

The fruit, like those of **C. rosea**, can be **poisonous**.[37] The roots are peeled, washed, split lengthwise and plaited to produce top-of-the-line baskets.

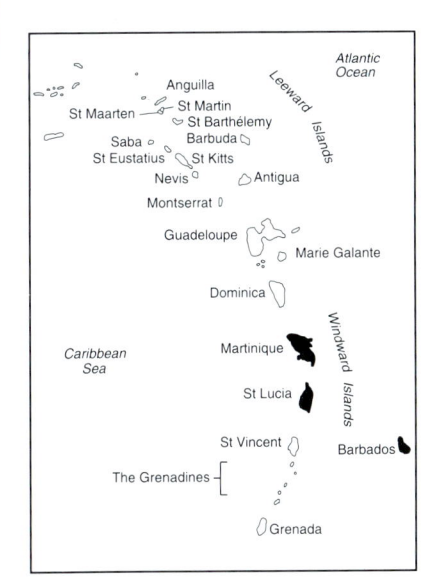

Endemic to the Lesser Antilles

Canellaceae

Canella winterana   (L.) Gaertner

pepper/wild cinnamon; cillament bush; *bwa kannèl*

Tree to 10 m high, the bark grey and aromatic, especially the inner bark. Leaves alternate, dark green and leathery, obovate to spatula-like, 2–10 cm long, round-tipped. Inflorescence usually terminal. Flowers with five red petals, 5 mm long, and staminal tube, 3 mm long. Fruit spherical to ovoid, 6 mm long, red to purple-black, sitting in the shallowly lobed, cup-like calyx.

In dry coastal forests.

The leaves are insecticidal and also poisonous to chickens. The bark, with volatile oils similar to those found in commercial cinnamon, makes a tea useful as a tonic[9],[44] and treatment for sore throat, indigestion and fever.[44] In the past a decoction was also used as a poultice for rheumatism and muscular pains.[31] With their red berries, sprigs make an effective Christmas decoration.

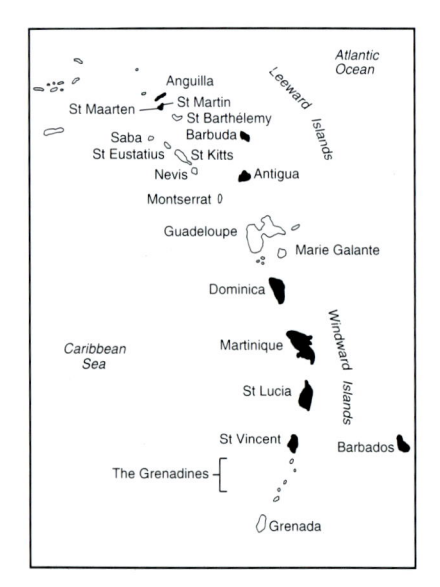

Canella winterana

Flacourtiaceae

Casearia decandra   Jacq.

wild honey tree; wild cherry; jumbie apple; *bwa jòn; jòn a zé; koko wavet; bwa koko kawet*

Small tree to 10 m high, young leaves often reddish. Leaves alternate, ovate to elliptic, 3–9 cm long, with a drip tip, margin shallowly and irregularly scalloped. Minute dots and dashes visible in leaf held up to the sun. Flowers white, in tight axillary clusters, appearing *en masse*, lasting a few days. Sepals five, oblong and petal-like. Petals absent. Stamens 10, 5 mm long. Fruit spherical, fleshy, 1 cm in diameter, orange to red.

In dry woods; sometimes cultivated.

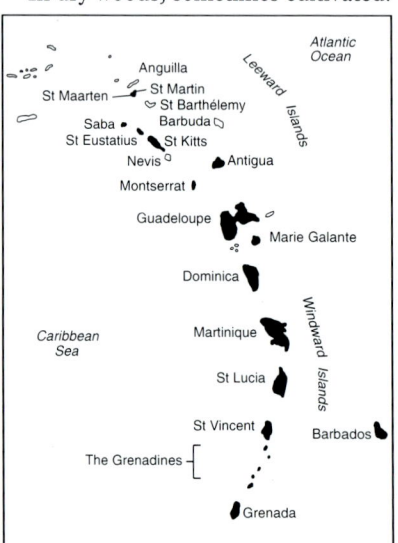

Casearia decandra

Passiflora suberosa

Passifloraceae – Passion fruit family

Passiflora suberosa   L.

ink vine; threft leaf; pop bush; *pòm lyann hazyé*

Slender climber. Leaves alternate, three-lobed, to 10 cm long. Petiole with glands near the middle. Flowers small, not showy, without bracts or petals, 3 cm across. Sepals five, slender, petal-like, creamish. Corona of outcurved filaments, purple at base. Berry ovoid, black, 2 cm long.

Wayside weed of the dry zone.

The French in St Lucia used the crushed leaves of this plant to treat venomous snake-bites.[31] A tea from the leaves is used to ease period pains[29] and as a cold/fever remedy.[56]

Greater Caribbean

Tropical America

Opuntia dillenii

Cactaceae – Cactus family

Opuntia dillenii (Ker Gawler) Haw.

flat hand dildo; cactus; casha; jumbie/sour prickle; prickle pear; *mal watjèt*; *watjèt (flè) jòn*

Much branched plant to 1.5 m high. Joints flattened and oval to 20 cm long with tufts of a few arching, yellowish spines, to 3 cm long, and numerous slender irritating bristles. Flowers yellow or orange, borne singly on the edges of the joints. Fruit reddish-purple, obovoid, to 4 cm long.

In dry, coastal areas.

The pads can be heated and applied to sprains, boils and tumours,[44] or a tea can be made from them to treat inflammation.[28],[44]

Pilosocereus royeni (L.) Byles & G. Rowley

(columnar/candelabra) cactus; pipe organ cactus; dildo; dul-dul; *syèj*

Erect plant, to 4 m high, unbranched but can form large clumps. Stems cylindrical, longitudinally grooved with clusters of needle-like spines along the ribs. Flowers, to 6 cm long, borne singly on the upper parts of the ribs, August–October. Perianth white. Fruit red, almost spherical, 4 cm across.

In dry areas near the coast.

A very variable species, once considered to be several species.[30] The fruit is edible.[18],[44] In Antigua the dead dried stems are used by children as fireworks; they crackle and pop when burnt.

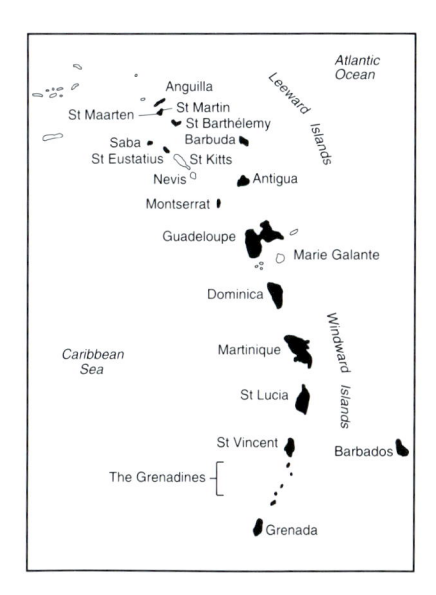

Pilosocereus royeni

Tropical America

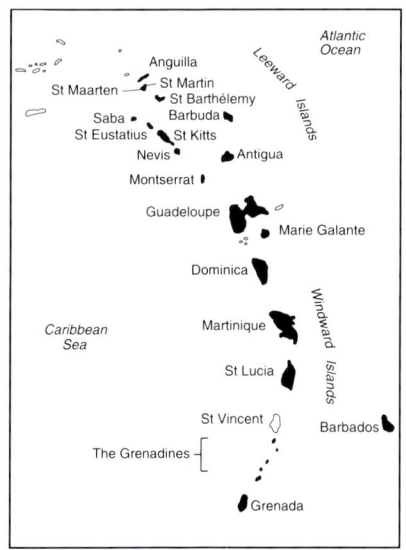

Southern USA, Greater and Lesser Antilles

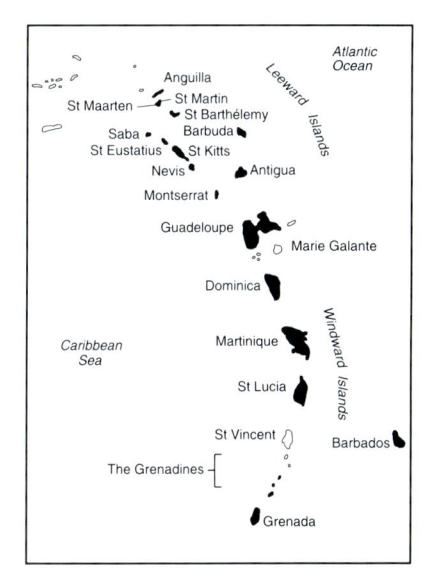

Lesser Antilles, Puerto Rico and the Virgin Islands

Ammannia coccinea

Lythraceae –
Queen-of-flowers family

Ammannia coccinea Rottb.

Herb to 1 m high, often branching near the base. Stem hairless, fleshy and often reddish. Leaves opposite, slender and pointed, the base clasping, to 10 cm long. Flowers deep pink, unstalked, in axillary clusters, the style protruding. Fruit a semispherical capsule, 4 mm long.

In freshwater swamps and marshy ditches.

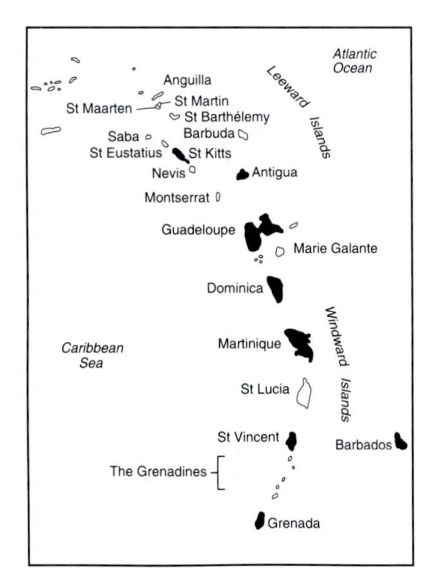

Southern USA and tropical America

Rhizophoraceae –
Mangrove family

Rhizophora mangle L.

red mangrove; *mang wouj*

Tree to 8 m high with numerous prop roots. Leaves opposite, elliptic, dark green and shiny above, to 12 cm long, long-petioled. Stipules narrow, to 4 cm long. Inflorescence of two or three flowers. Sepals yellowish, lanceolate, to 1.5 cm long, spreading. Petals yellow, woolly within, to 1 cm long. Fruit a leathery cone, to 3 cm long, germinating on the tree, the stake-like hypocotyl to 30 cm long.

The major component of Caribbean mangroves.

The bark can be used for tanning[24],[44] and, with its high astringency, is used to counter diarrhoea, haemorrhaging and dysentery.[9],[44] Growing at the fringes of mangrove swamps, it is an important builder of land and provides shelter for several juvenile marine species.

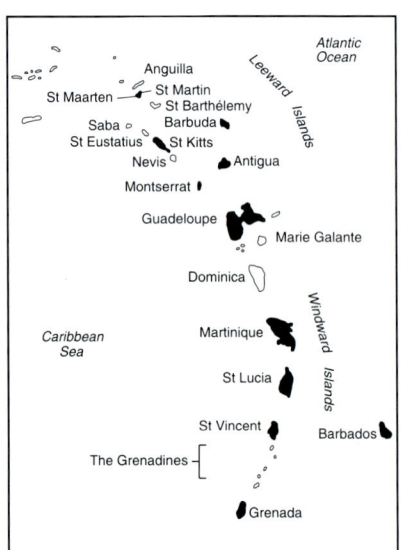

Southern USA, tropical America and West Africa

Combretaceae –
West Indian Almond Family

Conocarpus erectus L.

button bush/mangrove/wood; iron mang; *olivyé bò-lanmè; paltivyé wouj*

Shrub or small tree to 6 m high. Twigs winged or angled. Leaves alternate, elliptic to slightly obovate, to 9 cm long, with a pair of glands on the margin at the leaf base. Flowers small and creamish, bisexual or male, in ball-like heads, to 8 mm diameter, in terminal panicles. Fruits in an ovoid head, resembling a pine cone, to 1 cm long.

In sandy beachlands and the landward fringe of mangroves.

The wood makes high quality charcoal.[44] A tea from the bark is used to treat eye inflammation, prickly heat[44] and syphilis.[9] The introduced silver-leaved form, cv. Silver Dollar, makes a handsome hedge plant on seafront properties.

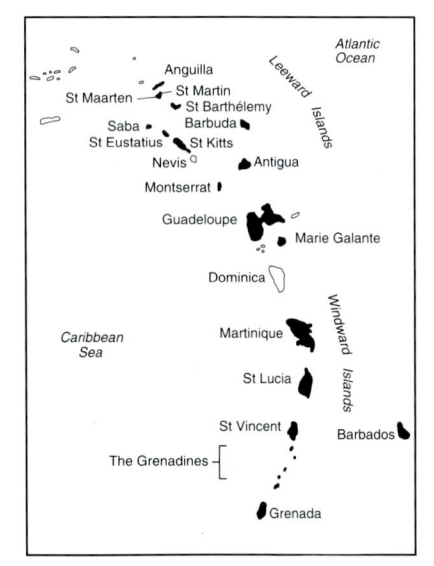

Tropical America, the Galapagos Islands and West Africa

Rhizophora mangle

Conocarpus erectus

Eugenia monticola

Myrtaceae –
Guava family

Eugenia monticola   (Sw.) DC.

rodwood; birds/black cherry; *gouyavyé*; *méwizyé (ti fèy)*

Shrub or small tree to 6 m high. Young branches finely pubescent. Leaves opposite, elliptic to ovate, 2–4 cm long, with a drip tip. Inflorescence axillary, bearing one or a few small white flowers. Petals four. Sepals four. Fruit spherical, 5 mm across, red to black, often with galls.

A common understorey shrub of forests at low to mid elevations.

The trunk grows erect and very straight, making it ideal for fashioning walking sticks and tool handles. The fruit is reportedly edible.[41]

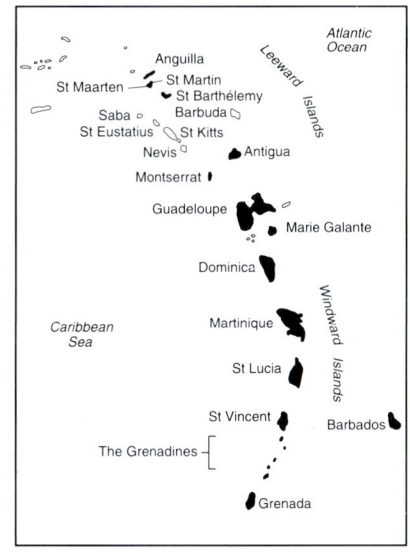

Greater and Lesser Antilles and northern South America

Myrcia citrifolia var. *citrifolia*

Myrcia citrifolia   (Aublet) Urban
var. *citrifolia*

(red) rodwood; black berry; *bwa gwiyé*; *méwizyé*; *bwa ti fèy*

Shrub or small tree to 6 m high. Leaves opposite, fleshy, shiny, often reddish, rounded to broadly elliptic, 3–6 cm long, sometimes with red, pimple-like galls. Flowers white and showy, in widely branched panicles. Sepals five. Petals five. Stamens numerous and twice as long as the petals. Fruit spherical, deep red, 1 cm in diameter, crowned by the calyx.

In full sun, at low to mid elevations.

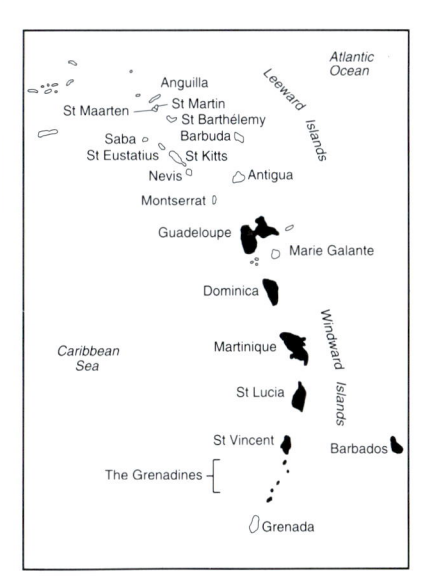

Greater and Lesser Antilles and northern South America

69

Melastomataceae – Melastome family

Miconia laevigata   (L.) D. Don

golden bush; candle/hog wood; *bwa sann/kòtlèt; (ti) kwékwé*

Shrub to 5 m high, young parts rusty-scaly. Leaves opposite, ovate to lanceolate, prominently five- or seven-veined, 8–15 cm long, with a drip tip and toothed margin, the teeth extending into tiny bristles. Inflorescence a terminal panicle, to 15 cm long. Flowers unstalked or on very short stalks. Calyx markedly five-lobed. Petals five, white or pink, to 5 mm long. Fruit a blue-black berry, 4 mm in diameter.

Understorey shrub of forests at low to mid elevations.

This is but one of the 21 *Miconia* species of the Lesser Antilles.[30]

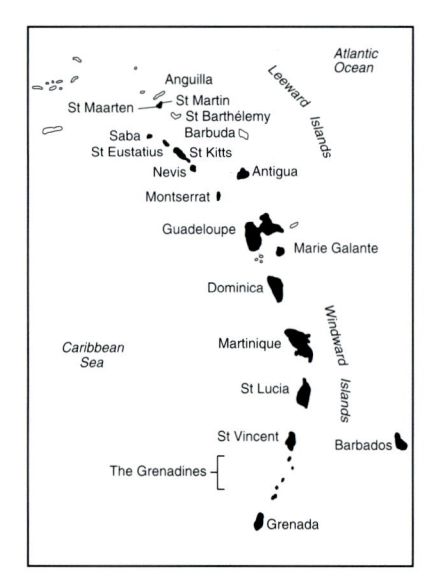

Miconia laevigata

Greater Caribbean

Onagraceae

Ludwigia octovalvis   (Jacq.) Raven

many-seed; wild clove; *jiwòf glo/ma; jèwonflé*

Shrubby herb to 1.5 m high, with minute scattered hairs. Leaves alternate, lanceolate, 4–10 cm long. Flowers yellow, 2 cm across, borne singly on stalks to 2 cm long, in upper leaf axils. Fruit cylindrical, tapering to base, eight-ribbed, 2–5 cm long, crowned with four sepals.

In wet or marshy places.

Used to make a tea to prevent miscarriages.

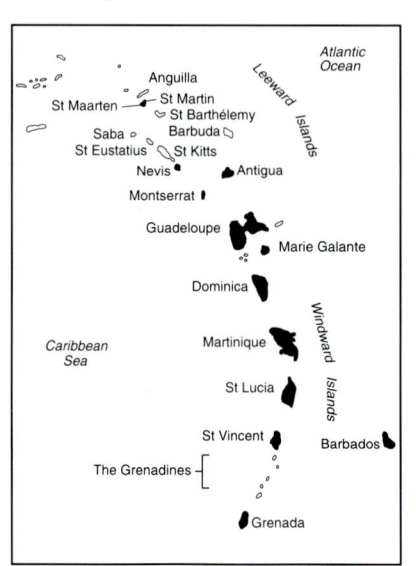

Ludwigia octovalvis

Throughout the Tropics

Apiaceae (Umbelliferae) – Carrot family

Eryngium foetidum   L.

fitweed; blessed thistle; cat claw; cla-cla; shado beni/vinni; *chadwon béni; zéb a fè*

Biennial herb to 40 cm high with a tap root. Stem with Y-shaped branching and conspicuous ribbing. Leaves of the basal rosette paddle-shaped, 3–20 cm long, the margin toothed and spiny. Leaves at the nodes deeply lobed and spiny. Inflorescence a thimble-like head, to 1.5 cm long, at the centre of a star-like whorl of slender, spiny, leaf-like bracts, each to 3 cm long. Flowers inconspicuous and unstalked. Fruit ovoid, to 2 mm long.

In damp, shady areas.

It is claimed the strong pungent odour exuding from the crushed plant can revive those suffering fits, convulsions and hysteria.[22],[25],[31] A tea made from the leaves or root is used to treat stomach problems,[23],[28],[47] fever,[9],[18],[28],[45],[51],[56] coughs and colds.[23],[25],[47],[56] With their celantro (coriander-like) flavour, the plant tops are also used to season meat dishes.[51] ▶

Eryngium foetidum

Jaquinia armillaris

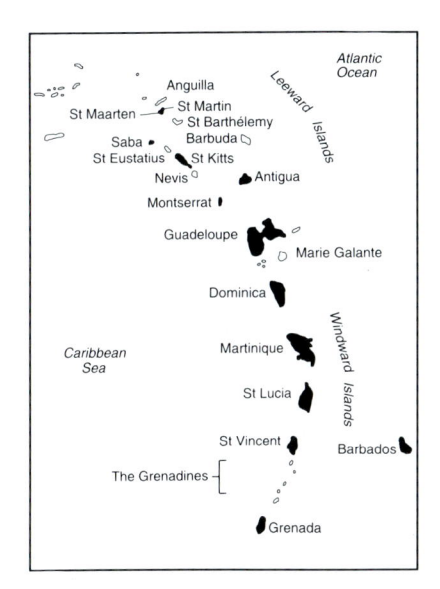

Theophrastaceae

Jaquinia armillaris   Jacq.

torchwood; pie crust (bark); *flanbo blan*; *bwa bwaslè/lafyèv*; *mal bwa chandèl*

Small tree to 6 m high, the trunk often greenish-yellow. Leaves in apparent whorls at the branch tips, leathery, pale green, obovate, 4–10 cm long, blunt and often notched at the tip. Inflorescence a terminal raceme. Flowers regular, bisexual. Calyx of five overlapping lobes. Corolla creamish, bell-shaped, five-lobed, to 5 mm long. Inner petal-like staminodes, alternating with the petals. Stamens five, clustered around the superior ovary and short style. Fruit almost spherical, 1 cm in diameter, orange.

In coastal woods and along exposed sea cliffs.

This makes an attractive, small tree when cultivated. The young shoots when crushed can be used to stupefy fish.[18] The Caribs used the seeds of this tree to make bracelets.[49]

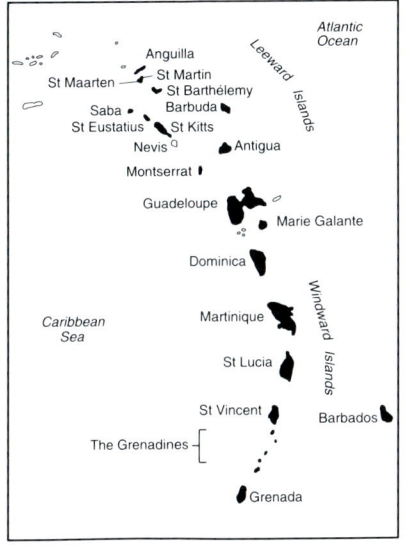

Ardisia solanacea

Myrsinaceae

Ardisia solanacea   Roxb.

Shrub or small tree to 4 m high. Leaves alternate, shiny, slightly fleshy, obovate to elliptic, 8–15 cm long, petioles and young leaves reddish. Inflorescence a drooping, axillary cluster. Calyx cup-like with five rounded lobes. Corolla of five pointed segments, pinkish and arching backwards. Anthers forming a column around the style. Fruit berry-like, red turning black, shiny, 1 cm in diameter.

In coastal areas.

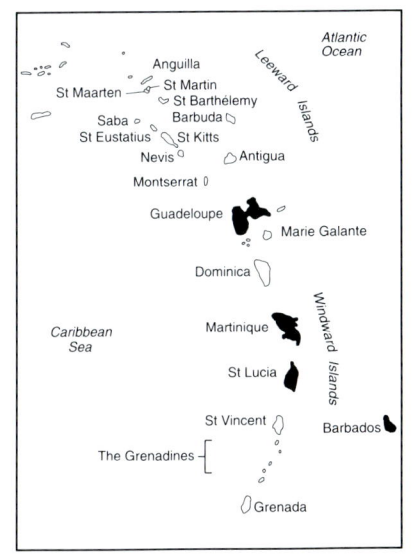

Throughout the Tropics

Greater and Lesser Antilles and northern South America

Native of Asia, naturalised

Plumbaginaceae – Plumbago family

Plumbago scandens L.

wild plumbago; Doctor John; old woman's bush; blister bush; *sinapis*; *mutad péyi*

Scrambling shrub. Leaves alternate, ovate to lanceolate or elliptic, 4–12 cm long, without stipules. Petiole to 1 cm long. Inflorescence a slender, terminal spike to 20 cm long. Calyx with conspicuous glandular hairs. Corolla white, a tube, 2–3 cm long, abruptly flaring out into five lobes. Flowers with long slender stamens and a short style or vice versa. Fruit oblong, brown and shiny, to 1 cm long.

Wayside weed.

The bruised leaves applied to the skin are an old remedy for rheumatism.[31]

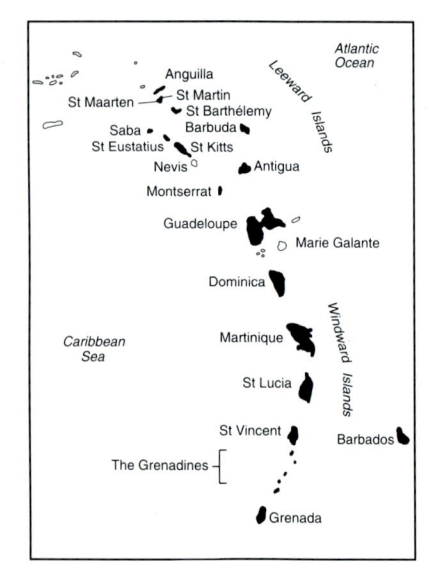

Tropical America

Plumbago scandens

Sapotaceae – Sapodilla family

Sideroxylon foetidissimum Jacq.

mastic; mast wood; *(a)koma (franc)*

Tree to 25 m tall, the trunk very straight. Leaves spirally arranged, elliptic, 6–10 cm long, margin wavy, petioles 3–4 cm long. Flowers yellow, slender-stalked, in axillary clusters. Fruit orange-yellow, single-seeded, plum-like, 2 cm long.

In forests at low to mid elevations.

Value as a timber led to its virtual extinction in Barbados.[11] Used medicinally to treat diarrhoea, fever, stomach pain and migraine.[45]

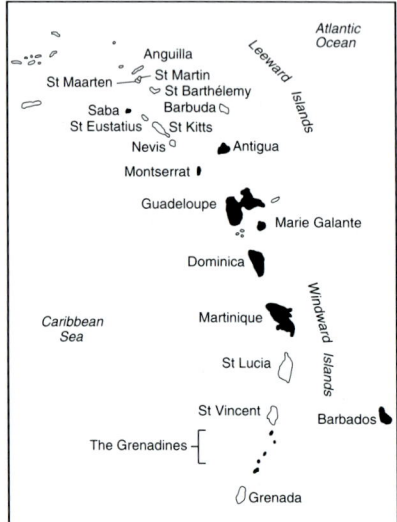

Greater Caribbean

Sideroxylon foetidissimum

Oleaceae – Olive family

Jasminum fluminense Vell.

wild jasmine; ink vine; *jasmen blan/boukè*

Slender scrambling vine, young stems with tiny hairs. Leaves opposite, compound of three roundly ovate to spade-shaped leaflets, each to 5 cm long or wide, with a short, abruptly pointed tip. Flowers white and fragrant, numerous, in loose axillary or terminal cymes. Corolla tube about 2 cm long, topped by five–nine slender lobes. Berries spherical, purplish to black, about 7 mm in diameter.

Wayside weed.

Four other ***Jasminum*** spp., all Old World natives, are cultivated in the region.[30] ▶

Jasminum fluminense

Spigelia anthelmia

Loganiaceae

Spigelia anthelmia L.

loggerhead/water weed; worm bush/ grass; bouvier; *zèb pwazon; (zèb) brenvilyé*

Erect annual herb to 30 cm high. Leaves opposite, clustered at the shoot tips, narrowly ovate to lanceolate, 3–11 cm long, without petioles. Inflorescence a terminal or axillary curved spike. Flowers with a calyx of five slender teeth and a pink five-lobed corolla. Fruit a bi-lobed, minutely warty capsule, about 5 mm across.

A common weed.

Contains spigeline, which is effective against worms, but the whole plant should be considered **poisonous**,[16],[23],[31],[37] even for cattle.[3],[25] Most members of this family contain poisonous alkaloids, strychnine being the best known of these.[26]

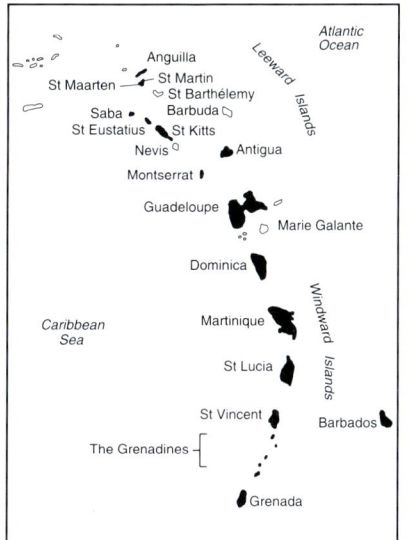

Gentianaceae – Gentian family

Enicostema verticillatum

(L.) Engler ex Gilg

part-of-man-life; *bal(y)é savann (bata); lang poul*

Herb to 50 cm high, stem square in cross-section. Leaves opposite, conspicuously three-nerved, lanceolate, 3–7 cm long. Flowers white, unstalked, clustered at the nodes. Calyx of five pointed lobes. Corolla longer, cigar-shaped, hardly open. Stamens five. Capsule ovoid, 5 mm long.

Weed of pastures.

A tea made from the leaves is considered highly effective against fevers.[29]

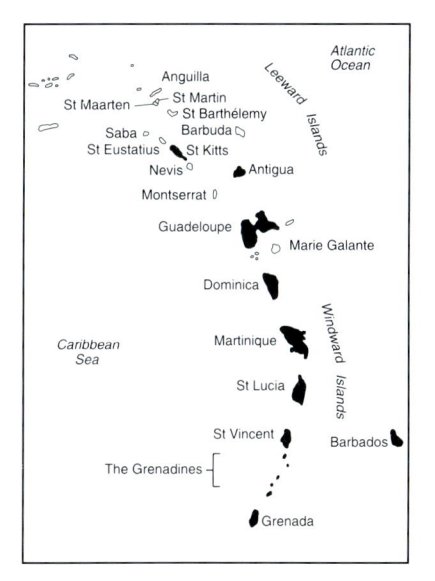

Enicostema verticillatum

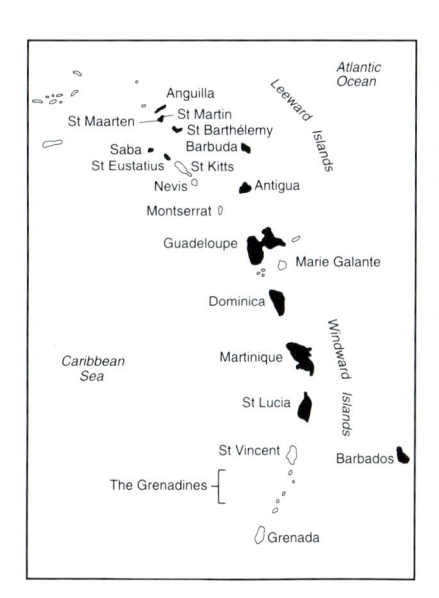

Native of Africa, naturalised

Greater Caribbean

Greater Caribbean

Rauvolfia tetraphylla

Apocynaceae – Oleander family

Rauvolfia tetraphylla L.

Shrub to 1 m high, with white latex throughout. Leaves mainly in whorls of four, ovate to elliptic, 3–10 cm long, minutely woolly beneath. Flowers white, in lateral clusters. Fruit a drupe, about 5 mm across, pink going red then black.

Wayside weed.

This plant is rich in reserpine,[3] a drug widely used in the treatment of hypertension.

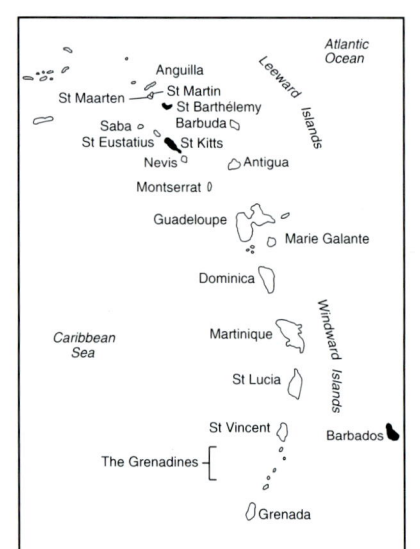

Asclepiadaceae – Stephanotis family

Asclepias curassavica L.

Indian root; red head/top; (poison) Johanna; sheep poison; wild ipecacuanha; *zèb Man Bwaven*; *ipéka bata*; *kóton kadwi*

Usually unbranched, hollow-stemmed herb to 60 cm high, with white latex. Leaves opposite, lanceolate, 5–12 cm long, with petiole about 1 cm long. Flowers several, in long-stalked umbels in the upper leaf axils. Corolla five-lobed, bright orange-red, forming a skirt below the central yellow column of the style, anthers and shielding corona. Fruit lanceolate in outline, 6–9 cm long.

Wayside weed, typically at mid elevations.

Named after the Greek god of medicine, appropriate for a former medicinal plant. It is effective against worms but is very dangerous to use and should be regarded as highly **poisonous**.[18],[45],[50] Important food source for Monarch butterfly larvae.

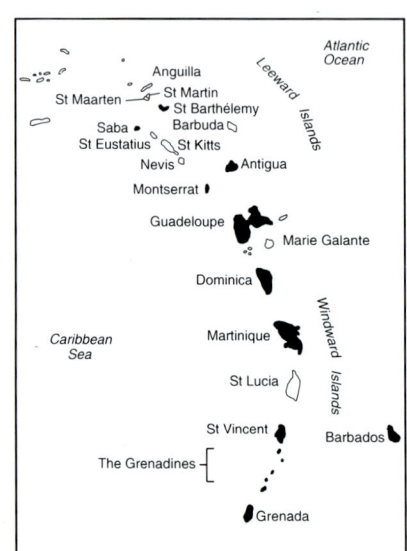

Asclepias curassavica

Calotropis procera

Greater Caribbean

Tropical America

74

Calotropis procera   (Aiton) Aiton f.

French cotton; monkey apple; cow heel; sprain leaf; milk bush; giant milkweed; *laswa*; *bwa kannon*; *bwa péta*

Grey-green, smooth-stemmed shrub, to 3 m high, with white latex. Leaves opposite, saucer-shaped to obovate, 12–24 cm long, with a short pointed tip. Flowers in large axillary umbels. Corolla, to 2.5 cm across, five-lobed, white with purple markings. Fruit green and sac-like, to 15 cm long, filled with silky-haired seeds.

In waste areas, especially near the coast.

This is a **poisonous** plant, rich in digitalis-like compounds, but with such an acrid sap that substantial quantities are not usually ingested.[37] The latex can be rubbed on the skin to treat rheumatism,[23],[45] although it may cause allergic skin reactions.[37] Furthermore, it is corrosive and depilatory[14] and is a centuries-old treatment for tumours, calluses and ringworm.[31] In Ghana the plant is regarded as an indicator of underground water.[1]

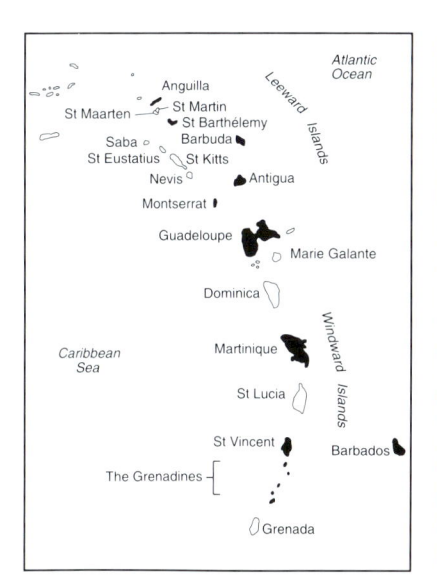

Metastelma barbadense

Metastelma barbadense   Schltr.

Slender climber with white sap. Stem often with minute scattered hairs. Leaves opposite, oval to ovate, 1–2 cm long, with an abrupt, sharply pointed tip. Flowers small, white and star-shaped, 2–5 per axillary umbel. Fruit not seen.

In dry woodland

The more widespread species, **M. parviflorum**, closely resembles this plant but the flower buds are club-shaped rather than globular.

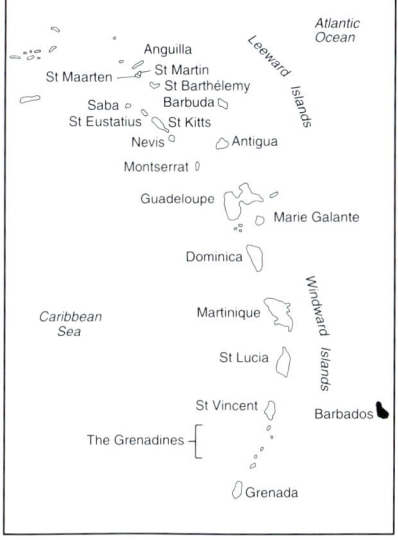

Evolvulus nummularius

Convolvulaceae –
Sweet potato family

Evolvulus nummularius   (L.) L.

véwonik

Creeping herb, rooting at each node. Stem with minute hairs. Leaves alternate, distinctly petioled, elliptic to rounded, to 1 cm long. Flowers white, occurring singly in the axils. Corolla flat and spreading, short-tubed, to 7 mm wide. Capsule globular, 3 mm across.

In pastures and semi-shade.

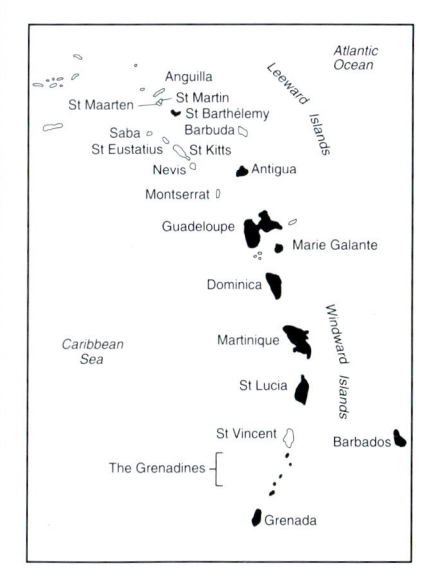

Native of Old World Tropics, naturalised

Endemic to Barbados

Throughout the Tropics

Ipomoea hederifolia

Ipomoea obscura

Ipomoea hederifolia L.

scarlet ipomoea; *liseron rouge*

Twining vine with slender, hairless stems. Leaves alternate, long-stalked, heart-shaped to three-lobed. Flowers several per cyme, produced November–January. Corolla scarlet, to 3 cm long, narrowly tubular, abruptly flaring outwards, the stamens and style protruding. Capsule ball-shaped, splitting at maturity, to 8 mm across.

In waste areas, especially roadside verges.

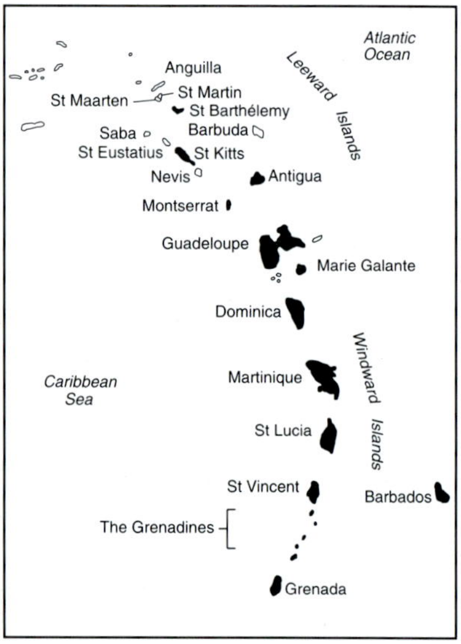

Ipomoea obscura (L.) Ker Gawler

Slender twiner. Stem with long hairs or with inconspicuous, minute hairs. Leaves alternate, roundly heart-shaped, to 6 cm long, with scattered hairs. Flowers one to a few together. Corolla funnel-shaped, about 2 cm long, white with a purple throat. Capsule dome-shaped and pointed, to 1 cm high, straw-coloured, splitting into four segments.

In waste areas.

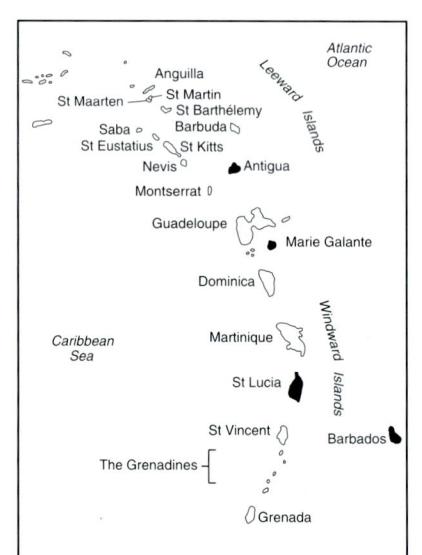

Ipomoea pes-caprae

Ipomoea pes-caprae (L.) R. Br. ssp. *brasiliensis* (L.) Ooststr.

seaside yam; seaside morning glory; sea vine/wiss; *patat bò-lanmè*

Creeping, fleshy vine with long, robust, purplish stems. Leaves alternate, roundish to oblong, to 8 cm long, bi-lobed or notched at the tip. Flowers usually borne singly. Corolla funnel-shaped, mauve, to 5 cm long. Capsule globular, 1 cm across, splitting into four segments.

On beaches and near the coast.

Young leaves applied to stings from marine animals provide relief,[45] apparently due to antihistaminic effects.[44] The plant also has purgative properties.[31],[45] ▶

Tropical America

Native of Old World Tropics

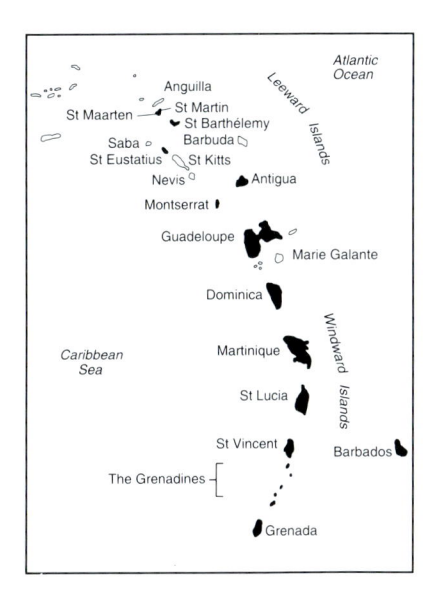

Jacquemontia pentantha

Merremia dissecta

Jacquemontia pentantha (Jacq.) Don

lyann blé; liseron bleu

Twining vine, young parts with scattered microscopic hairs. Stem often reddish-brown. Leaves alternate, narrowly heart-shaped, to 8 cm long. Flowers in axillary clusters. Corolla violet to pale blue with a white throat, broadly funnel-shaped, to 2 cm across, the stamens and style prominently exposed. Capsule globular, enclosed by the sepals.

Weed of roadside verges and waste places.

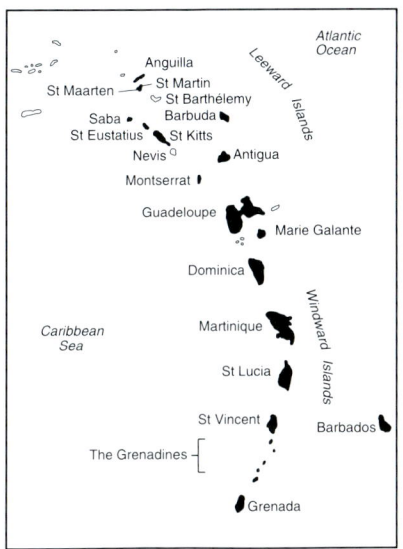

Merremia dissecta (Jacq.) H. Hallier

sprain bush; noyo vine; *lyann noyo; méné/mennen vini*

Twining vine. Stem usually smooth, often reddish. Leaves alternate, palmately lobed, almost to the base, into 5–7 segments, each lobed and coarsely toothed, to 7 cm long. Flowers with buds, triangular in outline, several per axillary stalk. Corolla funnel-like, white with a crimson throat, to 4 cm long and broad. Sepals translucent, boat-shaped, overlapping, to 2 cm long. Fruit a papery, dome-like capsule to 1 cm high, atop the outspread, persisting sepals.

Weed of waste places.

In the Grenadines a cough syrup for infants is prepared from the leaves.[29]

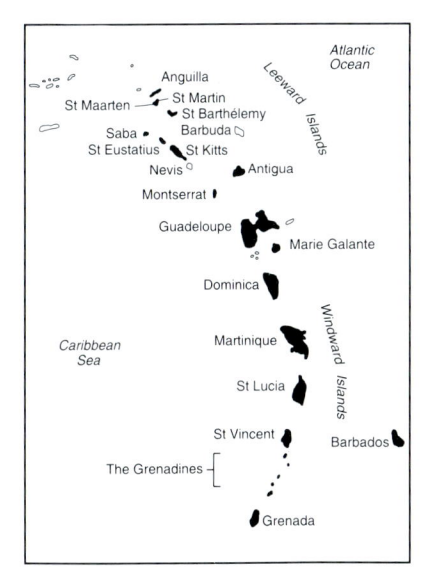

Tropical seashores

Tropical America

Tropical America

Nama jamaicensis

Hydrophyllaceae

Nama jamaicensis L.

herbe couchée

Flat, spreading annual herb. Leaves obovate, to 1.5 cm long, tapering into the base. Flowers regular, borne singly or in pairs. Corolla white, tubular, with five shallow lobes, about 7 mm long. Calyx segments, strap-like to 5 mm long. Capsule 5 mm long.

A weed; common in lawns.

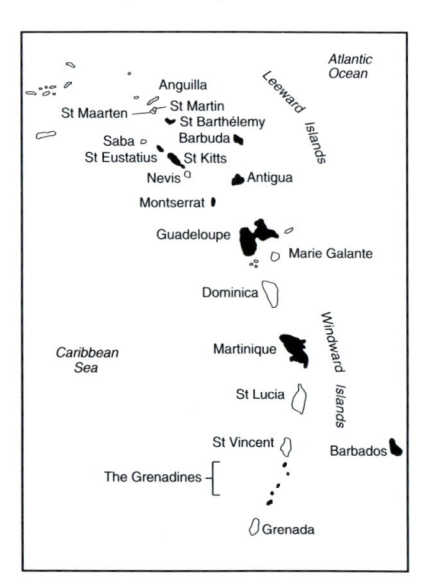

Southern USA, Central America and the Caribbean

Boraginaceae – Borage family

Argusia gnaphalodes (L.) Heine

seaside lavender/rosemary; iodine bush; *womaren*

Erect shrub to knee-height, greyish in colour due to dense silky hairs, lower parts of shoots bearded with dead leaves. Leaves alternate, linear to paddle-shaped, 4–8 cm long, to 1 cm wide, without a distinct petiole. Inflorescence a tight scorpioid cyme on a stalk 3–5 cm long. Corolla white, to 6 mm long; calyx about 5 mm long and woolly. Individual fruit green and succulent, four-lobed, to 1 cm in diameter, fusing to form a curved aggregate, drying to form black nutlets.

Seashore shrub.

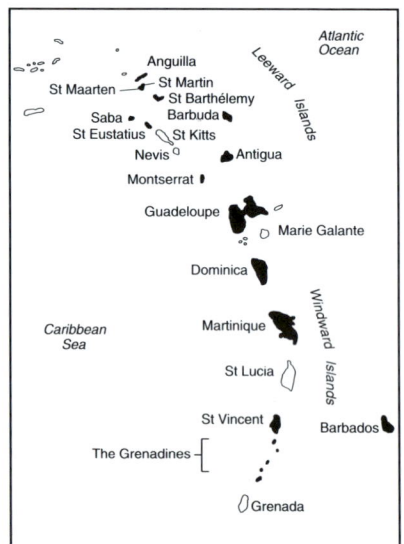

Native to the Greater and Lesser Antilles

Argusia gnaphalodes

Bourreria succulenta

Bourreria succulenta Jacq.

chink(swood); cutlass; strongback; *bwa kabwit bata*; *kòtlèt*

Shrub or small tree to 6 m high, stem and leaves hairless. Leaves alternate, lanceolate or elliptic, 5–15 cm long, 4–7 cm wide. Inflorescence a loose cyme. Calyx 4–5 mm long. Corolla white, tube to 6 mm long, flaring outwards into five rounded lobes. Flower 1 cm across, with stamens protruding. Fruit ovoid, about 1 cm in diameter, red, topped by fleshy sepals.

In dry, open habitats.

The berries are edible and an infusion of the leaves in rum is reputedly an aphrodisiac.[44]

Cordia curassavica

Cordia dentata

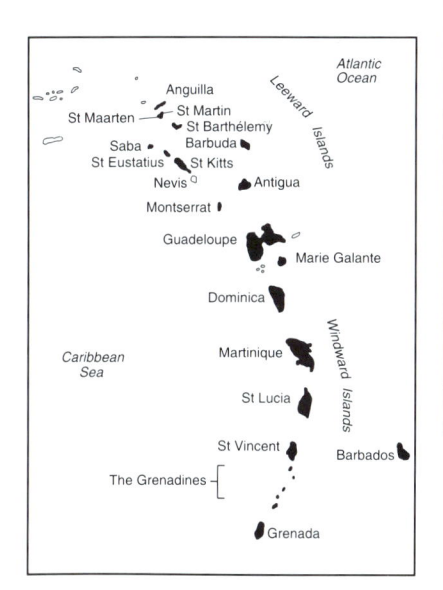

Cordia curassavica

(Jacq.) Roemer & Schultes

black/wild sage; *maho nwè/bò-lanmè*

Shrub to 2 m high. Branches almost black, covered in tiny curved hairs, giving a downy appearance. Leaves alternate, rough to the touch and aromatic when crushed, lanceolate to ovate, 5–15 cm long, 1–5 cm wide, margin shallowly toothed, blade tapering into the petiole. Inflorescence terminal, a scorpioid cyme with buds at the base, white flowers in the middle and rounded, fleshy red fruit, 5 mm diameter, towards the tip.

Weed of dry, sunny habitats.

A branch can be used as a yard broom,[22] while the leaves are rubbed on horses and dogs to improve the appearance of their coat.[11] A tea from the leaves promotes sweating[31] and is used to treat colds, flu, fever[56] and insomnia.[16],[51] The stem can be used as a toothbrush.[51] Fishermen in the Grenadines make cord from the bark.[29]

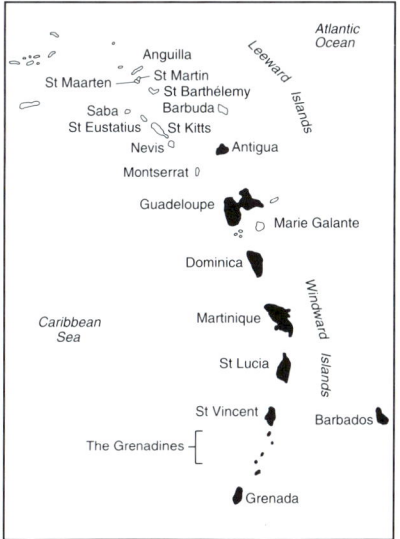

Cordia dentata Poiret

English/town clammy cherry; sticky cherry; *bwa zizi*; *lagli*

Small tree to 5 m high, with arching branches. Leaves alternate, broadly elliptic to roundish, 5–8 cm long and as broad, margin irregularly toothed, upper surface rough due to stiff hairs, petioles about 1 cm long. Flowers in conspicuous, showy heads. Corolla white to creamy, flaring outwards to 1.5 cm diameter. Fruit globular and white, 1 cm diameter.

Wayside tree.

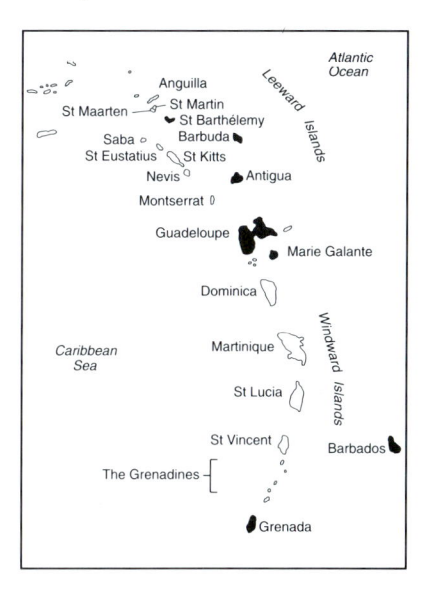

Greater Antilles to northern South America

Greater Caribbean

From Florida down through the Antilles to Venezuela

Heliotropium angiospermum

Heliotropium microphyllum

Tournefortia filiflora

Heliotropium angiospermum Murray

wild clary; eye bright; *ti kwèt a kòk*; *kwèt kodend*

Erect herb to 50 cm high, stem sparsely hairy. Leaves alternate, ovate to elliptic, 2–10 cm long, 1–5 cm broad, upper surface with scattered hairs. Inflorescence a scorpioid cyme, to 12 cm long. Calyx, 1.5 mm long. Corolla white, enclosed below by the calyx, flaring out above to 3 mm in diameter. Fruit, 2 mm in diameter, bi-lobed and dry.

Weed of open habitats.

All ***Heliotropium*** spp. are **poisonous**, causing liver failure if eaten.[37]

Heliotropium microphyllum Sw. ex Wikström

ti teny

Small but woody, cushion-forming plant, to a few centimetres high. Leaves hairy, greyish, elliptic, 4–5 mm long, about 1 mm broad, tightly arranged in rosette fashion on erect shoots. Flowers solitary. Corolla creamy-white with a yellow throat, 4 mm broad. Fruit of four nutlets, 1 mm in diameter.

A mat-forming plant of sea cliffs. Rare and in need of protection.[49]

Tournefortia filiflora Griseb.

zèb a chik

Small tree, trunk and branches almost black. Leaves alternate, elliptic to lanceolate, shiny, 15–30 cm long, 5–10 cm broad. Inflorescence a branched scorpioid cyme. Sepals 2 mm long. Corolla white, lower tubular portion slender to 1 cm long, flaring outwards at the top to 5 mm in diameter. Fruit white and pearl-like, 6 mm in diameter.

In forests at low to mid elevations.

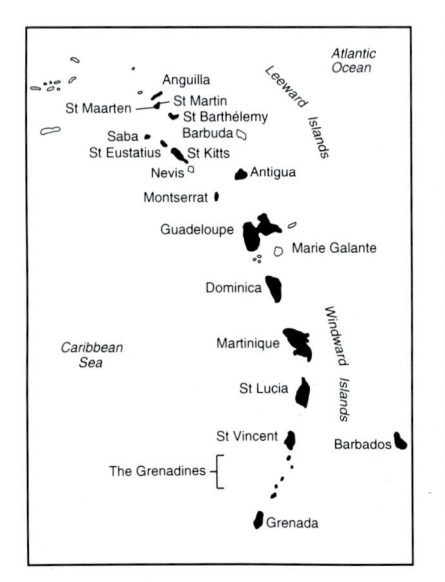

Tropical America

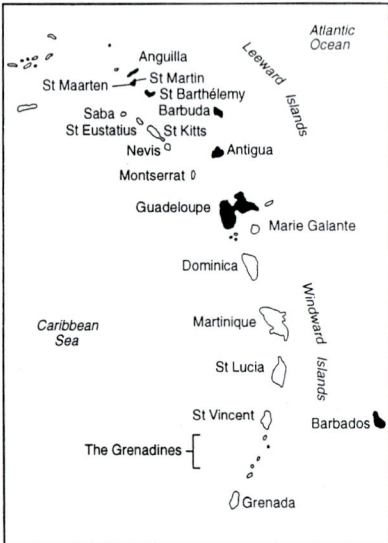

Endemic to the Lesser Antilles

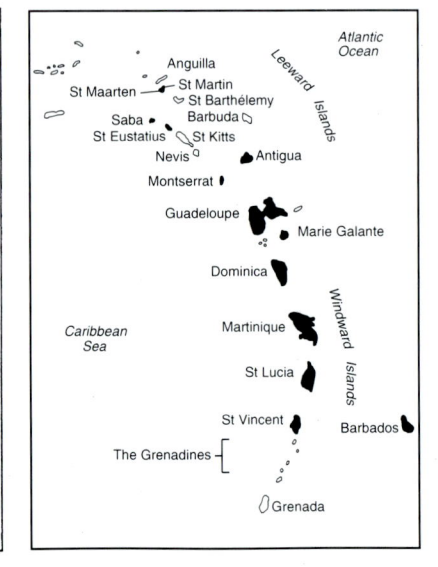

Puerto Rico and the Lesser Antilles

Tournefortia volubilis   L.

chigger nut; soldier bush; *ti chik*; *lyann nwè*

Woody vine or scrambling shrub, young branches finely pubescent. Leaves alternate, lanceolate to narrowly elliptic, 4–10 cm long, 1–3 cm broad. Inflorescence a branched scorpioid cyme. Calyx 1 mm long. Corolla greenish-yellow, tube 2 mm long, topped by slender lobes 1–2 mm long. Fruit, 5 mm in diameter, white and fleshy, with four black dots, separating later into four nutlets.

In dry forests and waste places.

The leaves were once used as a poultice on wounds and sores.[23],[31]

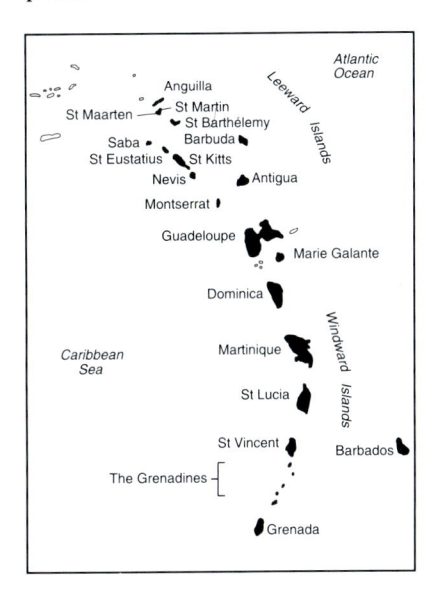

Tournefortia volubilis

Aegiphila martinicensis

Tropical America

Verbenaceae –
Vervain family

Aegiphila martinicencis   Jacq.

spirit weed; lance mahoe root; *bwa kabwit*

Shrub to 2 m high, young stems square in cross-section. Leaves opposite, oblong to elliptic, 8–16 cm long, 3–8 cm wide, generally with a drip tip. Petioles, about 1 cm long. Flowering branches arching over such that flowering/fruiting panicles hang. Corolla white or cream, tube 5–10 mm long, the stamens protruding. Fruit spherical, 1 cm in diameter, bright orange to red.

Shrub of roadside verges and forest margins at mid elevations.

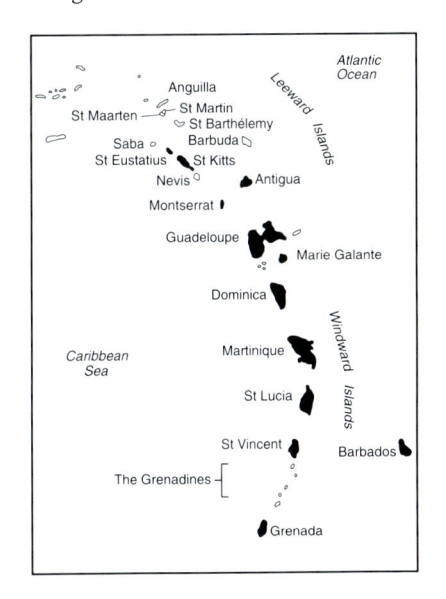

Greater Caribbean and South America

Citharexylum spinosum L.

fiddlewood; cutlet; susanna (berry); *bwa jòn/kòklet/kawé*

Tree to 18 m high. Petioles bright orange in colour, the entire leaf acquiring this colour prior to leaf fall in February–April. Leaves opposite, elliptic, 15–25 cm long. Flowers white, borne on elongated racemes, hanging from the axils and shoot tips. Corolla tube about 5 mm long. Fruit globular, to 1 cm in diameter, orange turning to black.

By the roadside and in forests at low to mid elevations.

Wood used to make charcoal, while the leaves provide a tea for chest pains[35] and asthma.[5] Juvenile leaves have toothed margins and this may explain the seemingly inappropriate specific epithet, **spinosum**.

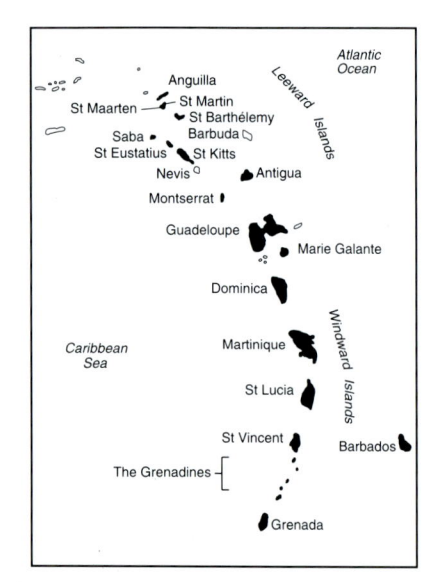

Lesser Antilles and northern South America

Clerodendrum aculeatum (L.) Schltr.

pibry; piri; privet; coffee/miracle/privy fence/hedge; hague bush; *zanmouwèt*; *té bò-lanmé*

Shrub to 3 m high, young branches covered in fine brown pubescence. Stem, cylindrical in cross-section, bearing opposite spines, to 8 mm long. Leaves opposite, very variable but more or less elliptic, 2–5 cm long. Flowers white in axillary clusters near the shoot tips. Corolla tube, to 2 cm long. Stamens four, prominently exerted, the filaments purple. Fruit spherical, to 8 mm in diameter, partly enveloped by the calyx.

Near the seashore and in dry places.

Sometimes planted as a hedge. The crushed leaves are applied as a poultice for skin disorders.[23],[44] A tea made from the leaves is fever-reducing and alleviates childbirth pain.[29]

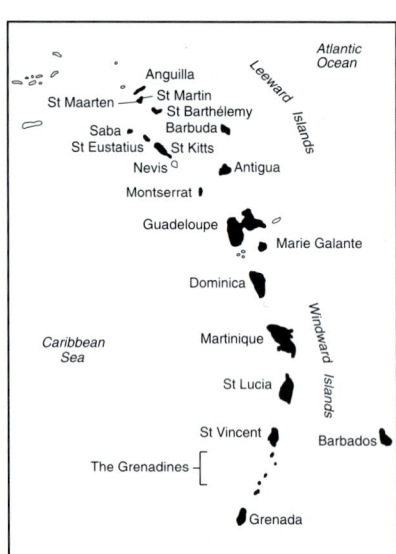

Greater Caribbean

Citharexylum spinosum

Clerodendrum indicum (L.) Kuntze

zèb à lon kou

Erect shrub to 1.5 m high, the stem furrowed. Leaves whorled, lanceolate or widest above the middle, 5–20 cm long, margin often irregular near the tip. Flowers in axillary cymes, several such cymes forming a terminal panicle. Calyx of five lobes, often purplish. Corolla white or cream, tube long and narrow, 8–11 cm long, with stamens protruding. Fruit spherical, black, 1 cm in diameter, prominent on the red, star-shaped calyx.

Roadside weed.

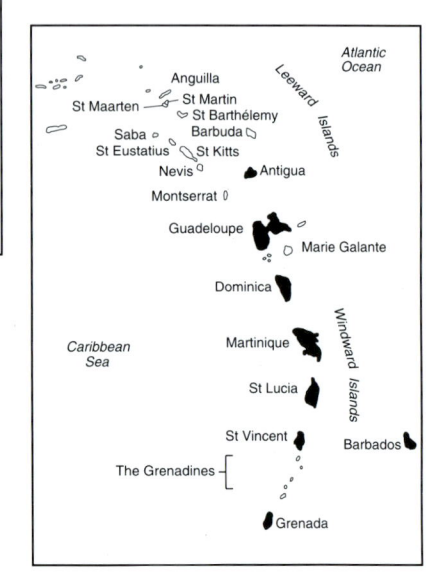

Native of Asia, naturalised garden escape

Clerodendrum aculeatum

Clerodendrum indicum

Lantana trifolia

Lantana trifolia L.

sage

Shrub to 1 m tall, stem pubescent and almost square in cross-section. Leaves in whorls of three, lanceolate, 4–10 cm long, margin shallowly toothed. Flowers mauve, in elongated spikes. Corolla tubular below, to 8 mm long, flat and spreading above, to 1 cm in diameter. Fruit spherical, to 4 mm across, purplish.

Weed of damp areas.

Six other **Lantana** species grow wild in the region, **L. camara** with its bicolor cream-pink or yellow-orange inflorescences being the most common. Despite a tradition of using the young shoots of these 'sages' to make bush teas to treat flu and fever,[28],[35],[45],[47],[51] human fatalities have resulted from eating the green berries[14] and so these plants should be considered **poisonous**.

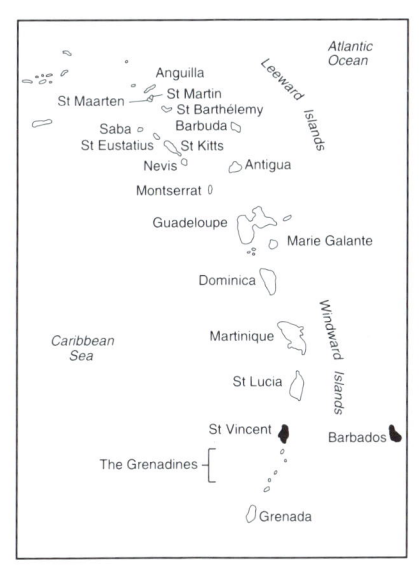

Greater Caribbean

Lippia strigulosa

Lippia strigulosa Martens & Galeotti

vèvenn kouwan

Creeping, perennial herb, rooting at the nodes. Leaves opposite, thick, almost succulent, often brown in colour, elliptic, 2–6 cm long, with distinct pinnate venation and the margin coarsely toothed, especially towards the tip. Flowers white, borne on ovoid heads, the latter held erect on stalks 2–6 cm long. Corolla tube about 3 mm long, spreading above to give the flower a lipped appearance.

Near the seashore.

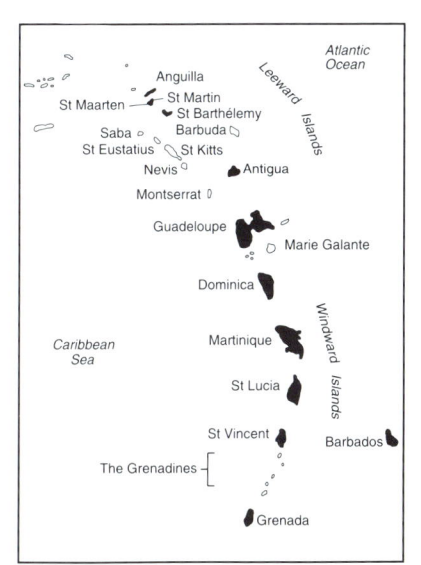

Greater Caribbean

Priva lappulacea

Priva lappulacea (L.) Pers.

clammy/velvet burr; white vervain; rabbit meat; *(ti) dayi*; *kòlan*; *géwitout*

Herb to 50 cm high, covered with scattered hairs. Leaves opposite, ovate to triangular, 3–10 cm long, margin toothed, petioles slender. Inflorescence a slender raceme, finely hairy, arching over. Corolla pale blue to violet, tubular below, 3 mm long, spreading out into lobes above. Calyx inflating around the fruit to form a sac, to 7 mm long, covered in hooked hairs which aid in fruit dispersal.

Weed of waste ground.

A tea made from the plant is regarded as a cure-for-all[45] and tonic.[29]

Tropical America

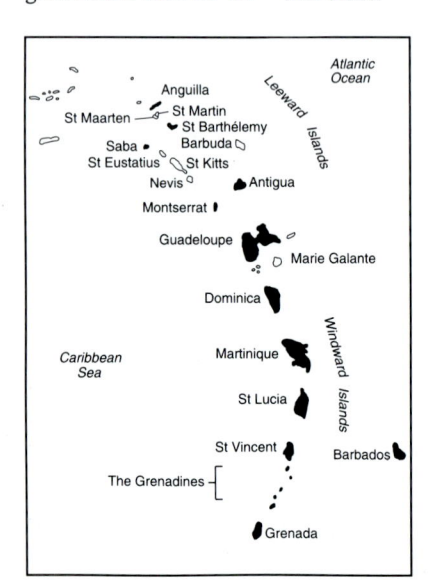

Stachytarpheta jamaicensis (L.) M. Vahl

vervain; verivine; *venvenn (blé)*; *vèvenn ké a rat*; *(venvenn) latjé wat*

Herb to 1 m high. Leaves opposite, ovate to elliptic, 2–7 cm long, margin toothed. Flowers deep violet to blue, on thickened, furrowed, erect spikes, to 20 cm long. Fruit cigar-shaped, about 4 mm long, the surrounding calyx completely embedded in the spike axis.

Near the coast and sunny, open habitats.

A plant considered a remedy for worms,[28],[35],[45] fungal infections of the skin,[51] nervousness,[45],[47] diabetes, diarrhoea,[56] hypertension,[16] colds, fever[31],[35],[56] and to 'purge' breast milk.[25],[29] Aptly described two centuries ago as 'a favourite and common medicine in the islands ... good for any ailment'.[31]

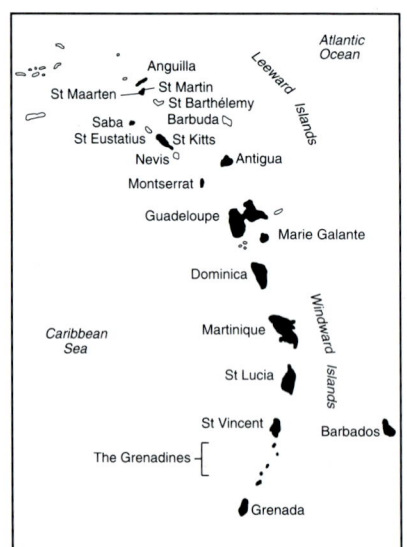

Southern USA and tropical America

Stachytarpheta jamaicensis

Hyptis pectinata

Leonotis nepetifolia

84

Lamiaceae (Labiatae) – Mint family

Hyptis pectinata   (L.) Poit.

piaba; *bòm*

Erect, usually shrubby, branching herb to 2 m high, not noticeably aromatic. Stem four-angled, minutely hairy. Leaves opposite, 2–6 cm long, margin irregularly toothed, long-petioled. Flowers appearing to be in erect spikes; in fact, in fan-shaped clusters at the nodes of the flowering shoot. Calyx sac-shaped, to 4 mm long at the fruiting stage, rimmed with bristles, minutely hairy. Corolla mauve.

Roadside weed of higher rainfall areas.

Considered a fever-reducing plant in Ghana[1] and Guyana.[16] It also goes by the name piaba in Ghana.[1]

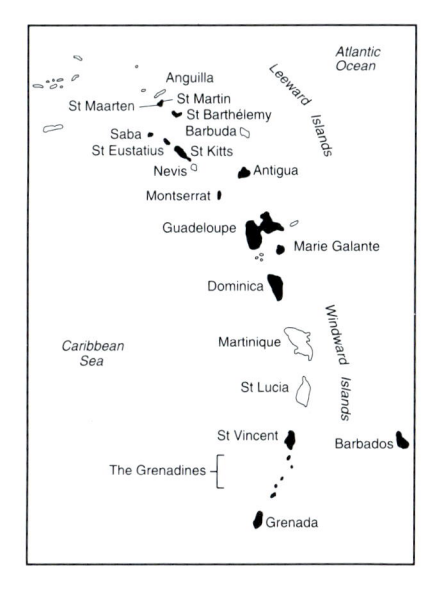

Tropical America

Leonotis nepetifolia   (L.) Aiton f.

ball bush/head; lion head/tail; button weed; rabbit food; man piaba; honeysuckle; Lord Lavington; cashie; *gwo ponpon/tèt*; *ponpon souda*; *zèb gwo bouton*

Annual, usually unbranched herb, to 2 m high. Stem square in cross-section, minutely hairy. Leaves opposite, ovate to spade-shaped, 3–8 cm long, roundly toothed. Flowers in ball-like clusters, to 6 cm across, at the nodes. Calyx curved and tubular, with bristle-tipped teeth, the upper the longest. Corolla orange, two-lipped.

Weed, especially of abandoned agricultural land.

A tea from the leaves is taken for coughs,[23],[51],[56] fever[5],[35],[55] and stomache ache,[29],[55] as well as applied as a salve for skin complaints.[5],[29],[35]

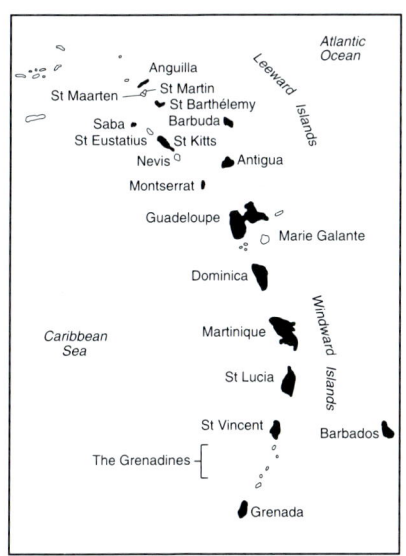

Native of tropical Africa, naturalised

Leonurus sibiricus

Leonurus sibiricus   L.

motherwort; *chandilyé*; *zèb Man Lali*

Erect herb to 60 cm high, the stem four-angled. Leaves opposite, deeply three-lobed, the lobes further cleft, 2–6 cm long. Flowers showy, in hemispherical clusters at the nodes. Calyx cup-shaped, the rim with five long spines. Corolla pink, two-lipped, the lower lip purplish.

Weed of well-watered areas.

Used as a cough remedy,[9],[28] consistent with the sedative properties of several members of this genus.[54]

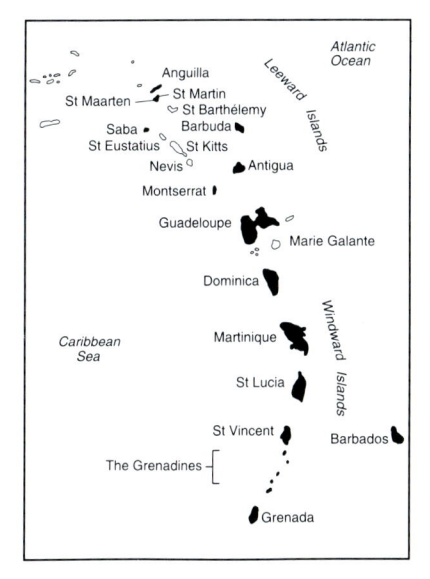

Native of Asia, naturalised

Salvia occidentalis

Salvia occidentalis Sw.

hopweed; *zèb a koulèv*; *ti vyòlèt*

Branched, semi-erect, sprawling herb, to 40 cm high, rooting at the nodes. Stem four-angled, with minute scattered hairs on the younger parts. Leaves opposite, ovate, 1.5–4 cm long, margin sharply toothed. Inflorescence terminal, 15–30 cm long, flowers in whorls at intervals on a vertical axis. Calyx with glandular hairs. Corolla pale blue with a white throat.

Weed of semi-shade, often near the coast.

Advocated for eye infections[9] and mouth sores.[33]

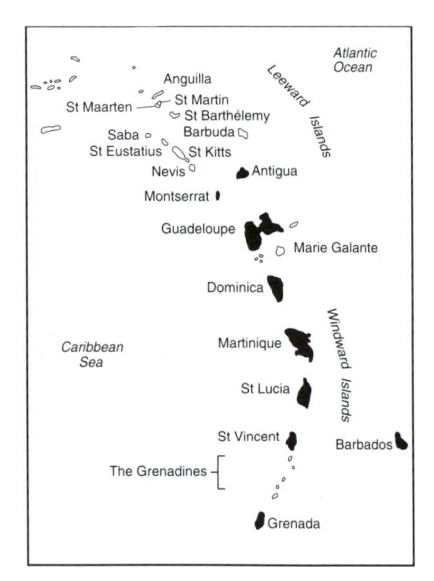

Tropical America

Solanaceae – Tomato family

Cestrum latifolium Lam.

wild jasmine; *jasmen sovaj*

Shrub to 2 m high, the young parts pubescent. Leaves alternate, ovate, 4–12 cm long, often with a drip tip. Flowers virtually unstalked, several per axillary cluster. Corolla slender, tubular, creamish, about 2 cm long, slit at the top to give five short, linear teeth. Fruit a black ovoid berry, 8 mm long, sitting in the cup-like, five-lobed calyx.

In woods at mid elevations.

The fruit and sap of most ***Cestrum*** spp. are **poisonous**.[37] The related **C. nocturnum** (Lady-of-the-night) is cultivated for its nocturnally fragrant flowers.

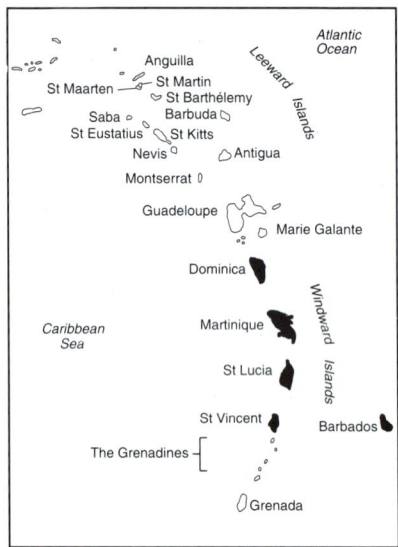

Greater Caribbean

Cestrum latifolium

Datura stramonium

Datura stramonium L.

thorn-apple; nightshade; belladonna; fireweed; joy juice; *konkonb chyen/dyab/zonbi*

Erect, branching, shrubby herb, to 1 m high, hairless. Leaves alternate, ovate, variously lobed and toothed, to 20 cm long, petiole half as long. Flower, with tubular, short-toothed calyx, to 5 cm long, and white, trumpet-shaped, five-toothed corolla, to 10 cm long, opening at dusk. Fruit an erect, spiky, ovoid capsule, to 4 cm long.

Weed of disturbed ground.

Leaves and seeds especially rich in dangerous alkaloids.[50] Formerly used as a painkiller.[45] The leaves are apparently smoked to give relief from asthma,[45],[47] but this is a **poisonous** plant not to experimented with. ▶

Physalis angulata L.

(cow) pops; poppers; pok (pok); *zèb a pòk*

Erect herb, to 1 m high, hairless. Leaves alternate, ovate, 5–15 cm long, margin with well-spaced, broad teeth, rarely entire. Flowers yellowish with purple markings, occurring singly in the forks. Calyx lobes initially triangular. Corolla bell-shaped, about 1 cm across. Calyx becoming like a paper lantern, 10-angled, about 3 cm long, enclosing an ovoid berry.

Wayside weed.

The unripe berries of several **Physalis** spp. are highly **poisonous** and have caused death in children.[37]

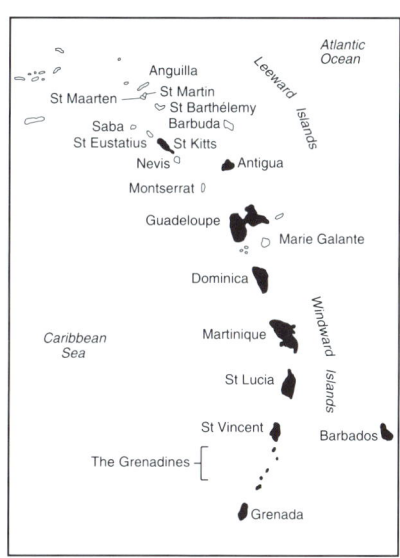

Physalis angulata

Tropics and subtropics worldwide

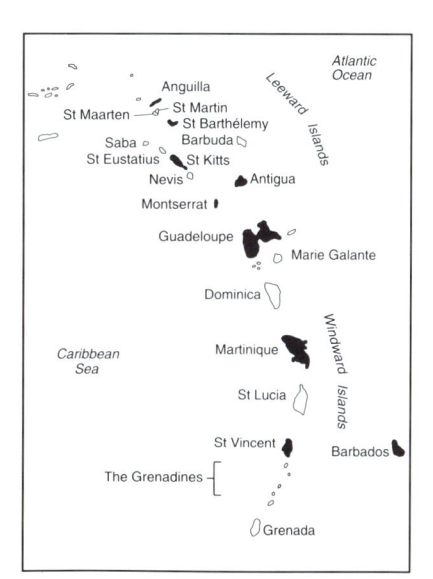

Native of Mexico, naturalised

Solanum americanum Miller

bird pepper; dolly tomato; kanker berry; spinach; ink balls; *agouma*; *zèb amè*

Annual, bushy herb to 60 cm high, stem often purplish, without prickles. Leaves alternate, ovate, 3–10 cm long, margin entire or slightly toothed. Flowers, about 5 mm wide, a few per umbel, borne along the stem. Flower resembling a shooting star, the five narrow white corolla lobes bent back, the central clump of yellow anthers sticking out from the centre. Fruit a shiny black berry, about 5 mm wide.

A common roadside weed.

Used in bush teas,[28] especially to treat shingles.[51] The leaves are also used in callalou soup.[35] The fruit is **poisonous** when green but edible when black.[8] The plant contains solanine glycoalkaloids, which may have little effect on adults but prove fatal to children.[37]

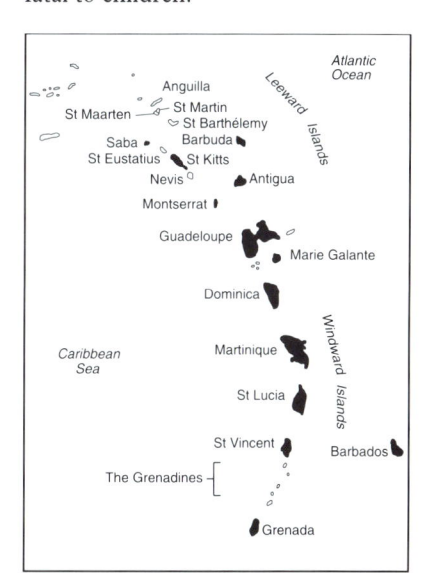

Solanum americanum

Throughout the Tropics

Solanum torvum

Solanum torvum Sw.

small red trubba; wild eggplant; susumba; *mélanjèn dyab*; *bélanjè bata/djab*

Tall shrub, to 3 m high, stem densely woolly and with a few scattered prickles or none at all. Leaves alternate, ovate, 7–20 cm long, margin slightly lobed, base unequal-sided. Flowers many per cluster. Corolla white, star-shaped, to 2 cm across, not bent backwards. Fruit a red, spherical berry, to 15 mm across.

Wayside weed in higher rainfall areas.

Used medicinally for kidney problems,[9] colds, diarrhoea[35] and asthma.[25] The fruit can be cooked as a vegetable.

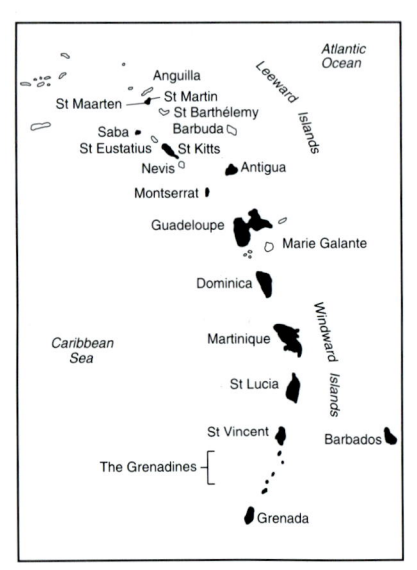

Tropical America

Scrophulariaceae – Snapdragon family

Bacopa monnieri (L.) Pennell

véwonik; *kwinin pavé*

Flat, spreading herb, rooting at the nodes, hairless and somewhat fleshy. Leaves opposite, obovate, 6–20 mm long, 2–4 mm wide, with virtually no petiole. Flowers occurring singly in the leaf axils. Corolla white, 1 cm across, spreading into five flat lobes. Fruit an ovoid capsule, to 5 mm long.

In swamps, submerged and along the margins.

Elsewhere known as water hyssop, cultivated in aquaria and regarded as being of medicinal value.[42]

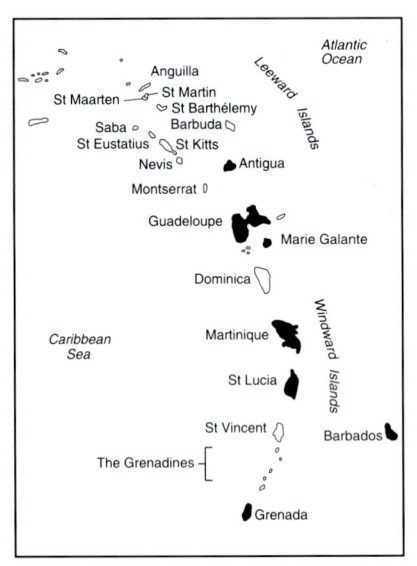

Throughout the Tropics

Bacopa monnieri

Capraria biflora

Capraria biflora L.

West Indian tea; wild tea; goat weed; tisane; *(di)té péyi*

Erect, woody herb to 1 m high. Leaves alternate, more or less elliptic, 3–6 cm long, the margin toothed above the middle. Flowers in clusters of 1–3 per leaf axil. Corolla white, regular and five-lobed, about 1 cm long. Fruit an ovoid capsule, to 5 mm long.

In dry, especially coastal, areas.

A tea made from the leaves is claimed to relieve a wide range of ailments.[9],[18],[28],[45],[51] ▶

Crescentia cujete

Tabebuia heterophylla

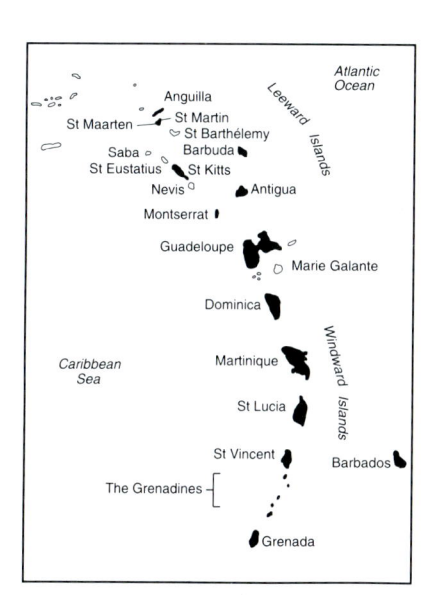

Bignoniaceae – Poui family

Crescentia cujete L.

calabash; *kalbas*

Small tree, trunk pale with an almost bleached appearance. Leaves simple, obovate, 4–20 cm long, to 6 cm wide, occurring as tight clusters from the old wood itself (in fact, dwarf shoots in the axils of fallen leaves). Flowers in clusters of 1–3, emerging from the old wood, the corolla buff-coloured with purple veins, bell-shaped and five-lobed, 4–7 cm long. Fruit more or less spherical and smooth, to 20 cm in diameter.

At low to mid elevations; occasionally cultivated.

This is the national tree of St Lucia.[5] It is probably an Amerindian introduction, the gourds used as bowls and utensils. The fruit pulp is highly **poisonous**,[47] but applied to the skin is soothing.[5],[45] The trunk makes a fine medium on which to grow certain orchids.[57]

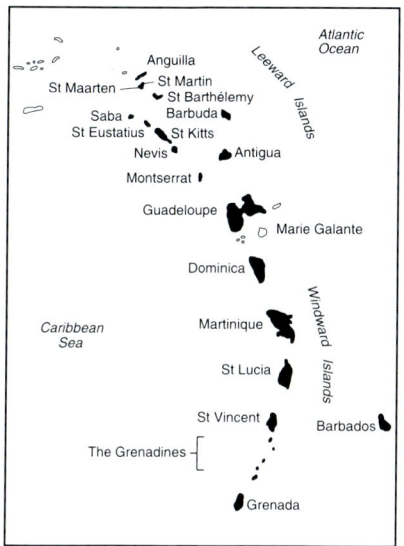

Tabebuia heterophylla (DC.) Britton

whitewood; (white) cedar; *powyé*

Tree to 20 m tall. Leaves opposite, with each pair at right angles to the next. Leaves compound of 3–5 leaflets, each more or less elliptic, extremely variable in size, 4–20 cm long, the terminal leaflet largest. Flowers borne in terminal clusters of a few flowers. Calyx, 1–2 cm long, irregularly lobed. Corolla funnel-shaped, 4–7 cm long, white or pale pink, usually yellow-throated. Fruit an elongated capsule, rounded in cross-section, pointed and hanging, to 20 cm long, splitting to reveal winged seeds.

In dry forests.

May drop its leaves in the dry season. Children make catapults from the Y-shaped forks.[22] A good timber for fishing boats, furniture and household items.[29],[35],[49] The Lesser Antillean endemic, **T. pallida**, is very similar but with simple leaves or up to three leaflets per leaf.

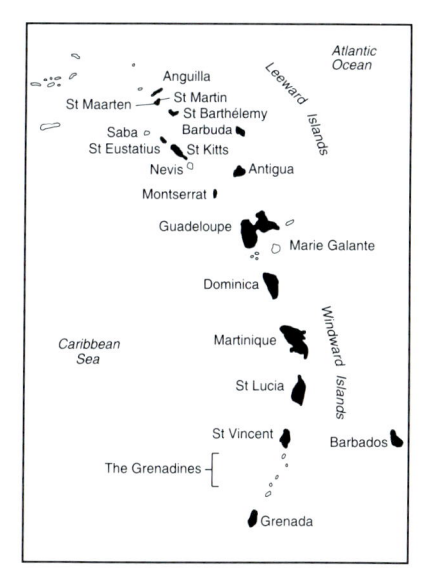

Tropical America

Native to northern South America

Greater and Lesser Antilles

Tecoma stans

Tecoma stans   (L.) A.L. Juss ex Kunth.

Christmas hope; elder bush; yellow blossom/elder; golden seal; *flè jòn*; *bwa pisanli/kawayib*

Shrub or tree to 10 m tall. Leaves opposite, each pair at right angles to the next, compound, odd-pinnate of 5–9 leaflets, each narrowly lanceolate, 3–14 cm long, with toothed margin. Flowers in terminal racemes produced year-round. Corolla yellow, tubular to bell-shaped, 3–5 cm long. Fruit an elongated, pointed capsule, 10–25 cm long, containing winged seeds.

In dry regions.

This is the national flower of the Bahamas.[13]

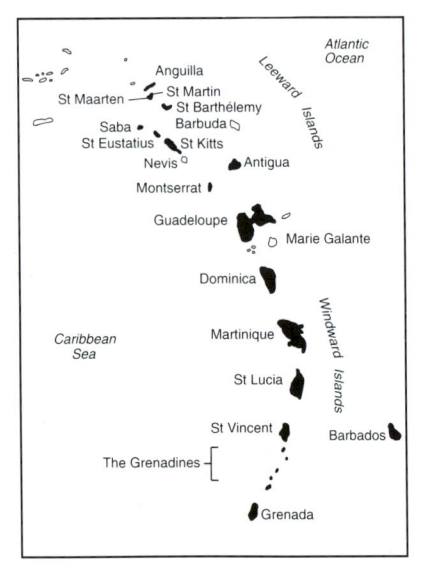

American Tropics and subtropics

Acanthaceae –
Acanth family

Andrographis paniculata
(Burm. f.) Wallich ex Nees

Erect, woody herb to 50 cm tall, stem squarish in cross-section. Leaves opposite, lanceolate, 6–10 cm long. Inflorescence a terminal panicle with flower-bearing branches arching outwards horizontally from the central stem. Flowers on erect stalks with minute bracts and bracteoles. Corolla two-lipped, white with purple markings. Capsule elongated, boat-shaped, grooved, to 2 cm long, splitting lengthwise into two.

Weed of dry areas, usually in semi-shade.

Its use in Trinidad to treat stomach cramps and fevers[50] was probably acquired from India, where it was used as a substitute for quinine in treating malaria.[42]

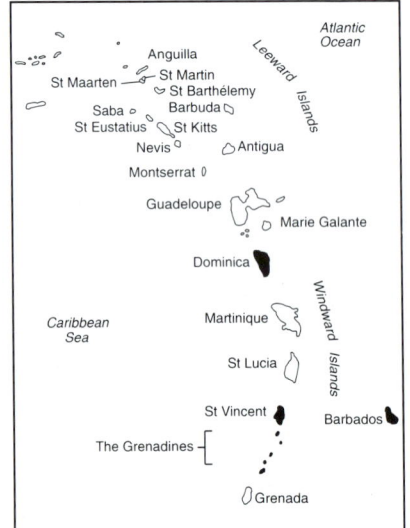

Native of tropical Asia

Andrographis paniculata

Asystasia gangetica

Asystasia gangetica (L.) T. Anders.

Demerara primrose

Scrambling, perennial herb to 1 m or more, young stem squarish in cross-section and finely ribbed. Leaves opposite, ovate to spade-shaped, 3–7 cm long. Flowers in terminal racemes with minute linear bracts. Sepals free, narrow and pointed, to 8 mm long. Corolla funnel-shaped, to 4 cm long, five-lobed, each lobe to 1 cm long and wide. Throat of corolla white or cream, remainder white, cream, pink or purple. Fruit a club-shaped capsule, to 2.5 cm long.

Garden escape, now a wayside weed.

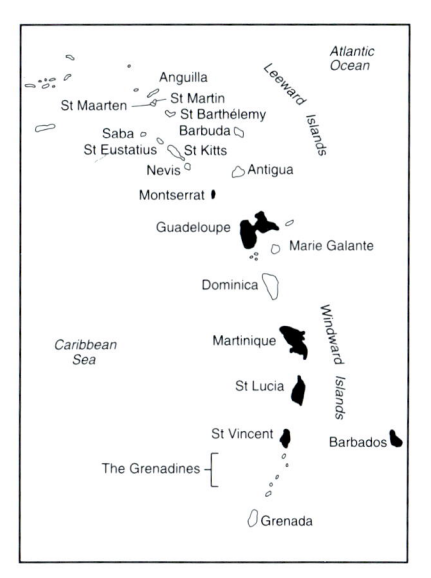

Native of Asia

Barleria prionitis

Barleria prionitis L.

dog bush; *pikannyé jòn*

Shrubby plant to 1 m high, with 3–5 needle-like spines in each leaf axil. Leaves opposite, elliptic, 5–10 cm long, to 4 cm wide, tapering into or winging the petiole. Flowers in clusters in the axils of the upper leaves and at shoot tips. Bracts surrounding flowers, green, not showy, to 2 cm long, broad at the base, tapering to a sharp point. Corolla orange-yellow to cream, five-lobed, two-lipped. Fruit an ovoid capsule, 2 cm long.

Weed of roadsides and pastures.

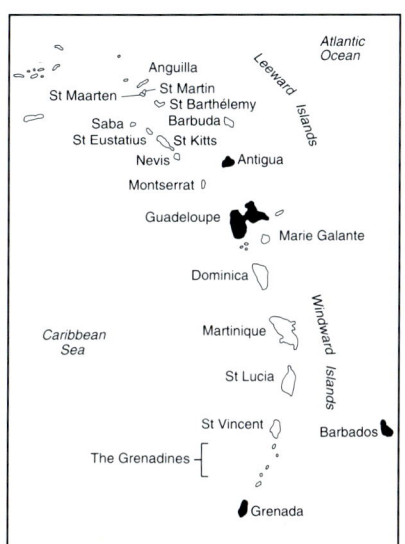

Native of tropical Asia and Africa

Justicia secunda

Justicia secunda M. Vahl

St John's bush; blood root

Shrub to 1 m high, stem distinctly ribbed. Leaves opposite, lanceolate to ovate, margin entire to gently scalloped, 10–20 cm long. Petioles slender, to 6 cm long. Inflorescence a terminal, narrow panicle with many two-lipped red flowers, each about 2 cm long. Fruit a slender capsule, 1 cm long.

Wayside or forest shrub at mid elevations.

Makes a red infusion used as a cooling tea, a bath for skin rashes[51] and an afterbirth douche.

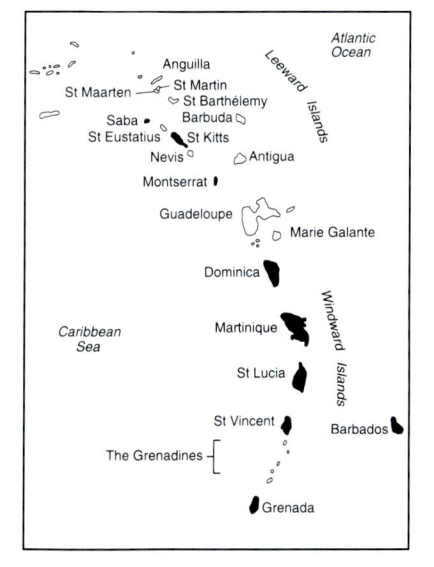

Lesser Antilles and northern South America

Odontonema nitidum

Thunbergia fragrans

Myoporaceae

Bontia daphnoides L.

sea/wild olive; *olivyé bò-lanmè*

Shrub or small tree. Leaves alternate, without stipules, narrowly elliptic, 6–9 cm long, 1–2 cm wide, tapering into the petiole. Flowers distinctly lipped, occurring singly in the leaf axils. Corolla yellowish, the lower lip with purple hairs. Fruit globular, to 15 mm long, the free end pointed.

Coastal plant, also cultivated as a hedge or windbreak.

Unrelated to the Mediterranean olive. The only member of this Old World family to be found in this hemisphere. It is claimed the leaves can be used to kill poultry lice. A tea is made from the leaves and used to treat a range of ailments.[44],[51]

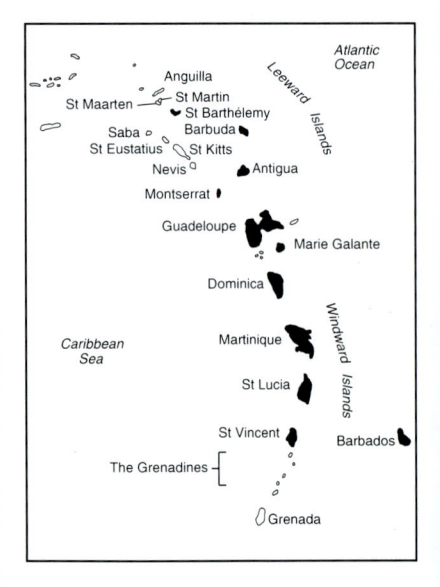

Odontonema nitidum (Jacq.) Kuntze

bwa jounou/kwapo/zendyen; *chapantyé gwan bwa*

Shrub to 2 m high, often rooting at the swollen, bent nodes. Leaves opposite, elliptic, 8–20 cm long. Inflorescence a narrow, terminal panicle. Flowers with white or purple, two-lipped corolla, about 1 cm long, bracts inconspicuous, linear to 5 mm long. Fruit a capsule, to 2 cm long.

Understorey shrub of forests at low to mid elevations.

Thunbergia fragrans Roxb.

Slender twining vine. Leaves opposite, ovate to lanceolate, 4–11 cm long, margin with a few broad teeth towards the base. Flowers axillary, borne singly on a stalk to 6 cm long. Corolla white, 4 cm across. Fruit a rounded, beak-tipped capsule.

Garden escape, now a wayside vine at low to mid elevations.

The related **T. alata**, (black-eyed Susan), with orange, dark-throated flowers, is also naturalised throughout the region. A form of this, with a white centre and known as golden bells, is the national flower of Saba.[30]

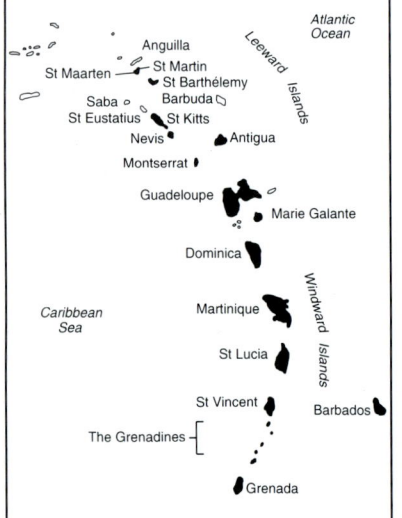

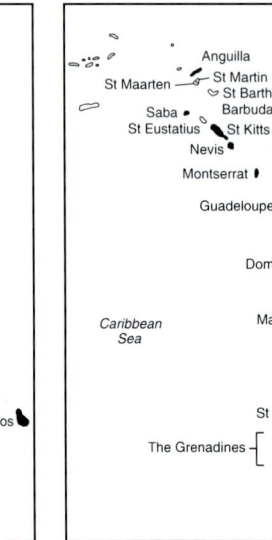

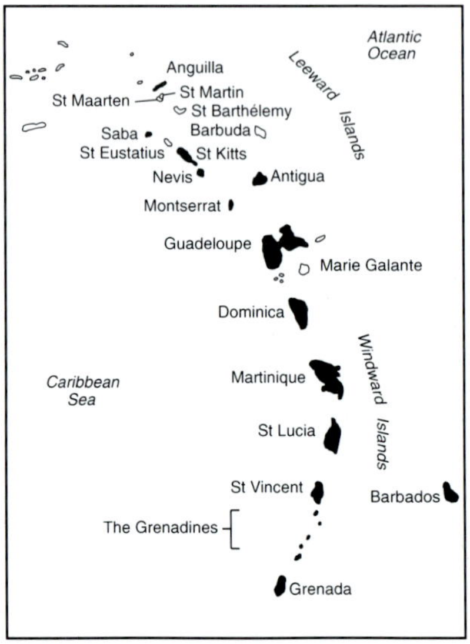

Greater and Lesser Antilles and Virgin Islands

Native of India, naturalised

The Bahamas down through the island arc to Venezuela

Bontia daphnoides

Chiococca alba

Chomelia fasiculata

Rubiaceae – Coffee family

Chiococca alba (L.) Hitchc.

snowberry; buck/David's root; *bwa bwanda*; *lyann (a) sòsyé*

Scrambling viny shrub. Leaves opposite, elliptic to lanceolate, 5–8 cm long, 2–3 cm wide, margin wavy. Stipules triangular and sharp-pointed, about 2 mm long. Flowers and fruit hanging in loose axillary racemes. Corolla yellow, bell-shaped and five-lobed, to 8 mm long. Fruit white, globular and fleshy, to 7 mm diameter, often crowned by the calyx.

In woods at low to mid elevations.

The root is used as a male aphrodisiac[32] and has long been used to treat venereal diseases and sores.[9],[31]

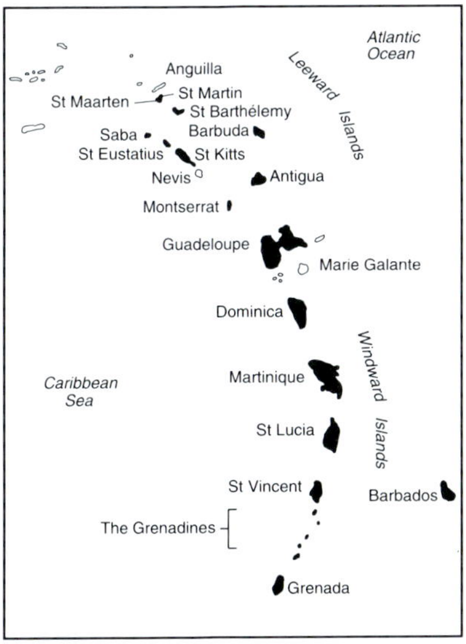

Chomelia fasiculata (Sw.) Sw.

dartwood

Shrub to 3 m high, with pairs of opposite, angled spines. Stipules triangular and pointed, to 3 mm long, often shed from older parts of the stem. Leaves opposite, often appearing as a tight whorl, elliptic, ovate or rounded, to 4 cm long. Flowers creamish, the corolla tube long and narrow, about 1 cm long, the five lobes flaring out abruptly. Flower stalk threadlike, to 3 cm long, 2–4 flowers attached directly to the end of this. Fruit oblong to 8 mm long, purplish black, crowned by the calyx.

In woods to mid elevations.

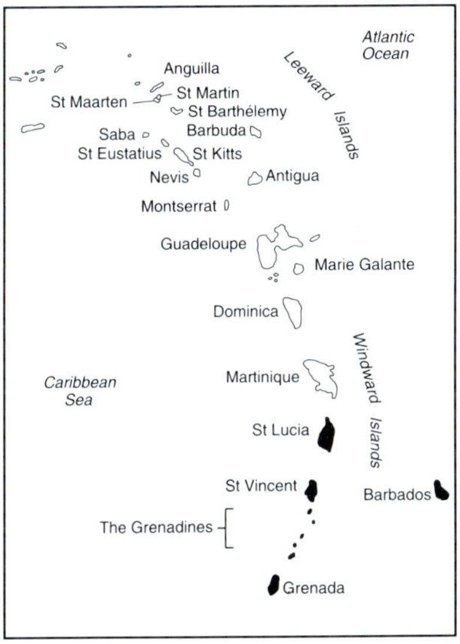

Greater Caribbean

Endemic to the Lesser Antilles

Erithalis odorifera   Jacq.

candlewood; black torch; *bwa chandèl/flanbo*

Shrub or small tree to 5 m tall. Stipules, broad and sheathing with a central point, persisting even after leaves are shed. Leaves opposite, shiny and fleshy, obovate and blunt-tipped, to 12 cm long and 6 cm wide. Flowers white, fragrant and numerous in short axillary panicles. Corolla lobes 8 mm long. Calyx cup-like, about 3 mm long, distinctly lobed. Fruit globular and black, to 4 mm in diameter.

On sea cliffs and in coastal woods. Virtually indistinguishable from **E. fruticosa**, which has smaller flowers. The wood contains an inflammable resin and can be used to make torches.[28]

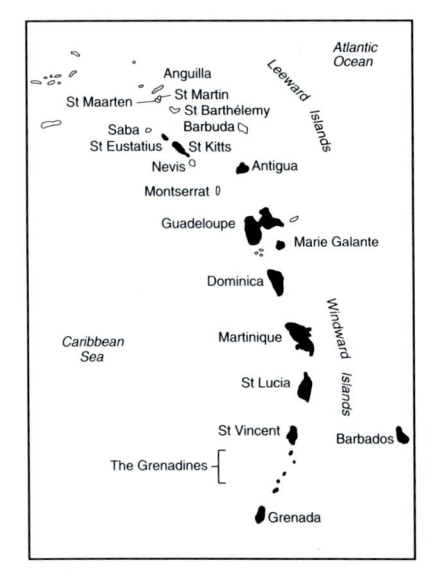

Erithalis odorifera

Puerto Rico, the Lesser Antilles and Venezuela

Gonzalagunia hirsuta   (Jacq.) Schum.

blueberry; ink bush; *bwa foufou; (bwa) kilibwi*

Shrub to 4 m tall. Stem covered in short brown hairs. Stipules between the petioles, broad below, bristle-like above, to 1 cm long. Leaves opposite, elliptic, lanceolate or ovate, 5–20 cm long, 2–6 cm wide, with conspicuous pinnate venation. Inflorescence spike-like, drooping, to 40 cm long. Flowers with white, tubular four-or five-lobed corolla. Fruit fleshy and globular, to 4 mm in diameter, purplish-blue when ripe.

In disturbed forests and by roadsides to mid elevations.

The fruit is not known to be edible.

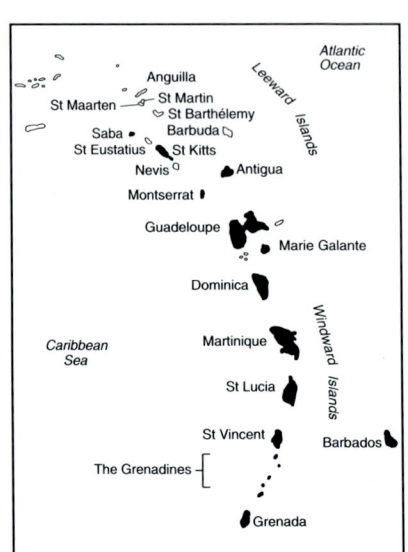

Gonzalagunia hirsuta

Greater and Lesser Antilles down to Brazil

Morinda citrifolia

Morinda citrifolia   L.

forbidden fruit; dog/monkey dumpling; jumbie breadfruit/soursop; pain killer; joy juice; *kòwòsòl zombi; kòsòl chyen; bilimbi; pòm makak*

Small tree to 6 m high. Stipules broad and flap-like, sheathing the stem between the petioles. Leaves opposite, dark and shiny, ovate or elliptic, often unequal-sided, 10–30 cm long, 8–15 cm wide. Flowers white, in tight globular heads. Fruit fleshy, to 10 cm long, 5 cm wide, cream to greenish, vaguely resembling a small, misshapen pineapple.

In coastal and dry woods.

Leaves are applied to the temples to relieve headache and reduce fever or placed on any painful area of the body.[23],[28],[51] The fruit is not poisonous[44] and is used as crab bait. Red and yellow dyes can be obtained from the flowers and root respectively.[42] ▶

Oldenlandia corymbosa

Oldenlandia corymbosa L.

lang poul; *mil gwenn*

Annual herb to 15 cm tall, branches often semi-erect. Stipules broad, sheathing the stem between the petioles, with one or more bristles. Leaves opposite, linear to narrowly lanceolate, to 2 cm long and 3 mm wide, the midrib a prominent furrow. Flowers white, on a slender branched stalk, in clusters of 1–4 at the nodes. Fruit a cup-shaped, horn-rimmed capsule.

A weed along the edges of roads and paved areas.

The dried plant, steeped in white wine, provides a drink considered an aphrodisiac.[45] A tea is also made from the plant and taken for colds[28] and fever.[9]

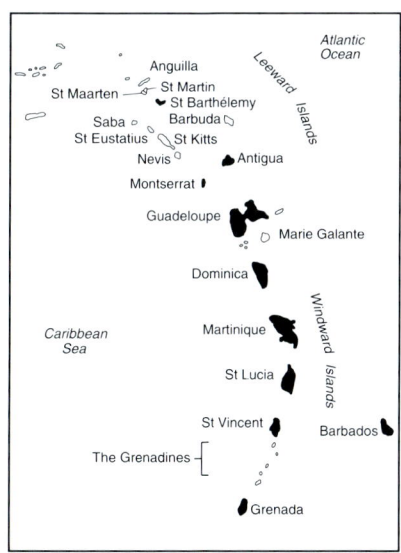

Palicourea crocea (Sw.) Roer & Schultes

red palicorea; *bwa kabwit (nwè)*; *bwa lank*

Shrub or small tree, typically 2 m high. Stipules two-lobed, about 2 mm long, between the petioles. Leaves opposite, elliptic, 7–14 cm long, with a drip tip. Inflorescence pyramidal, axes typically red. Corolla typically yellow, the tube to 1 cm long, rimmed by short lobes. Fruit globular, to 6 mm diameter, blue to purple.

Used medicinally to induce vomiting.[9]

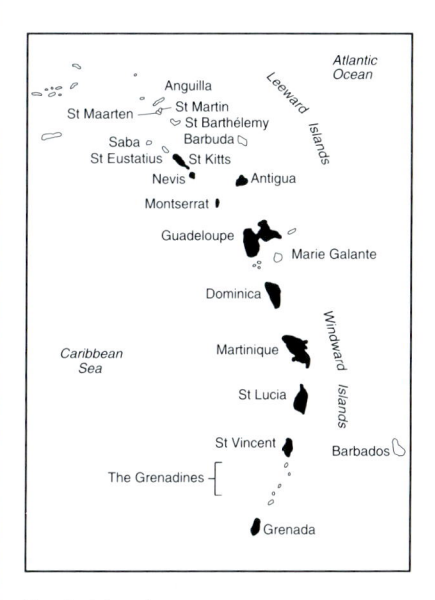

Palicourea crocea

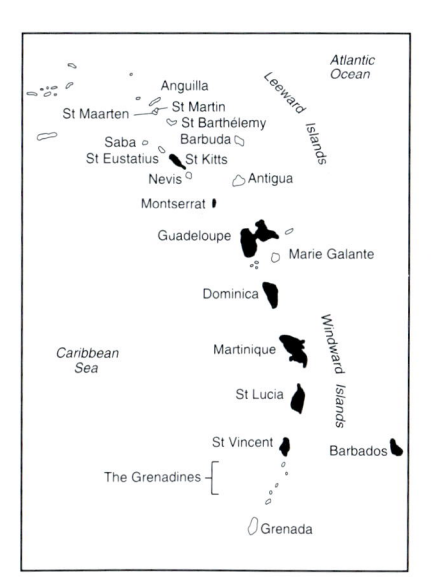

Native of tropical Asia and Australia

Tropics worldwide

Tropical America

Psychotria nervosa

Psychotria nervosa Sw.

St John's bush; bastard cankerberry; *ti kafé bata/mawon*

Shrub to 1.5 m high. Stipules brown and papery, blunt-tipped, sheathing the stem between petioles, about 1 cm long, lost from all but the youngest parts of the stem. Leaves opposite, elliptic or lanceolate, 6–12 cm long, 2–4 cm wide, with prominent pinnate venation. Flowers white, in tight, terminal panicles. Fruit globular to slightly elongated, red and fleshy to 7 mm in diameter.

In forests at mid elevations.

Leaves used in a bush tea for colds, fever, stomach ailments[23] and anaemia.[29]

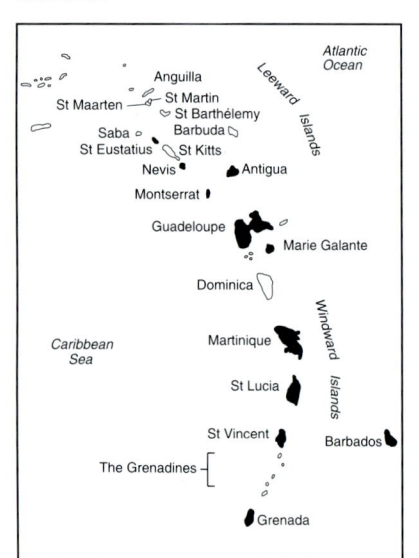

Greater Caribbean

Spermacoce confusa Rendle

buttonweed; *zèb makònèt; zèb akwe*

Annual herb to 60 cm high. Stem distinctly square in cross-section, corners ridged. Hairless or with short conspicuous stiff hairs, especially on the ridges of the stem. Stipule difficult to discern in fertile plants, sheath very short, topped by bristles, 2 mm long. Leaves opposite, lanceolate to linear, 2–4 cm long, 3–10 mm wide, often with stiff, low-lying hairs. Clusters of a few whitish flowers at every node.

Weed of waste places.

Twelve species of **Spermacoce** occur in the Lesser Antilles,[30] most quite difficult to tell apart.

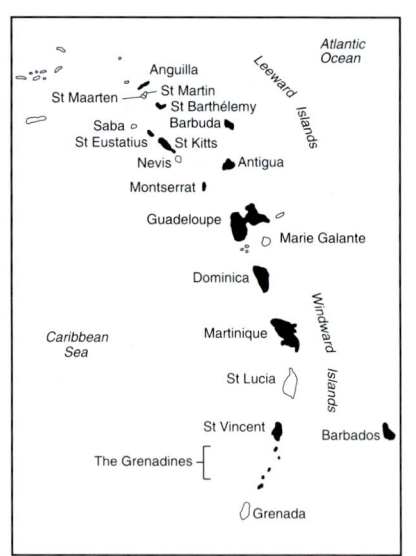

Tropical America

Spermacoce confusa

Strumpfia maritima

Strumpfia maritima Jacq.

womaren bò-lanmè

Low shrub, typically 20 cm high, stem ringed by remains of stipules. Stipules triangular, the sheathing bases persisting. Leaves in whorls of three, linear, 1–2 cm long, 1–2 mm wide. Flowers in short axillary racemes. Corolla pale pink and five-lobed with a yellow column of fused anthers conspicuous in the centre. Fruit globular, white and fleshy to 4 mm in diameter.

On rocky sea cliffs.

A weak tea made from the leaves is taken for colds and to aid in the passing of kidney stones, while a strong tea is an abortifacient and leads to sterility.[44] ▶

Sambucus canadensis

Coccinia grandis

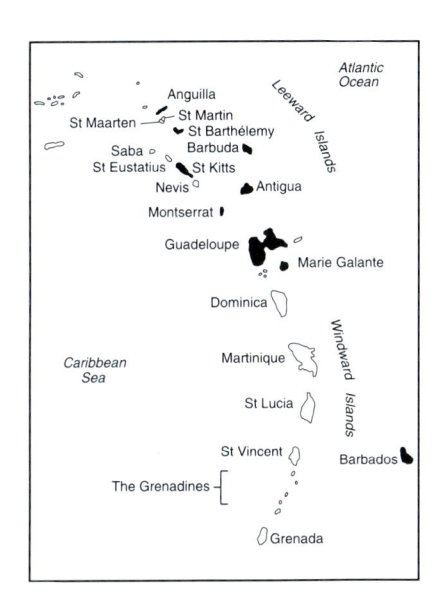

Caprifoliaceae –
Honeysuckle family

Sambucus canadensis L.

(West Indian) elder; elderberry; *siyo*; *flè siwo*

Shrub to 3 m tall. Leaves opposite, superficially odd-pinnate but the lowest pair of leaflets themselves divided into two or three leaflets. Leaflets narrowly elliptic or ovate, 3–8 cm long, with a drip tip, margin sharply toothed. Inflorescence a showy cyme of white flowers, to 12 cm across. Fruit blue-black, spherical, 3 mm across.

Wayside shrub, commonly cultivated.

This is the elderberry used in the USA to make jellies and pies.[42] The plant (not the ripe, cooked fruit) is apparently **poisonous**,[37] yet throughout the Caribbean a syrup made from the flowers is used to treat coughs and a tea from the leaves taken to reduce fever.[18],[28],[45],[51] In St Kitts an extract of the leaves is applied for back pain.[56]

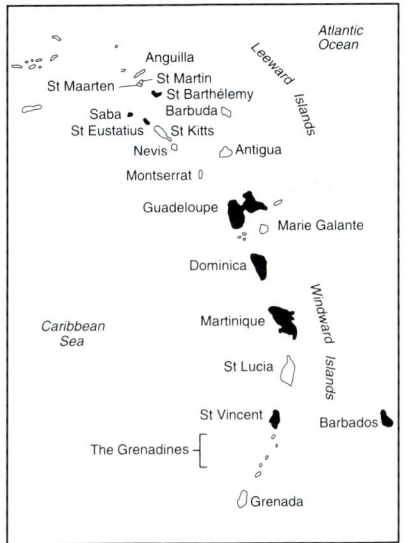

Florida, Mexico and the Greater and Lesser Antilles

Native of the south-eastern USA

Cucurbitaceae –
Cucurbit family

Coccinia grandis (L.) Voigt

jumbie/wild cucumber; susumba

Perennial vine, without hairs, climbing by means of slender, unbranched tendrils. Leaves alternate, vaguely heart-shaped to five-lobed and angular, 4–8 cm long, on slender petioles. Flowers borne singly. Corolla white, five-lobed, bell-shaped, about 2 cm long. Fruit ovoid, turning red, about 6 cm long.

A rampant weed.

The green fruit can apparently be eaten.

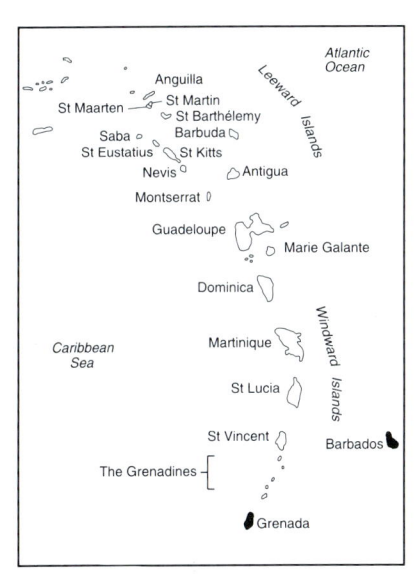

Native of Africa, naturalised

Momordica charantia L.

cerasee; carila; miraculous vine; balsam/maiden/pear apple; lizard food; *pòm kouli*; *koukouli*; *konkonb kouli*

Low-climbing vine with unbranched tendrils and angular stems. Leaves alternate, roundish in outline, 3–7 cm in diameter, deeply five- to seven-lobed, the lobes themselves roundly toothed. Flowers yellow, 2–3 cm across, with five blunt-tipped corolla lobes. Fruit 4–6 cm long, tapering at both ends, ridged and warty, orange-yellow, splitting lengthwise into three to reveal seeds individually embedded in a red, fleshy aril.

Wayside weed.

A very bitter tea made from the leaves is used to treat flu,[6],[23] fever,[9],[45],[47] inflammation[35] and diabetes.[47],[51] The fresh crushed leaves can be applied to skin disorders.[56] The seeds are **poisonous**[37] and the fruit is an abortifacient.[29]

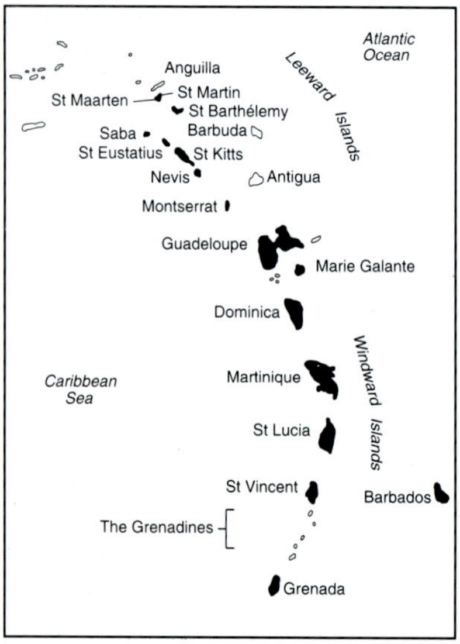

Old World Tropics

Lobeliaceae – Lobelia family

Hippobroma longiflora
(L.) G. Don

star of Bethlehem; pipeshank; *pip zonbi*; *zèb pwazon*

Unbranched herb to 50 cm high, with a blistering, white latex. Leaves spirally arranged in a dense manner, narrowly elliptic to obovate, to 15 cm long, margin with coarse teeth as well as regular minute spurs. Flowers occurring singly in the upper leaf axils. Corolla white, a long, slender tube to 10 cm long, topped by five slender, spreading lobes, each about 15 mm long. Fruit an ovoid capsule, embedded in the remains of the flower.

Roadside weed.

An extremely **poisonous** plant, causing convulsions when ingested.[37]

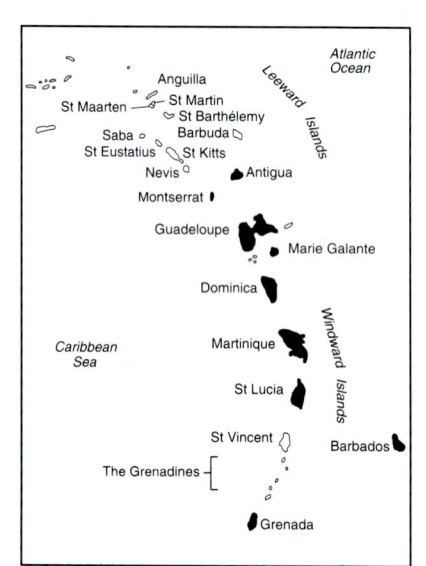

Tropical America

Momordica charantia

Hippobroma longiflora

Ambrosia hispida

Asteraceae (Compositae) – Daisy family

Ambrosia hispida Pursh

wild/seaside geranium; bay tansy; *tapi (vè)*

Perennial, creeping, highly aromatic plant, rooting at the nodes. Leaves opposite or alternate, thrice-pinnate, fleshy yet lacy in appearance, 4–8 cm long. Inflorescence an upright spike, to 8 cm high. Flowers inconspicuous, in cup-like, unstalked heads, 4 mm across, male on the upper parts of the spike, female below. Fruit 3 mm across.

A seaside ground cover.

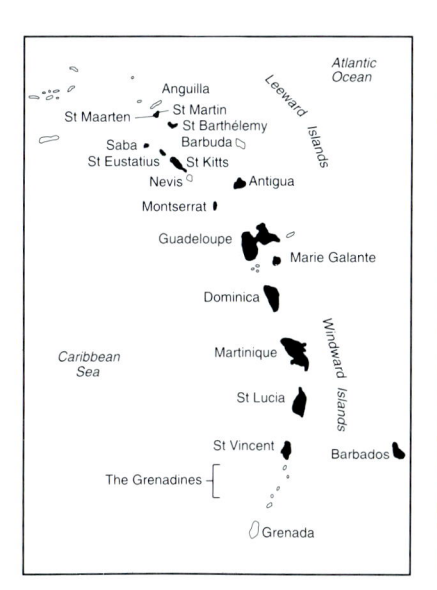

Conyza canadensis

Conyza canadensis (L.) Cronq.

Erect herb to 1.5 m high, only the upper half branched, the plant with a broom-like appearance. Leaves alternate, linear, 2–3 cm long, indistinguishable from the bracts of the inflorescence. Heads small and numerous, 5 mm across, with white rays and yellow disc, in slender panicles. Fruit 1 mm long, topped by a plume of bristles.

Roadside weed.

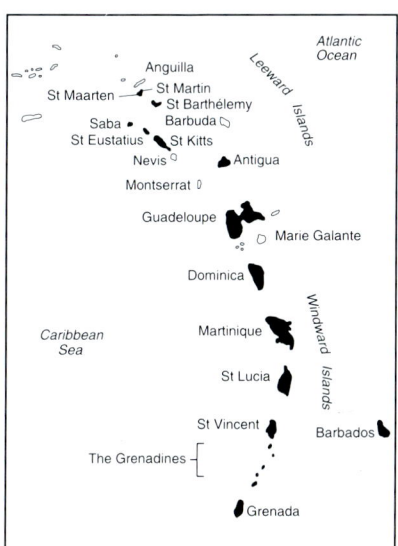

Eclipta prostrata

Eclipta prostrata (L.) L.

conga lala; *zèb a lank*

Spreading, branched, semi-erect herb to 50 cm high. Stem and leaves rough, with stiff hairs. Leaves opposite, narrowly lanceolate, 4–8 cm long, virtually without petioles, margin shallowly toothed. Heads white, hemispherical, not obviously rayed, to 8 mm across, borne on individual axillary stalks, to 5 cm long. Fruit dry, 2 mm, without a plume of hairs or scales.

In moist, semi-shade conditions.

An extract of the plant is applied for treatment of athlete's foot.[51] Plant extracts kill nematodes.[42] In India a black dye for colouring the hair or for use by tatooists is made from the plant.[42]

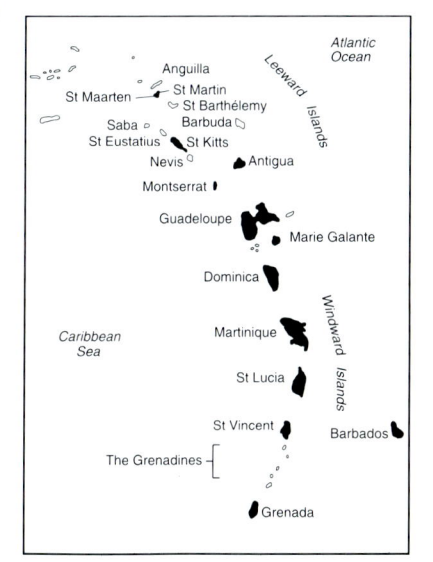

Greater and Lesser Antilles and the Bahamas

Temperate and tropical regions

Worldwide

Emilia fosbergii

Emilia fosbergii Nicholson

cupid's paintbrush; red/soldier's tassel; rabbit meat; jack oats; *ti léton*; *salad a lapen*

Herb to 80 cm high, with scattered hairs. Leaves alternate, lower ones ovate, 3–8 cm long, with winged petiole and toothed margin, stem leaves oblong, to 12 cm long, with toothed margin and clasping the stem. Heads bright red, tassel-like, on tall, branched stalks. Involucre of linear bracts which cup the florets, 9–14 mm long, 3–6 mm wide. Heads silky-hairy in fruit.

Wayside weed.

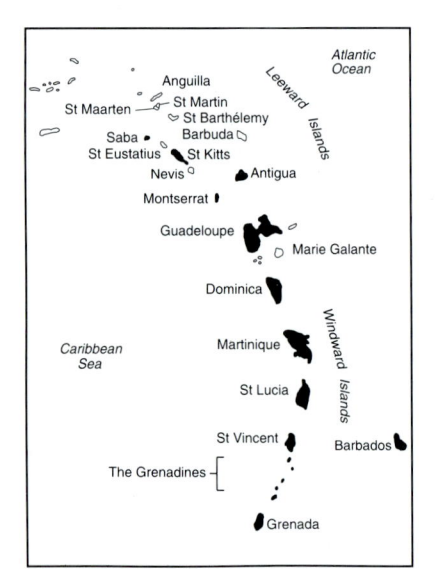

Old World native, naturalised

Eupatorium odoratum L.

Christmas bush; *fléwi Nwèl*; *lang (a) chat*

Scrambling shrub to 2 m high, branches wide apart. Leaves opposite, ovate to lanceolate, 4–10 cm long, prominently three-veined, margin entire to sharply toothed, petioles to 2 cm long. Flowering heads, white to mauvish, non-rayed, in showy, terminal corymbs, appearing around December. Fruiting heads evident as tufts of silky-white hairs.

Roadsides and waste places.

The leaves are used in a bush tea to treat coughs and colds[18],[24],[29],[47],[51] and are also applied as a poultice to wounds.[24],[47],[51]

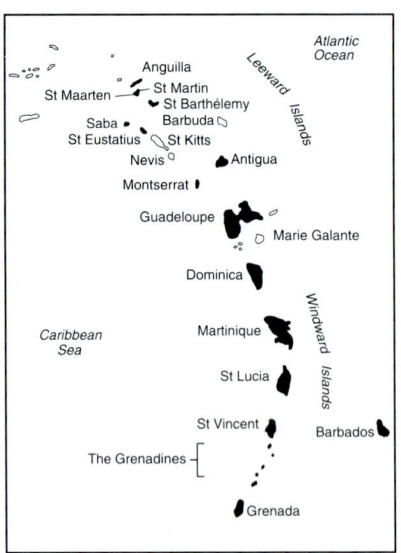

Southern USA down to South America

Eupatorium odoratum

Parthenium hysterophorus

Parthenium hysterophorus L.

whitehead (bush); *matwikè*; *zèb a pyan*

Erect, tap-rooted herb, with ribbed stem, branching freely, typically 50 cm high. Leaves alternate, to 15 cm long, deeply twice-pinnately cut into slender segments. Heads white, about 5 mm across, dome-shaped, in loose panicles.

Weed of dry areas.

Once used as an abrasive for scrubbing wooden floors, especially at Christmas time. In Asia the plant is claimed to cause dermatitis,[51] yet in several Caribbean islands it is used to prepare a bath for treating skin disorders.[23],[45],[51],[56] In the French islands it is steeped in rum to prepare a bitter aperitif and reputed fever reducer.[45] It is also considered a painkiller and tranquilizer.[9]

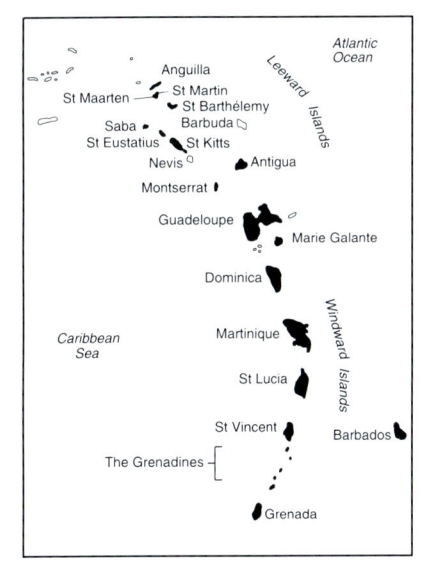

Tropical America

Pectis humifusa

Pectis humifusa Sw.

duckweed; *ti mawgwit*

Creeping, mat-forming perennial. Leaves opposite, obovate, to 1 cm long, margin with bristles towards the base. Heads, about 6 mm across, with yellow disc and yellow rays, borne singly at the shoot tips. Fruit dry, 2 mm long, topped by equally long bristles.

Seaside ground cover.

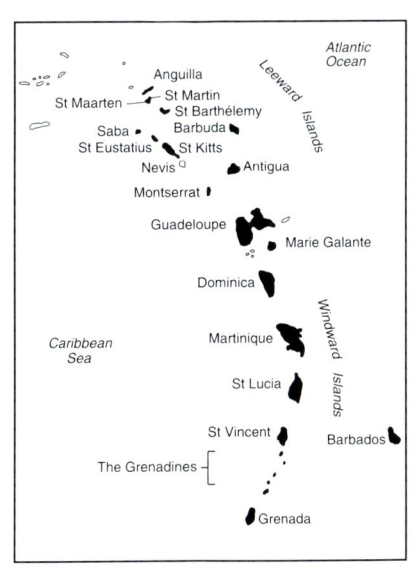

Greater and Lesser Antilles

Pseudogynoxys chenopodioides

Pseudogynoxys chenopodioides (Kunth) Cabrera

Trinidad vine; *flè jòn*; *marguerite à tonnelles*

Climbing, woody vine with ribbed stem. Leaves alternate, ovate to lanceolate, 4–8 cm long, margin with broad, triangular, spur-tipped teeth. Heads showy, to 3 cm wide, with yellow-orange disc and orange-red rays, in branched terminal clusters. Fruiting heads with tufts of silky-white hair.

Garden escape, naturalised as a roadside weed.

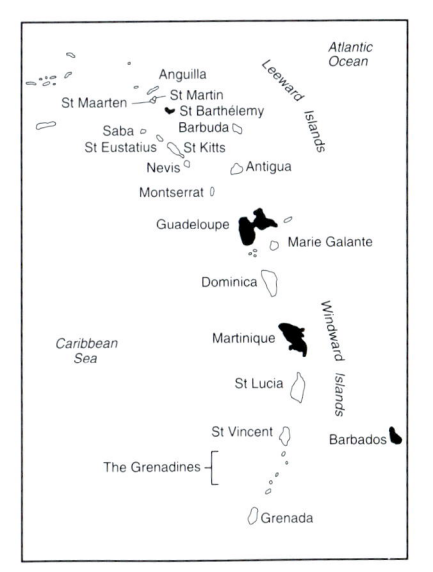

Native of Mexico

Spilanthes urens

Tridax procumbens

Wedelia trilobata

Spilanthes urens   Jacq.

bouton blan

Creeping, branched herb. Leaves opposite, narrowly elliptic to lanceolate, 2–8 cm long, without petioles. Heads non-rayed, white, mound-shaped, 1.5 cm wide and high, borne singly on a tall, erect stalk, to 15 cm long. Fruit black, dry, 3 mm long.

Damp areas in full sunlight.

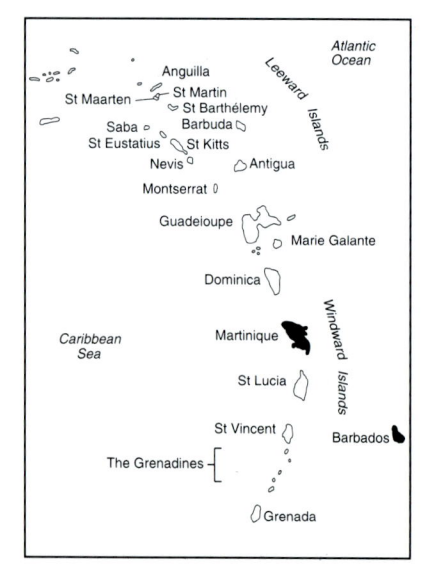

Greater Caribbean

Tridax procumbens   L.

rabbit thistle; graveyard daisy; *bouton blan*; *mawgwit blan*

Creeping, semi-erect herb. Stem rough to touch, with long scattered hairs. Leaves opposite, ovate in outline but sharply toothed, often appearing three-lobed, 2–7 cm long, petiole 1 cm long. Heads to 15 mm across, with yellow disc and squat cream rays, borne singly on an erect stalk, to 25 cm long. Fruiting head a chaffy ball.

Roadside weed.

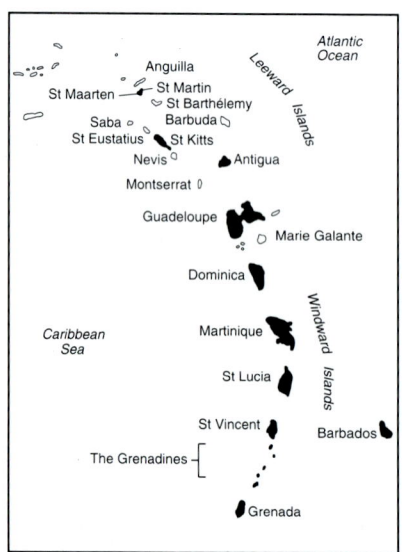

Native to tropical America, widely naturalised

Wedelia trilobata   (L.) Hitchc.

carpet/graveyard daisy; marigold; piss-weed; *venvenn kawayib*; *pàt a kanna*; *zèb a fanm*

Creeping herb, rooting at the nodes. Leaves opposite, three-lobed, the two lateral lobes small, 2–6 cm long, margin shallowly toothed, both surfaces rough with scattered hairs. Heads to 3 cm across, disc and rays yellow, occurring singly on erect stalks to 10 cm high. Fruit oblong, 4 mm long, topped by a scaly cup.

In full sun in coastal and damp areas.

A leaf tea prevents bed wetting,[56] induces abortion and facilitates passage of the placenta after childbirth.[28],[44]

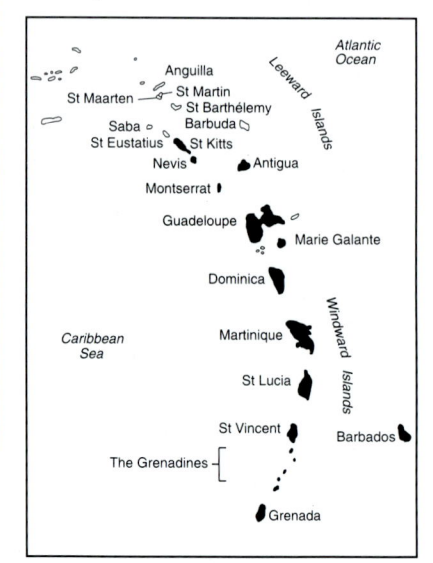

Tropical America

Glossary of Botanical Terms

achene small, dry, one-seeded fruit which does not split open

adventitious occurring in an atypical location, eg roots on the stem

alternate borne singly, not opposite or whorled

angled not rounded, angular in cross-section

anther tiny sac bearing pollen at the top of the stamen

annual plant completing its life cycle (germination, flowering, fruiting, dying) in one year

aril discrete fleshy material covering a seed within a fruit

axil upper angle between a leaf and the stem

axillary occurring in the axil

bisexual having both male and female sex organs

berry fleshy fruit with many seeds rather than a central stone, eg tomato

bract leaf-like structure associated with a flower or inflorescence

bracteole small leaf-like structure usually associated with a flower stalk

bulbil plantlet developing at the leaf margin or axil or on an inflorescence. This can fall off and grow into a new plant

calyx outermost whorl of the flower, usually green in colour. The collective term for the sepals

capsule dry fruit made up of more than one carpel, the seeds released through holes, splits or the lid

carpel basic unit of the flower's female sex organ. The pistil may comprise a single carpel or several fused together

club-shaped cylindrical but swollen or becoming wider towards the top

compound leaf one made up of two or more leaflets attached to the stem via a single stalk

corolla flower parts, usually white or coloured, surrounding the sex organs but enclosed by the sepals. The collective name for the petals

corona a crown-like ring, often showy, between the petals and stamens

corymb flat-topped, open inflorescence of the raceme type, outer flowers having longer stalks than inner ones

cultivar (cv.) a particular cultivated form of a plant; often what the layman calls a variety

cyathium cup-like inflorescence structure

cyme an inflorescence in which the flower at the tip (or centre in a broad inflorescence) opens first while the younger flowers develop at axillary positions further back on the inflorescence

deciduous readily shed, not remaining on the plant for extended periods

dehiscent splitting

drip tip narrow leaf tip, pinched in abruptly

drupe fleshy fruit with a central, stony seed, eg mango

elliptic roughly ellipse-shaped, oval with narrowed ends

endemic known only from that area

entire (of leaves) where the margin or edge is smooth and without teeth or lobes

epiphyte plant rooted on another plant

even-pinnate compound leaf with paired leaflets on opposite sides of the axis, without an unpaired tip leaflet

filament column, usually threadlike, of the male sex organ, on which the anther sits

floret individual tiny flower making up a densely packed inflorescence, especially in the Asteraceae

free not fused or joined to any other organ

fruit part of the plant containing seed(s), typically formed from the ovary

gall localised swelling on plant, usually following penetration by an egg-laying insect

genus a group of species which share important flower, fruit and even vegetative features

gland secretory structure, often a protuberance

gland-dotted used to describe leaves with tiny light dots which are visible when the leaf is held up to the light

glandular hair hair with a swollen tip, as if bearing a drop of fluid

gynophore stalk on which an ovary is borne

herb plant which is not woody

hypocotyl the portion of a seeding shoot below the cotyledons or seed leaves

indehiscent not splitting

inferior ovary ovary is below the point of attachment of the sepals and petals; the rest of the flower sits on the ovary

inflorescence group or cluster of flowers

involucre whorl or collar of bracts (leaf-like structures) at the base of a flower or flower head

irregular flower having only one plane of symmetry or bilaterally symmetrical; usually having petals of varying shape and size

juvenile leaves unlike those produced by the mature plant, usually of a different shape and size; not simply young leaves

keel portion of pea-type flowers which sticks out, generally curved

labellum lip-like portion of perianth of an orchid flower

lanceolate lance-shaped; long and narrow, broadest at the base, gently tapering towards the tip

liana large woody vine, often with trunk-like stems

linear long, thin, parallel-sided

margin edge or border, usually of a leaf

microscopic not readily visible with the naked eye

midrib the main central leaf vein

naturalised introduced, but self-seeding and surviving without apparent human assistance

net-veined with a network of veins; not parallel-veined

node point on a stem where a leaf (or pair or whorl of leaves) is attached

oblong parallel-sided, rounded at the ends, 2–4 times longer than wide

obovate broadest above the middle; reverse of ovate

ochrea tubular sheath occurring at the node, derived from stipules

odd-pinnate compound leaf with paired leaflets on opposite sides of the axis with an unpaired tip leaflet

opposite said of leaves occurring in pairs, one opposite the other across the stem

ovate egg-shaped in outline; broadest below the middle

ovoid three-dimensional structure, ovate in outline

paddle-like resembling the blade of an oar

palmate leaf lobes or leaflets radiating outwards from a central point, like the digits of a spread hand

panicle inflorescence which is a branched raceme, usually cone-shaped like a Christmas tree

parallel-veined main and subsidiary veins running lengthwise as in the leaves of grasses

peltate said of leaves where the petiole or leaf stalk joins the leaf blade towards the centre, not at the edge

perennial plant which lives longer than two or three years

perianth collective name for the two whorls of modified leaves (sepals and petals) which surround and protect the sex organs in the flower; used especially to collectively describe sepals and petals when these are indistinguishable

petal one of the inner whorl of modified leaves of the flower, often white or coloured

petiole stalk connecting the stem to a leaf blade or compound leaf

phylloclade flattened branch, appearing and functioning as a leaf

pinna leaflet of a once-pinnate compound leaf or first division of a twice-pinnate leaf

pinnate compound leaf with leaflets in pairs on opposite sides of the axis. Once-pinnate leaves have a single axis with paired leaflets on either side while twice-pinnate leaves are further divided with side axes bearing pairs of leaflets. (See **odd-pinnate** and **even-pinnate**)

pinnate venation with lateral veins roughly at right angles to the midrib

pinnule leaflet of a twice-pinnate leaf

pistil female sex organ in the flower, made up of one or more carpels and comprising stigma, style and ovary

pollinium clump of pollen grains, dispersed as such

pubescent bearing pubescence or a covering of short soft hairs

raceme elongated inflorescence with the main axis bearing stalked flowers, the oldest at the bottom, the youngest at the top

rachis central axis of an inflorescence or compound leaf

receptacle swollen tip of the flower stalk to which the flower parts are attached

regular flower one that is radially symmetrical or with more than one plane of symmetry; in essence, having petals of about the same size and shape

rhizome creeping, underground stem, often fleshy

schizocarp dry fruit splitting at maturity into dry, one-seeded segments

sepal one of the outermost leaf-like whorls of the flower

shrub woody, perennial plant, smaller than a tree and often branched from the ground

simple leaf one not divided into leaflets

spadix thick, fleshy spike, covered with minute flowers

spade-like roughly deltoid to hemispherical

spatula-like paddle-shaped

spathe leafy structure, often coloured, sheathing or enclosing an inflorescence

species (sing. sp. and pl. spp.) the basic unit of biological diversity and its classification; individuals which are the same species usually look alike and are able to successfully produce offspring

spike elongated inflorescence bearing unstalked flowers, the youngest at the tip

stamen male sex organ of the flower

staminode non-functional or sterile stamen

standard upright, flat, flag-like portion of pea-type flowers

stipel leafy or bristle-like appendage at the base of a leaflet

stipule leafy or bristle-like appendage at the base of a leaf

style stalk-like portion between the stigma and ovary

subspecies (ssp.) form of a recognised species differing from the latter in one or more significant ways

succulent fleshy, juicy

superior ovary ovary sitting above and within the whorls of stamens, petals and sepals

terminal situated at the tip

umbel flat-topped, parasol-shaped inflorescence; all flower stalks or branches arising from a single point at the top of the main stem

unisexual having either male or female sex organs but not both

vegetative reproduction propagation of a plant not utilising the sexual process which leads to seed production. Results in exact copies of the parent plant

variety (var.) minor variant of the typical species, differing in a minor trait such as leaf variegation

winged bearing one or more broad flanges along its length

Glossary of Creole and French common names of plants

Creole names are given in bold italics,
French names in italics.

agouma derived from ogomo, a Guinean word for this and related plants
annanna bata wouj *ananas bâtard rouge* (bastard) wild red pineapple
annanna mawon *ananas marron* maroon (runaway) pineapple
awali *aralie* unknown origin/meaning
balizyé (wouj) *balisier (rouge)* balisier is the common name of some **Heliconia** and **Canna** species
bal(y)é midi *balai midi* midday broom
bal(y)é onzè *balai onze heures* 11 o'clock broom
bal(y)é savann (bata) *balai savane (batârd)* (bastard) wild broom
bélanjè bata *bélangère bâtard* bastard eggplant
la belle mexicaine the beautiful mexican girl
bilimbi of Asian origin. Applied to several acid fruit (eg carambola, gooseberry)
bòm *baume* balsam
boukousou *boucoussou* of unknown origin/meaning
bouton blan *bouton blanc* white button
boyo chat *boyau chat* cat gut
boyo djab *boyau diable* devil gut
brenvilyé *Brinvilliers* name for this poisonous plant specific to the French islands. Madame de Brinvilliers was a famous poisoner at Versailles in the reign of Louis XIV.[20]
bwa *bois* tree, wood, bush or, as an adjective, forest
bwa annizèt *bois anisette* anise-scented bush
bwa bwanda *bois branda* branda is a word of unknown origin/meaning
bwa bwaslè *bois bracelet* bracelet bush/tree
bwa chandèl *bois chandelle* candle wood
bwa chanpinyon *bois champignon* mushroom bush
bwa dowanj *bois d'orange* orange wood. St Lucian name for this dyewood tree
bwa flanbo *bois flambeau* torch wood
bwa foufou *bois foufou* hummingbird bush. Onomatopoeic, referring to the sound of the whirring wings or perhaps to the erratic flight (*fou* is French for mad)
bwa gwiyé *bois grillé* scorched wood/tree
bwa jòn *bois jaune* yellow wood
bwa jounou *bois genou* knee bush (the swollen nodes resemble knees)
bwa kabwit (bata) *bois-cabrit (bâtard)* (bastard) goat bush/tree
bwa kabwit (nwè) *bois cabrit (noir)* (black) goat bush/tree
bwa kannèl *bois cannelle* cinnamon tree
bwa kannon *bois canon* cannon tree

bwa kawayib   *bois caraïbe*   Caribbean bush/tree
bwa kawé   *bois carré*   square-stemmed tree
bwa kilibwi   *bois colibri*   hummingbird bush
bwa kòklèt   *bois côtelette*   ribbed-stemmed tree
bwa koko kawet   *bois coco carette*   literally 'loggerhead turtle's testes tree'
bwa kòtlèt   *bois côtelette*   ribbed trunk bush/tree
bwa koulèv   *bois couleuvre*   snake wood
bwa kwab   *bois crabe*   crab wood
bwa kwapo   *bois crapaud*   toad bush
bwa lafyèv   *bois la fièvre*   fever wood
bwa lajan   *bois d'argent*   silver bush
bwa lank   *bois l'encre*   ink bush
bwa mòwtèl   *bois immortel*   literally 'immortal tree/wood', but called *immortelle* in the English-speaking Caribbean
bwa nwè   *bois noir*   black bush/wood
bwa péta   *bois pétard*   firecracker tree
bwa pisanli   *bois pissenlit*   dandelion bush
bwa pouant   *bois puant*   stinking tree
bwa sann   *bois cendre*   ash bush
bwa syèj   *bois cierge*   candle bush
bwa ti fèy   *bois petites feuilles*   small-leaved bush
bwa zendyen   *bois indien*   Indian wood
bwa zizi   *bois zizi*   zizi bush. Zizi is the name of a bird
bwa zowtolan   *bois ortolans*   ground dove bush
bwi   *buis*   box tree
chadwon (mawbwé)   *chardon (marbré)*   (mottled) thistle
chadwon béni   *chardon béni*   blessed thistle
chandilyé   *chandelier*   candlestick
chans   *chance*   luck
chapantyé gwan bwa   *charpentier grand bois*   big carpenter bush
chapo dlo/glo   *chapeau d'eau*   water hat
chou pikan   *chou piquant*   prickly cabbage
danday   *dent d'ail*   garlic tooth, referring to the smell of the plant
dayi   of unknown origin/meaning
dimwazèl   *demoiselle*   unmarried woman
dité péyi   *thé pays*   country tea
douvan(t) nèg   *devant de nègre*   literally 'in front of a black person'
dyotin   *diotine*   of unknown origin/meaning
endigo bata   *indigo bâtard*   wild indigo
fawin cho   *farine chaude*   hot flour. Duss (1837) claimed the smell of the flowers could be likened to cassava flour[20]
fawin zombi (zonbi)   *farine à zombi*   zombie flour. See previous entry
fèy chofi   *feuilles à échauffures*   ground itch (athlete's foot) leaf
fèy douvan   *feuille devant*   literally 'in front of the leaf', probably because you smell this pungent plant before you see it
flanbo blan   *flambeau blanc*   white torch
flè jòn   *fleur jaune*   yellow flower
flè siwo   *fleur sirop*   syrup flower

fléwi Nwèl *fleurit (à) Noël* Christmas flower
géwitout *guérit tout* cure-all
gimòv *guimauve* marsh mallow
glouglou (wouj) *glouglou (rouge)* (red) glouglou – origin/meaning unknown
go(n)myé modi *gommier maudit* cursed gum tree
go(n)myé wouj *gommier rouge* red gum tree
gonbo bata *gombo bâtard* bastard okra
gonbo fwansèz *gombo français* French okra
gonbo savann *gombo savan* wild okra
gouyavyé *goyavier* guava tree
gwan fèy *grande feuille* large leaf
gwan folet *grand follet* Virtually untranslatable. *Follet* means frolicsome, merry, elf, sprite
gwan kouzen *grand cousin* big cousin
gwan twèf *grand trèfle* large trefoil/clover. See also *twèf*
gwenn amba fèy (blan) *graines-en-bas feuille (blanc)* (white) seed-under-leaf
gwenn zowtolan *graine ortolans* ground dove seed
gwif chat *griffe chat* cat claw
gwigwi of unknown origin/meaning.
gwo bal(y)é *gros balai* big broom
gwo mov *grosse mauve* big mallow
gwo ponpon *grosse pompon* big pompom
gwo tèt *gros tête* big head
gwo zowèy *grosse oreille* big ear
hazyé/razyé/wazyé a woody plant but not a tree. Also used for a plant generally as in the creole proverb 'tout hazyé sé rimèd' – every plant is a remedy
herbe couchée prostrate herb
hontèz *honteuse* ashamed girl
ipéka bata *ipéca bâtard* wild ipecacuana
jasmen blan *jasmin blanc* white jasmine
jasmen boukè *jasmin à bouquets* bouquet jasmine
jasmen sovaj *jasmin sauvage* wild jasmine
jòn a zé *jaune d'oeuf* egg yolk
jéwonflé *géronflé* gilly flower (name of a temperate plant)
jiwòf glo *girofle gl'eau* water clove
jiwòf ma *girofle mare* pond clove
kach-kach noise made by the seeds in the pod
kaka béké/bétjé *caca béké* white man's faeces
kalbas *calebasse* calabash
kampèch *campèche* name alluding to the State of Campeche, Mexico, where the plant is native
kannik of unknown origin/meaning
karatas Duss states this is derived from the Brazilian name, *karaguata-acanga*.[20]
kaya blan *acaya à fleurs blanches* white kaya. Kaya is a name for marijuana and probably signifies the digitately compound leaves of the plant rather than any narcotic qualities
kilibwi see **bwa kilibwi**.
kiwaj *curage* literally, refuse from the drains
kòd a vyélon *corde de violon* violin string
kòd gwaté *corde gratter* itch rope

kòklya   *Cochléaria*   scurvy grass
koko chat   *coco chat*   cat's testes
koko wavet   *coco ravet*   literally 'cockroach testes'
kòlan   *collant*   sticky material
koma (franc)   *acomat (franc)*   (the real) mastic
konkonb chyen   *concombre à chien*   dog cucumber
konkonb dyab   *concombre diable*   devil cucumber
konkonb kouli   *concombre (des) coolies*   coolie cucumber
konkonb zonbi   *concombre zombi*   zombie cucumber
kòsòl chyen   *corossol (de) chien*   dog soursop
kòtlèt   *côtelette*   ribbed-stemmed tree
kóton kadwi   *coton quadrille*   literally 'quadrille cotton'. Cotton refers to the silky seeds while the flowers evoke the image of dancers, hence quadrille
koukouli   perhaps a contraction of *konkonb kouli*
koupayou (bata)   *copahu (bâtard)*   (bastard) copaiba
koupyé   see *poupyé*
kouzen maho   *cousin mahot*   mahoe cousin
kouzen wouj   *cousin rouge*   red cousin
kòwòsòl zombi   *corossol de zombie*   zombie soursop
kwèson kouwan   *cresson courant*   creeping cress
kwèson savann   *cresson de savane*   wild cress
kwèt kodend   *crête de coq d'Inde*   turkey's comb
kwinin pavé   *quinine (des) pavés*   paving stone quinine
lagli   *(arbre à) la glu*   glue tree
lamowi   *Morue*   salt fish. In Dominica, children playing shop pretend the leaves of this plant are pieces of salted cod
lang (a) bèf   *langue boeuf*   cow's tongue
lang (a) chat   *langue de chat*   cat's tongue
lang poul   *langue poule*   fowl's tongue
lanvè jòn   *l'envers jaune*   literally 'yellow reverse'. May refer to how the outer petal-like segments are bent back
lanvè mal   *l'envers mâle*   literally 'male reverse'. See previous entry
lapit(te)   derived from *pita*, the Spanish word for *Agave*. Pointe à Pitre, Guadeloupe, may well be named after this plant[20]
laswa   *(arbre à) la soie*   silk tree
latjé wat   *la queue de rat*   rat's tail
lépini (blan/wouj)   *l'épineux (blanc/rouge)*   (white/red) thorny tree
lis blan   *lis blanc*   white lily
lis jòn savann   *lis jaune savane*   wild yellow lily
lis wouj   *lis rouge*   red lily
liseron bleu   blue bindweed
liseron rouge   red bindweed
lyann   *liane*   vine
lyann (a) bawik   *liane à barriques*   barrel vine
lyann (a) dlo   *liane à eau*   literally 'water vine', ie succulent
lyann a si   *liane à scie*   saw vine
lyann a sòsyé   *liane à sorciers*   witch's vine
lyann blan   *liane blanc*   white vine

lyann blé   liane bleu   blue vine
lyann bwanda   liane branda   bwanda is a word of unknown origin/meaning
lyann bwilan   liane brûlante   stinging vine
lyann mang   liane mangle   swamp vine
lyann mòl   liane molle   soft (fleshy) vine
lyann noyo   liane noyau   stone (kernel) vine. Perhaps alluding to the smell of bitter almond
lyann nwé   liane noire   black vine
lyann Pak   liane Pâques   Easter vine
lyann pèsi   liane persil   parsley vine
lyann savon   liane savon   soap vine
lyann wòz   liane rose   pink vine
mabi   mauby
mabouj   mabouge   lizard (gecko). Probably of Amerindian origin
maho (bò-)lanmè   mahot bord-de-mer   seaside mahoe. Maho is a Carib name for a plant with a bark that can be made into rope
maho nwè   mahot noir   black mahoe
makata (bous)   worm purse. Makata is probably a word of African origin like the Jamaican word *macaca*, meaning worm or grub. Bous is from the French *bourse*, meaning purse
mal bwa chandèl   mâle bois chandelle   male candle wood
mal dòmi   mal dormi   literally 'badly slept'
mal èstomak   mal estomac   bad stomach (used to treat stomach ache)
mal tèt   mal tête   (used to treat) headache
mal watjèt   mâle rachette   male racquet
malenmbé   malimbé   of unknown origin or meaning
malonmé vwè   malnommé vraie   literally 'the true misnamed' (plant). Alternatively, *malonmé* could be of African or Amerindian origin
mang wouj   mangle rouge   red mangrove
mannjini   manchineel (Dominica)
mansniyé   mancellier   manchineel (French islands)
mapou (ti fèy)   mapou (petites feuilles)   small leaf mapou. Mapou is an Amerindian name
marguerite à tonnelles   arbour daisy
matwikè   matricaire   feverfew (name of a temperate plant)
mawgwit blan   marguerite blanche   white daisy
Mawi hont   Marie honte   shy Marie
Mawi Jann   Marie-Jeanne   Mary-Jane
Mawi lopital   Marie l'hôpital   Probably a contraction of 'Miss Mary behind the hospital' (in creole), a name also heard
médsinyé (bata)   médicinier (bâtard)   (bastard) medicine plant
médsinyé (modi)   médicinier (maudit)   (cursed) medicine plant
médsinyé wouj   médicinier rouge   red medicine plant
mélanjèn dyab   mélongène diable   devil's eggplant
mennen/méné vini   méné vini   literally 'to compel to comeback'. This famous magical plant is used in baths to cause an unfaithful lover to return
méwizyé (ti fèy)   merisier (petites feuilles)   (small-leaved) wild cherry tree
mèzè mawi   from a Dominican creole incantation used before touching the plant to trigger leaf closure – 'Miss Mary, close your door, the devil is coming'
mil gwenn   mille-graines   thousand seeds
miwèt   murette   (a vine growing on a) wall

monval   of unknown origin/meaning
mutad péyi   *moutarde du pays*   wild mustard
mouzanbé blan   *mouzambé blanc*   white mouzambé. Of unknown origin but seemingly applied to plants with digitately compound leaves
mòv   *mauve*   mallow
mòv gwi   *mauve grise*   grey mallow
mòv savann   *mauve des savanes*   wild mallow
mòwtèl   *immortel*   literally immortal, but it is the French word *immortelle* that is used in the English-speaking Caribbean
mûrier pays   local mullberry
nénuphar   water lily
olivyé bò-lanmè   *olivier du bord de mer*   seaside olive
paltivyé wouj   *palétuvier rouge*   red mangrove
pantouf   *pantoufle*   slipper
pàt a kanna   *patte de canard*   duck foot
patagon (wouj)   *patagon (rouge)*   red patagon. Patagon is a word of unknown origin/meaning
patat bò-lanmè   *patate bord de mer*   seaside potato
pengwen   not from the French *pingouin*, meaning an auk. Hughes (1750) claimed this was from the gaelic for white head.[33] It is more likely compounded from pine and whyn, the latter being an old English word for thorny shrub.[22]
pèsi bata   *persil bâtard*   wild parsley
pèsi nwè   *persil noir*   black parsley
pikan kouzen   *piquant cousin*   prickly cousin
pikannyé jòn   *picanier jaune*   yellow picanier. Of unknown origin, probably meaning prickly
pip zonbi   *pipe zombi*   zombie pipe
plòk   from the sound made when the flower is hit
pòm kouli   *pomme coolie*   coolie apple
pòm lyann hazyé   *pomme-liane-hallier*   literally 'apple vine plant'. See *hazyé*
pòm makak   *pomme macaque*   monkey apple
ponpon jòn   *pompon jaune*   yellow pompom
ponpon souda   *pompon soldat*   soldier pompom
poupyé (bata)   *pourpier (bâtard)*   (wild) purslane
poupyé bò-lanmè   *pourpier-bord-de-mer*   seaside purslane
poupyé kouwan   *pourpier courant*   creeping purslane
powyé   *poirier*   pea tree
pwa   *pois*   pea
pwa bò-lanmè   *pois bord de mer*   seaside pea
pwa boukousou   *pois boucoussou*   Bookoosoo pea. See *boukousou*
pwa dou   *pois doux*   sweet pea
pwa gwaté   *pois gratter*   itching pea
pwa hazyé   *pois hallier*   pea plant
pwa jòn   *pois jaune*   yellow pea
pwa mabouya   *pois margouillat*   lizard pea. See *mabouj*
pwa pijon   *pois de pigeon*   pigeon pea
pwa pwazon   *pois poison*   poison pea
pwa savann   *pois de savane*   wild pea
pwa vonvon   *pois à vonvons*   bumble-bee vine. See *vonvon*
pwa wouj   *pois rouge*   red pea

pwa zonbi   *pois zombie*   zombie pea
pwa zwèzo   *pois des oiseaux*   bird pea
salad a lapen   *salade à lapin*   rabbit salad
salspawèy   *salsepareille*   sarsaparilla
simen kontwa   Dominican name for this worming agent, from the Latin *semen contra*, meaning 'seed against' (in this case, worms)
sinapis   *sinapisme*   mustard plaster (due to the taste of the plant)
siyo   *sureau*   elder
sonnèt   *sonnette*   rattle or hand-bell
soumaké   possibly from *sou marqué*, a marked coin
syèj   *cierge*   candle
tamawen bata   *tamarind bâtard*   bastard tamarind
tapi (vè)   *tapis (vert)*   (green) carpet
té bò-lanmè   *thé bord-de-mer*   seaside tea
té péyi   *thé pays*   country tea
teny wouj   *teigne rouge*   red scurf
tèt à nèg   *tête à nègre*   negro head
ti bal(y)é   *petit balai*   small broom
ti bòm   *petit baume*   little balsam
ti chik   *petite chique*   small chigger (bush)
ti kafé bata   *petit café bâtard*   small bastard coffee
ti kafé bwa   *petit café des bois*   small forest coffee
ti kafé mawon   *petit café marron*   small maroon (runaway) coffee
ti kwékwé   *petit crécré*   little crécré. Crécré is a Martiniquan word of unknown origin/meaning
ti kwèt a kòk   *petite crête à coq*   little cock's comb
ti léton   *petit laiteron*   little milk thistle
ti lis jòn   *petit lis jaune*   little yellow lily
ti Mawi   *petite Marie*   little Mary
ti mawgwit   *petite marguerite*   small daisy
ti pwa   *petit pois*   small pea
ti tanmawen   *petit tamarin*   small tamarind
ti teny (won)   *ti teigne (rond)*   small (round) scurf
ti twèf   *petit trèfle*   small trefoil/clover
ti vyòlèt   *petite violette*   little violet
twèf   *trèfle*   trefoil, referring to the three-lobed leaf (*trèfle* being French for the clubs of playing cards)
twèf jòn   *trèfle jaune*   yellow trefoil
valéryàn   *valériane*   valerian (common name of a plant in Europe)
vèdégwi   *vert de gris*   verdigris, ie green tarnish that develops on weathered copper and brass
venvenn/vèvenn (blé)   *verveine (bleu)*   (blue) vervain
vèvenn kawayib   *verveine caraïbe*   Caribbean vervain
vèvenn ké a rat   *verveine queue à rat*   rat tail vervain
vèvenn kouwan   *veveine courante*   creeping vervain
vèvenn latjé wat   see ***latjé wat***
véwonik   *véronique*   veronica or speedwell (name of a European weed)
vonvon   bumble bee (onomatopoeic)
vyé fiy   *vieille fille*   old maid

watjèt (flè) jòn   *raquette à fleurs jaunes*   yellow-flowered racquet
wézen   *raisin*   grape
wézinyé lanmè   *raisinier du bord-de-mer*   seaside grape tree
womaren (bò-lanmè)   *romarin (du bord-de-mer)*   (seaside) rosemary
(l)yàn(n) sèpan   *liane serpent*   snake vine
zakasya   acacia
zanmouwèt   *amourette*   from the name of an exotic *Acacia* used in marquetry
zèb   *herbe*   non-woody plant
zèb a albumin   *herbe à albumine*   albumin weed. Medicinal plant used to treat 'albumine', a creole medical term unconnected with albuminuria
zèb (a) chans   *herbe à la chance*   luck plant
zèb a chik   *herbe à chiques*   chigger bush, ie used against chiggers, skin-burrowing fleas
zèb a kò   *herbe à cors*   corn weed, ie used to remove corns
zèb a fanm   *herbe à femme*   woman herb, ie used by women
zèb a fè   *herbe à fer*   iron weed
zèb a koulèv   *herbe à couleuvre*   snake bush
zèb a lank   *herbe à l'encre*   ink weed
zèb a lon kou   *herbe à long cou*   long neck bush
zèb a pòk   from the popping sound made when the calyx is squeezed
zèb a pyan   *herbe à pian*   yaws herb (presumably for treating yaws, a skin disease)
zèb a vè   *herbe à vers*   worm weed
zèb akwè   *herbe à croix?*   possibly cross weed
zèb a(n)mè   *herbe amère*   bitter herb
zèb blan   *herbe blanche*   white herb
zèb bwilan   *herbe brûlante*   stinging herb
zèb dwagon   *herbe dragon*   dragon herb
zèb gwa   *herbe grasse*   fat herb
zèb gwo bouton   *herbe gros bouton*   big button/knob bush
zèb kouwès   *herbe à couresse/couleuvrel*   snake weed
zèb makònèt   *herbe à macornet*   of unknown origin/meaning
zèb malonmé   *herbe mal nommé*   see **malonmé**
zèb malotèt   *herbe mal-à-la-tête*   headache bush
zèb Man Bwaven   *herbe Madame Boivin*   Mrs Boivin's plant
zèb Man Lali   *herbe à Madame Lalie*   Mrs Lalie's plant
zèb pwazon   *herbe poison*   poison bush
zèb sèk   *herbe sêche*   dry bush
zèb sémityè   *herbe cimetière*   cemetery bush
zépina (péyi)   *épinard (pays)*   (country) spinach
zikak   *icaquel*   Amerindian name for the fruit
zingting   of unknown meaning/origin
ziyanm bwa   *igname bois*   forest yam
ziyanm kochon   *igname cochon*   pig yam
ziyanm mawon   *igname marron*   maroon (runaway) yam
zouti (bwilan)   *ortie (brûlante)*   (stinging) nettle
zouti bwa   *ortie-bois*   woody nettle
zyé a chat   *yeux de chat*   cat eyes
zyé a kwab   *yeux de crabe*   crab eyes

References

[1] Abbiw, D. (1990) *Useful plants of Ghana* Intermediate Technology Publications, London & Royal Botanic Gardens, Kew

[2] Adams, C.D. (1972) *Flowering plants of Jamaica* University of the West Indies, Mona, Jamaica

[3] Adams, D., Magnus, K. & Seaforth, C. (1963) *Poisonous plants in Jamaica* University of the West Indies, Mona, Jamaica

[4] Austin, D.F., Bourne, G.R. (1992) 'Notes on Guyana's medical ethnobotany' *Economic Botany* **46**, 293–298

[5] Barlow, V. (1993) *The nature of the islands*, Cruising Guide Publications, Dunedin, Florida

[6] Bayley, I. (1949) 'The bush-teas of Barbados' *Journal of the Barbados Museum & Historical Society* **16**, 103–113

[7] Beard, J.S. (1949) 'The natural vegetation of the Windward & Leeward islands' *Oxford Forestry Memoirs* **21**, 1–192

[8] Bell, C.R. & Taylor, B.J. (1982) *Florida wild flowers and roadside plants*, Laurel Hill Press, Chapel Hill

[9] Beuze, R. (1973) *La santé par les plantes des Antilles Françaises*, Emile Désormeaux, Fort-de-France

[10] Borchsenius, F. & Bernal, R. (1996) *Flora Neotropica Monograph 70, Aiphanes (Palmae)*, New York Botanical Garden, New York

[11] Carrington, S. (1993) *Wild plants of Barbados*, Macmillan Education Ltd., London & Basingstoke

[12] Coomans, H.E. & Coomans-Eustatia, M. (1988) *Flowers from St. Martin*, De Walburg Pers, Zutphen

[13] Correll, D.S. & Correll, H.B. (1982) *Flora of the Bahama Archipelago*, J. Cramer, Vaduz

[14] Duke, J.A. (1985) *CRC handbook of medicinal herbs*, CRC Press, Boca Raton, Florida

[15] Feldmann, P. & Barré, N. (1993) 'Les orchidées des Petites Antilles liste commentée actualisée' *L'Orchidophile* **106**, 68–80

[16] Feng, P.C. (1956) 'A preliminary survey of the medicinal plants of British Guiana' *West Indian Medical Journal* **5**, 265–270

[17] Fiard, J.-P. (1992) *Arbres rares et menacés de la Martinique* Société des Galeries de Géologie et la Botanique de Fort de France, Fort-de-France

[18] Fournet, J. (1978) *Flore illustrée des phanérogames de Guadeloupe et de Martinique* Institut National de la Recherche Agronomique (INRA), Paris

[19] Fournet, J. & Hammerton, J.L. (1991) *Weeds of the Lesser Antilles/Mauvaises herbes des petites antilles* INRA, Paris. CARDI, Bridgetown

[20] Fournet, J. personal communication

[21] Francis, J., Rivera, C. & Figueroa, J. (1994) *Toward a woody plant list for Antigua and Barbuda: past and present* General Technical Report SO–102, USDA, New Orleans

[22] Fraser, H., Carrington, S., Forde, A., Gilmore, J. (1990) *A–Z of Barbadian Heritage* Heinemann Publishers (Caribbean) Ltd., Kingston, Jamaica

[23] Gooding, E.G.B. (1939–1942) 'Facts and beliefs about Barbadian plants' *Journal of the Barbados Museum & Historical Society* **7**, 170–74; **8**, 32–35, 103–106, 194–97; **9**, 17–19, 84–88, 126–129, 192–94; **10**, 3–6

[24] Gooding, E.G.B., Loveless, A.R. & Proctor, G.R. (1965) *Flora of Barbados* H.M.S.O., London

[25] Groome, J.R. (1970) *A natural history of the island of Grenada W.I.* Caribbean Printers Ltd., Arima, Trinidad

[26] Heywood, V.H. (ed.) (1978) *Flowering plants of the world* Oxford University Press, Oxford, London, Melbourne

[27] Honychurch, P.N. (1978) *Dominica's National Park Vegetation* Dominica National Park Service, Roseau, Dominica

[28] Honychurch, P.N. (1986) *Caribbean wild plants and their uses* Macmillan Caribbean, London & Basingstoke

[29] Howard, R.A. (1952) 'The vegetation of the Grenadines, Windward Islands, B.W.I.' *Contributions from the Gray Herbarium of Harvard University* **174**, 1–129

[30] Howard, R.A. (1974–1989) *Flora of the Lesser Antilles Vols. 1–6* Arnold Arboretum, Jamaica Plain, Massachusetts

[31] Howard, R.A. (1994) '18th Century West Indian pharmaceuticals' *Harvard Papers in Botany* (5) 69–91

[32] Howard, R.A. personal communication

[33] Hughes, G. (1750) *The natural history of Barbados* London, 1972 reprint, Arno Press, New York

[34] James, A.A. (1985) *Flora and fauna of the Cabrits peninsula* Forestry & Wildlife Division, Ministry of Agriculture, Dominica

[35] James, A.A. (1986) *Cabrits plants and their uses* Forestry & Wildlife Division, Ministry of Agriculture, Dominica

[36] Kenny, J. (1988) *Native orchids of the Eastern Caribbean* Macmillan Caribbean, London & Basingstoke

[37] Lampe, K.F. & McCann, M.A. (1985) *AMA handbook of poisonous and injurous plants* American Medical Association, Chicago

[38] Lawrence, G.H.M. (1951) *Taxonomy of vascular plants* Macmillan, New York

[39] Ligon, R. (1657) *A true and exact history of the island of Barbadoes* 1970 reprint, Frank Cass & Co. Ltd., London

[40] Little, E.L. & Wadworth, F.H. (1964) *Common trees of Puerto Rico and the Virgin Islands* United States Department of Agriculture (USDA), Washington, DC

[41] Little, E.L., Woodbury, R.O. & Wadsworth, F.H. (1974) *Trees of Puerto Rico and the Virgin Islands* USDA, Washington, DC

[42] Mabberley, D.J. (1987) *The plant-book* Cambridge University Press, Cambridge, New York, New Rochelle, Melbourne, Sydney

[43] Magras, M. (1989) *Caribbean flowers/Fleurs des Antilles* Les editions du Latanier, Saint Barthélemy

[44] Nellis, D.W. (1994) *Seashore plants of South Florida and the Caribbean* Pineapple Press, Sarasota

[45] Ouensanga, C. (1983) *Plantes médicinales et remèdes créoles. Tome I. Plantes médicinales* Emile Désormeaux, Paris

[46] Poole, R. (1753) *The beneficient bee: or, a traveller's companion. Containing each day's observation, in a voyage from London, to Gibralter, Barbadoes, Antigua, Barbuda, Mountserrat, Nevis. Containing a summary account of the said places* London

[47] Robineau, L. (ed.) (1991) *Hacia una farmacopea caribeña* Enda-Caribe & Universidad Nacional Autónoma de Honduras, Santo Domingo

[48] Rollet, B. (1992) 'Comments on and additions to the Flora of the Lesser Antilles by R.A. Howard and Flora of Dominica by D.H. Nicholson', *Bulletin du Museum national d'histoire naturelle* (4e sér.) **14**, 279–296.

[49] Sastre, C. & Portecop, J. *Plantes fabuleuses des Antilles* Editions Caribéennes, Paris

[50] Seaforth, C.E. (1988) *Natural products in Caribbean folk medicine* University of the West Indies, Trinidad

[51] Seaforth, C.E., Adams, C.D. & Sylvester, Y. (1983) *A guide to the medicinal plants of Trinidad & Tobago* Commonwealth Secretariat, London

[52] Simpson, B.B., Ogorzaly, M.C. (1986) *Economic botany: plants in our world* McGraw-Hill Book Co., New York

[53] Stoffers, A.L. (ed.) (1966–1984) *Flora of the Netherlands Antilles. Spermatophyta Dicotyledonae* **II**, 1–96 & 97–209; **III**, 1–60, 61–142, 143–409, Natural Science Study Group of the Netherlands Antilles, Utrecht

[54] Stuart, M. (1979) *The encyclopedia of herbs and herbalism* Macdonald & Co. (Publishers) Ltd., London

[55] Tirimanna, S. (1987) *Medicinal plants of Suriname* Westfort Publishers, Paramaribo

[56] Whittaker, M.C. (1992) *Medicinal plants of St. Kitts & Nevis Part I* College of Further Education, Basseterre, St Kitts

[57] Williams, R.O. & Williams, R.O. (1969) *The useful and ornamental plants of Trinidad and Tobago* Government Printery, Trinidad

[58] Zomlefer, W.B. (1994) *Guide to flowering plant families* University of North Carolina Press, Chapel Hill & London

Index

Family names are given in capitals, scientific names in bold italics, common names in normal type face and French creole names in italics.

Aaron's beard   29
Abutilon hirtum   62
Acacia farnesiana   42
Acacia tortuosa   42
Acalypha poiretii   53
ACANTH FAMILY   11, 90
ACANTHACEAE   11, 12, 90
ACKEE FAMILY   58
Aechmea lingulata   17
Aegiphila martinicencis   81
AGAVACEAE   21
Agave barbadensis   21
Agave caribaeicola   21
Agave dussiana   21
AGAVE FAMILY   21
Agave karatto   21
Agave schuermaniana   21
Agave van grolae   21
agouma   87, 106
Aiphanes minima   16
AIZOACEAE   36
akoma (franc)   72
Albizia lebbeck   42
Alternanthera tenella   33
Alysicarpus vaginalis   44
AMARANTH FAMILY   33
AMARANTHACEAE   33
Amaranthus dubius   33
Amaranthus spinosus   33
Amaranthus viridis   33
AMARYLLIDACEAE   8, 19
amaryllis   20
AMARYLLIS FAMILY   8, 19
Ambrosia hispida   99
Ammannia coccinea   68
Andrographis paniculata   90
annanna bata wouj   18, 106
annanna mawon   17, 106
anodyne   63
Anthurium willdenowii   16
Antigonon leptopus   31
APIACEAE   70
APOCYNACEAE   10, 74
ARACEAE   8, 16
Ardisia solanacea   71
ARECACEAE   8, 16
Argemone mexicana   37
Argusia gnaphalodes   78

Argythamnia polygama   54
ARISTOLOCHIACEAE   30
Aristolochia trilobata   30
AROID FAMILY   8, 16
ASCLEPIADACEAE   10, 74
Asclepias curassavica   74
ASTERACEAE   9, 10, 99
asthma plant   54
Asystasia gangetica   91
awali   65, 106

baby bush   39
baby eye   56
Bacopa monnieri   88
balé see *balyé*
balizyé (wouj)   22, 106
ball bush   85
ball head   85
ballard bush   64
balloon vine   58
balsam   59, 64, 65
balsam apple   98
BALSAM FAMILY   59
BALSAMINACEAE   59
balyé   61
balyé midi/onzè   63, 106
balyé savann (bata)   41, 61, 63, 73, 106
barbed wire   22
Barleria prionitis   91
barricado   56
bay tansy   99
bat tree   38
bastard cankerberry   96
beach apple   56
beef steak   44
beefwood   34
BEET FAMILY   32
bélanjè bata   88, 106
bélanjè dyab   88
belladonna   86
belle mexicaine   31, 106
bellyache bush   56
bhaji   33
BIGNONIACEAE   89
bilimbi   94, 106
billbush   57
binairy   63
birch gum   52
bird pepper   87
birds cherry   69
bitter shrub   54
bitter tamarind   57
black berry   69

black bush   61
black cherry   69
black loblolly   34
black sage   79
black torch   64, 94
black widow   64
black willow   38
black-eyed Susan   92
blackbead tree   60
blessed thistle   70
blister bush   72
blood root   91
bloodberry   35
blue fifi   45
blue vine   45
bluebell   45
blueberry   94
Blutaparon vermiculare   33
blydog   41
boater bush   65
Boehmeria ramiflora   29
Boerhavia coccinea   34
bòm   85, 106
bonavist   48
Bontia daphnoides   92
BORAGE FAMILY   12, 78
BORAGINACEAE   12, 78
bottle brush   38
bottle cod   46
BOUGAINVILLEA FAMILY   34
boukousou   48, 106
Bourreria succulenta   78
bouton blan   102, 106
bouvier   73
bower   33
boyo chat/djab   19, 106
BRASSICACEAE   38
bread   46
bread and cheese   44, 59
BREADFRUIT FAMILY   28
brenvilyé   73, 106
broadback   34
broken skull   38
Bromelia plumieri   18
BROMELIACEAE   8, 17
BROMELIAD FAMILY   8, 17
broom   61, 63, 64
broom broom   54
broom cassia   41
broomweed   61, 63
brush William   43
Bryophyllum pinnatum   39
buck root   93

116

bud grass   46
buff coat   65
burn-mouth vine   49
burn-tongue vine   49
burr mallow   64
Bursera simaruba   52
BURSERACEAE   10, 52
button bush   68
button mangrove   68
button weed   85, 96
button wood   68
bwa   106
bwa annizèt   27, 106
bwa bwanda   93, 106
bwa bwaslè   71, 106
bwa chandèl   27, 94, 106
bwa chanpinyon   64, 106
bwa dowanj   28, 106
bwa flanbo   94, 106
bwa foufou   94, 106
bwa gwiyé   69, 106
bwa jòn   66, 82, 106
bwa jounou   92, 106
bwa kabwit   81, 95, 106
bwa kabwit bata   78, 106
bwa kabwit nwè   95, 106
bwa kannèl   66, 106
bwa kannon   28, 75, 106
bwa kawayib   90, 107
bwa kawé   82, 107
bwa kilibwi   94, 107
bwa kòklèt   82, 107
bwa koko kawet   66, 107
bwa kòtlèt   70, 107
bwa koulèv   38, 107
bwa kwab   44, 107
bwa kwapo   92, 107
bwa lafyèv   71, 107
bwa lajan   54, 107
bwa lank   95, 107
bwa mòwtèl   47, 107
bwa nwè   38, 42, 107
bwa péta   75, 107
bwa pisanli   90, 107
bwa pouant   38, 107
bwa sann   70, 107
bwa syèj   27, 107
bwa ti fèy   69, 107
bwa zendyen   92, 107
bwa zizi   79, 107
bwa zowtolan   56, 107
bwi   30, 107

CABBAGE FAMILY   38
CACTACEAE   67
cactus   67
CACTUS FAMILY   67
Caesalpinia bonduc   40
CAESALPINIACEAE   9, 40
calabash   89
Calotropis procera   75
Canavalia rosea   45
candelabra cactus   67
candle bush   27

candlewood   70, 94
candlewood tree   58
Canella winterana   66
CANELLACEAE   66
CAPER FAMILY   38
CAPPARACEAE   38
Capparis cynophallophora   38
Capparis flexuosa   38
Capraria biflora   88
CAPRIFOLIACEAE   97
Cardiospermum microcarpum   58
carila   98
carpet daisy   102
CARROT FAMILY   70
Casearia decandra   66
casha   42, 67
cashie   85
CASSIA FAMILY   9, 40
cassie   42
cat claw   70
cat's blood   35
catalpa   63
Cecropia schreberiana   28
cedar   89
cemetery vine   31
Centrosema virginianum   45
cerasee   98
Cestrum latifolium   86
Cestrum nocturnum   86
chadwon béni   70, 107
chadwon (mawbwé)   37, 107
Chamaecrista glandulosa var.
   swartzii   41
Chamaesyce hirta   54
chandilyé   85, 107
chans   16, 107
chapantyé gwan bwa   92, 107
chapo dlo   37, 107
chapo glo   27, 107
chaw stick   60
checkweed   54
CHENOPODIACEAE   32
Chenopodium ambrosoides   32
chew stick   60
chigger nut   81
children weed   57
chink   78
chinkswood   78
Chiococca alba   93
Chomelia fasiculata   93
chou pikan   16, 107
Christmas bush   41, 100
Christmas hope   90
CHRYSOBALANACEAE   40
Chrysobalanus icaco   40
cillament bush   66
Cissus verticillata   61
Citharexylum spinosum   82
CITRUS FAMILY   52
cla-cla   70
clammy burr   84
Cleome gynandra   39
Clerodendrum aculeatum   82
Clerodendrum indicum   82

Clitoria ternatea   45
Clusia plukenetii   65
Clusia rosea   65
CLUSIACEAE   65
Coccinia grandis   97
Coccoloba pubescens   31
Coccoloba uvifera   32
cockroach grass   19
coco plum   40
COCOA FAMILY   64
COFFEE FAMILY   11, 93
coffee fence   82
colic bush   39
Colubrina arborescens   60
columnar cactus   67
COMBRETACEAE   68
Commelina elegans   19
COMMELINACEAE   8, 19
COMPOSITAE   99
conga lala   99
conga root   35
Conocarpus erectus   68
CONVOLVULACEAE   10, 11, 75
Conyza canadensis   99
coralila   31
coralita   31
Corchorus siliquosus   61
Cordia curassavica   79
Cordia dentata   79
cossie   42
cotton   3
cow heel   75
cowheel (bush)   27
cow pops   87
cowitch   49
crab wood   44
crapaud bones   27
CRASSULACEAE   39
crata   21
creeping Charlie   29
Crescentia cujete   89
Crinum bulbispermum   19
Crotalaria retusa   46
croton   55
Croton flavens   54
Croton lobatus   55
CRUCIFERAE   38
CUCURBIT FAMILY   11, 97
CUCURBITACEAE   10, 11, 97
cudjoe root   35
Cupania americana   58
cupid's paintbrush   100
cure-for-all   53
cutlass   78
cutlet   82
CYMODOCEACEAE   15

dagger   21
DAISY FAMILY   10, 99
Dalbergia ecastaphyllum   46
danday   35, 107
dartwood   93
Datura stramonium   86
David's root   93

117

dayi 84, 107
Demerara primrose 91
Dendropemon caribaeus 30
Desmodium incanum 46
devil tree 47
dildo 67
dimwazèl 35, 107
Dioscorea altissima 22
DIOSCOREACEAE 22
dité péyi 88, 107
doctor bush 27
Doctor John 72
dog berry/blood 35
dog bush 41, 91
dog dumpling 94
dog wood 38
dolly tomato 87
donkey rub-down 49
douvan(t) nèg 35, 107
dry juice 37
ducana leaf 31
duck weed 17, 101
DUCKWEED FAMILY 17
dul-dul 67
DUNK FAMILY 60
Dutch casha 42
dutchman's butter 41
DUTCHMAN'S PIPE FAMILY 30
dyotin 41, 107

Easter lily 20
Easter vine 53
Eclipta prostrata 99
elder 97
elder bush 27, 90
elderberry 97
Emilia fosbergii 100
endigo bata 48, 107
English clammy cherry 79
Enicostema verticillatum 73
Epidendrum ciliare 24
Erithalis fruticosa 94
Erithalis odorifera 94
Eryngium foetidum 70
Erythrina variegata 47
Eugenia monticola 69
Eupatorium odoratum 100
Euphorbia cyathophora 55
EUPHORBIACEAE 10, 53
Evolvulus nummularius 75
eye bright 80
eyelash orchid 23

FABACEAE 9, 10, 11, 44
fat pork 40
FAT PORK FAMILY 40
fawin cho/zombi (zonbi) 57, 107
fèy chofi 39, 107
fèy douvan 35, 107
fiddlewood 82
fifi 45
fireman 58
fireweed 86
fitweed 70

FLACOURTIACEAE 66
flanbo blan 71, 107
flat hand dildo 67
flè jòn 90, 101, 107
flè siwo 97, 107
Flemingia strobilifera 47
fléwi Nwèl 100, 108
forbidden fruit 94
FRANKINCENSE FAMILY 52
French cotton 75
French weed 19
fustic 28

garden balsam 59
Garfield bush 50
garlic root 35
GENTIAN FAMILY 73
GENTIANACEAE 73
géwitout 39, 84, 108
gimòv 65, 108
giant milkweed 75
glouglou (wouj) 16, 108
goat meat 43
goat weed 88
goat wiss 19
golden bells 92
golden bush 70
golden seal 90
gomyé see *gonmyé*
gonbo bata 62, 108
gonbo fwansèz 55, 108
gonbo savann 62, 108
gonbo zonbi 62
gonmyé wouj/modi 52, 108
Gonzalagunia hirsuta 94
Gossypium barbadense 3
Gouania lupuloides 60
gouyavyé 69, 108
GRAPE VINE FAMILY 61
graveyard daisy 102
GUAVA FAMILY 11, 69
gully balsam 65
gully root 35
gum tree 52
gumbo limbo 52
gutter lily 21
GUTTIFERAE 65
gwan fèy 31, 108
gwan folet 37, 108
gwan kouzen 64, 108
gwan twèf 51, 108
gwenn amba fèy (blan) 57, 108
gwenn zowtolan 56, 108
gwif chat 44, 108
gwigwi 16, 108
gwo balyé 41, 108
gwo mov 62, 108
gwo ponpon/tèt 85, 108
gwo zowèy 56, 108

Haematoxylon campechianum 41
hague bush 82
Halodule wrightii 15
hazyé 108

heart seed 58
Helianthus annuus 10
Heliconia bihai 22
HELICONIA FAMILY 22
HELICONIACEAE 22
Heliotropium angiospermum 80
Heliotropium microphyllum 80
herbe couchée 78, 108
herringbone 57
Hibiscus 3
HIBISCUS FAMILY 12, 62
hibiscus tree 63
Hippeastrum puniceum 20
Hippobroma longiflora 98
Hippomane mancinella 56
hog bhaji 36
hog butter 34
hog feed/food 34
hog meat 36
hog weed 34
hog wood 70
honeysuckle 85
HONEYSUCKLE FAMILY 97
hontèz 43, 108
hoop wiss 35
hoop wood 46
hopweed 86
horse bean 45
horse eye 40
horse nickel/nicker 40
horse purslane 36
horse rub-down 49
HYDROCHARITACEAE 15
HYDROPHYLLACEAE 78
Hymenocallis caribaea 20
Hyptis pectinata 85

immortel 47
impatience 59
Impatiens balsamina 59
Indian mallow 64
Indian root 74
indigo 48
Indigofera suffruticosa 48
information bush 27
Inga laurina 43
ink balls 87
ink bush 94
ink vine 66, 72
iodine bush 78
ipéka bata 74, 108
Ipomoea hederifolia 76
Ipomoea obscura 76
Ipomoea pes-caprae ssp.
  brasiliensis 76
IRIDACEAE 22
IRIS FAMILY 22
iron mang 68

jack oats 100
Jacquemontia pentantha 77
Jaquinia armillaris 71
jasmen blan 72, 108
jasmen boukè 72, 108

jasmen sovaj 86, 108
Jasminum fluminense 72
Jatropha gossypiifolia 56
jèwonflé 70, 108
jiwòf glo 70, 108
jiwòf ma 70, 108
Johanna 74
John Bull tree 63
joint bush 27
jòn a zé 66, 108
joy juice 86, 94
Judas tree 47
jug plum 34
jumbie apple 66
jumbie basil 35
jumbie breadfruit 94
jumbie cucumber 97
jumbie earring 46
jumbie pepper 35
jumbie prickle 67
jumbie soursop 40, 94
Justicia secunda 91
JUTE FAMILY 61

kach-kach 40, 108
kafé bwa 30
kaka béké 41, 42, 108
kaka bétjé 41, 108
kalbas 89, 108
KALLANCHOE FAMILY 39
Kallstroemia pubescens 51
kampèch 41, 108
kanker berry 87
kannik 40, 108
karatas 18, 108
kaya blan 39, 108
kilibwi 94, 108
kiwaj 19, 108
kòd a vyélon 46, 108
kòd gwaté 61, 108
kòklya 27, 109
koko chat 22, 109
koko wavet 66, 109
kòlan 46, 84, 109
koma (franc) 72, 109
konkonb chyen/dyab 86, 109
konkonb kouli 98, 109
konkonb zonbi 86, 109
kòsòl chyen 94, 109
kòtlèt 78, 109
kòton kadwi 74, 109
koukouli 98, 109
koupanyi 54, 109
koupayou (bata) 54, 109
koupyé 36, 109
koupyé bata 51
kouzen maho 64, 109
kouzen wouj 64, 109
kòwòsòl zombi 94, 109
kwékwé 70
kwèson kouwan 51, 109
kwèson savann 38, 109
kwèt kodend 80, 109
kwinin pavé 88, 109

LABIATAE 85
Lablab purpureus 48
lady's slipper 56
lady-of-the night 86
lady-shame 43
lagli 79, 109
LAMIACEAE 11, 12, 85
lamowi 39, 109
lance mahoe root 81
lang a bèf 21, 109
lang a chat 57, 100, 109
lang poul 73, 95, 109
Lantana camara 83
Lantana trifolia 83
lanvè jòn 22, 109
lanvè mal 22, 109
lapit 21, 109
Laportea aestuans 29
laswa 75, 109
latjé wat 84, 109
leaf-of-life 39
leather coat (tree) 31, 65
Lemna perpusilla 17
LEMNACEAE 17
lent tree 47
Leonotis nepetifolia 85
Leonurus sibiricus 85
Lepianthes peltata 27
Lepidium virginicum 38
lépini (blan/wouj) 52, 109
Leucaena leucocephela 43
lignum vitae 51
LIGNUM VITAE FAMILY 51
lilac bush 55
LILIACEAE 8
lily 19
lion head 85
lion tail 85
Lippia strigulosa 83
lis blan 20, 109
lis jòn savann 22, 109
lis wouj 20, 109
liseron bleu 77, 109
liseron rouge 76, 109
lizard food 98
LOBELIA FAMILY 98
LOBELIACEAE 98
LOGANIACEAE 73
loggerhead weed 73
logwood 41
LORANTHACEAE 30
Lord Lavington 85
love bush 39
luck bush 47
Ludwigia octovalvis 70
lyann a bawik 35, 46, 109
lyann a dlo 61, 109
lyann a si 59, 109
lyann a sosyé 93, 109
lyann blan 35, 109
lyann blé 77, 110
lyann bwanda 53, 110
lyann bwilan 58, 110
lyann mang 46, 59, 110

lyann mòl 61, 110
lyann noyo 19, 77, 110
lyann nwè 81, 110
lyann Pak 53, 110
lyann pèsi 58, 110
lyann savon 60, 110
lyann wòz 53, 110
LYTHRACEAE 68

mabi 60, 110
mabouj 38, 110
macaw palm 16
Maclura tinctoria 28
Macroptilium lathyroides 48
maho (bò-)lanmè 63, 79, 110
maho nwè 79, 110
mahoe 61, 63
maiden apple 98
makata (bous) 43, 110
mal bwa chandèl 71, 110
mal dòmi 27, 110
mal èstomak 27, 110
mal tèt 27, 110
mal watjèt 67, 110
Malachra alceifolia 62
malenmbé 27, 110
malgoj 51
malonmé vwè 54, 110
MALPIGHIACEAE 53
MALVACEAE 12, 62
Malvastrum americanum 62
MAMMEY APPLE FAMILY 65
man piaba 85
man 'pon tree 30
man-of-war bush 38
man-to-man 46
manatee grass 15
manchineel 56
mang wouj 68, 110
MANGROVE FAMILY 68
manicou feed 40
mannjini 56, 110
mansniyé 56, 110
many-seed 70
mapou (ti fèy) 34, 110
marguerite à tonnelles 101, 110
marigold 102
marsh mallow 65
masambay 39
mast wood 72
mastic 72
matwikè 101, 110
mauby 60
mawgwit blan 102, 110
Mawi hont 43, 110
Mawi Jann 43, 110
Mawi lopital 62, 110
maypole 21
médsinyé 56, 110
médsinyé modi 56, 110
médsinyé wouj 56, 110
mélanjèn dyab 88, 110
MELASTOMATACEAE 70
MELASTOME FAMILY 70

119

Melochia nodiflora 64
Melochia tomentosa 64
méné vini 77, 110
mennen vini 77, 110
Merremia dissecta 77
MESEMBRYANTHEMUM
 FAMILY 36
Metastelma barbadensis 75
Metastelma parviflorum 75
méwizyé 69, 110
méwizyé ti fèy 69
Mexican poppy 37
mèzè Mawi 43, 110
miamossi 43
Miconia laevigata 70
mil gwenn 95, 110
milk bush 56, 75
milk grass 54
milk weed 54
milky bush 54
milky-milky 54, 55
mimosa 43
MIMOSA FAMILY 9, 42
Mimosa pudica 43
MIMOSACEAE 9, 42
MINT FAMILY 11, 85
miracle fence 82
miraculous vine 98
mistletoe 30
MISTLETOE FAMILY 30
miwèt 35, 110
Momordica charantia 98
money bush 41, 44
monkey apple 75
monkey banana 17, 18
monkey dumpling 94
monkey hand 27
monkey spoon 57
monkey tamarind 41
monval 43, 111
MORACEAE 10, 28
Morinda citrifolia 94
mother sigil 50
mother-in-law's tongue 42
motherwort 85
mouzanbé blan 39, 55, 111
mòv 64, 111
mòv gwi 65, 111
mòv savann 62, 111
mòwtèl 47, 111
Mucuna pruriens 49
mùrier pays 28, 111
mutad péyi 72, 111
mutton porridge 57
MYOPORACEAE 92
Myrcia citrifolia var. *citrifolia* 69
MYRSINACEAE 71
MYRTACEAE 11, 12, 69

naked indian 52
Nama jamaicensis 78
nénuphar 37, 111
Neptunia plena 44
nettle 29
NETTLE FAMILY 29

nightshade 86
noyo vine 77
NYCTAGINACEAE 34
NYMPHACEAE 37
Nymphaea ampla 37

Odontonema nitidum 92
OLACACEAE 30
old woman's bush 72
Oldenlandia corymbosa 95
OLEACEAE 72
OLEANDER FAMILY 74
OLIVE FAMILY 72
olivyé bò-lanmè 68, 92, 111
ONAGRACEAE 70
Opuntia dillenii 67
ORCHID FAMILY 8, 23
ORCHIDACEAE 8, 23
OXALIDACEAE 51
Oxalis debilis var. *corymbosa* 51
OXALIS FAMILY 51

pain killer 94
Palicourea crocea 95
PALM FAMILY 8, 16
PALMAE 16
paltivyé wouj 68, 111
pantouf 56, 111
PAPAVERACEAE 37
part-of-man-life 73
Parthenium hysterophorus 101
Passiflora suberosa 66
PASSIFLORACEAE 10, 11, 66
PASSION FRUIT FAMILY 11, 66
pàt a kanna 102, 111
patagon wouj 34, 111
patat bò-lanmè 76, 111
Paullinia cururu 59
PEA FAMILY 9, 11, 44
pear apple 98
pearwood tree 58
Pectis humifusa 101
Pedilanthus tithymaloides 56
pengwen 18, 111
Peperomia pellucida 27
pepper cinnamon 66
PEPPER FAMILY 27
pèsi bata 58, 111
pèsi nwè 59, 111
Petiveria alliacea 35
Phyllanthus amarus 57
Phyllanthus epiphyllanthus 57
Physalis angulata 87
PHYTOLACCACEAE 35
piaba 85
pibry 82
pickle ash 37
pie bark/crust 71
pig weed 19
pikan kouzen 64, 111
pikannyé jòn 91, 111
Pilea nummularifolia 29
Pilosocereus royeni 67
pingwing 18
pip zonbi 98, 111

pipe organ cactus 67
Piper dilatatum 27
Piper nigrum 27
PIPERACEAE 27
pipeshank 98
piri 82
Pisonia fragrans 34
piss-weed 102
pissabed 41, 43
Pistia stratiotes 16
Pitcairnia angustifolia 18
Pithecellobium unguis-cati 44
plòk 39, 111
PLUMBAGINACEAE 72
PLUMBAGO FAMILY 72
Plumbago scandens 72
POINSETTIA FAMILY 53
poison apple 56
poison Johanna 74
pok (pok) 87
police macca 51
polycrozier 16
POLYGALACEAE 53
POLYGONACEAE 31
pòm kouli 98, 111
pòm lyann hazyé 66, 111
pòm makak 94, 111
pond grass 19
pond weed 17
ponpon jòn 42, 44, 111
ponpon souda 85, 111
poor man's pepper 38
pop-a-gun 28
pop bush 66
poppers 87
POPPY FAMILY 37
pops 87
Portulaca oleracea 36
PORTULACACEAE 36
POUI FAMILY 89
poupyé 36, 111
poupyé bata 51, 111
poupyé bò-lanmè 36, 111
poupyé kouwan 36, 111
powyé 89, 111
prickle pear 67
prickly yam vine 22
Priva lappulacea 84
privet 82
privy fence 82
privy hedge 82
*Pseudogynoxys
 chenopodioides* 101
Psychotria nervosa 96
pudding bush/wiss 61
purple fifi 39
purslane 36
PURSLANE FAMILY 36
pussley 36
pwa bò-lanmè 45, 111
pwa boukousou 48, 111
pwa dou 43, 111
pwa gwaté 49, 111
pwa hazyé 49, 111
pwa jòn 50, 111

pwa mabouya 38, 111
pwa pijon 48, 111
pwa-pwa 45, 111
pwa pwazon 48, 51, 111
pwa savann 45, 112
pwa vonvon 45, 111
pwa wouj 48, 111
pwa zonbi 46, 48, 50, 51, 112
pwa zwèzo 49, 112
pwi-pwi 43

QUEEN-OF-FLOWERS FAMILY 68

rabbit food 85
rabbit meat 84, 100
rabbit thistle 102
rabbit weed 33
rata sugar 41
Rauvolfia tetraphylla 74
razyé 108
red dialthaea 64
red head 74
red mangrove 68
red palicorea 95
red rodwood 69
red tassel 100
red top 74
red wood 43
RHAMNACEAE 60
Rhizophora mangle 68
RHIZOPHORACEAE 68
Rhynchosia minima 49
river lily 19
river tamarind 41, 43
Rivina humilis 35
rock bush 27
rock sage 54
rodwood 69
roselle 3
RUBIACEAE 11, 12, 93
RUTACEAE 10, 52

sage 83
sailor's broom 64
salad a lapen 100, 112
salspawèy 21, 112
salt fish 39
Salvia occidentalis 86
sambo 39
Sambucus canadensis 97
SAPINDACEAE 10, 58
SAPODILLA FAMILY 72
SAPOTACEAE 10, 72
SARSAPARILLA FAMILY 19
sarsparilla 22
scarlet ipomoea 76
Schoepfia schreberi 30
scratch wiss 61
SCROPHULARIACEAE 88
sea bean 45
sea grape 32
SEA GRAPE FAMILY 31
SEA GRASS FAMILY 15
sea olive 92
seaside bean 45

seaside geranium 99
seaside lavender 78
seaside mahoe 63
seaside morning glory 76
seaside rosemary 78
seaside sage 54
seaside samphire 36
seaside vine 76
seaside wiss 76
seaside yam 76
Securidaca diversifolia 53
seed-under-leaf 57
Senna bicapsularis var.
   bicapsularis 41
sensitive plant 43
Sesuvium portulacastrum 36
shado beni 70
shado vinni 70
shak-shak 42, 46
shame bush 43, 44
shame lady 43, 44
shame weed 43
shame-lady-shame 43
shameful 43
shamrock 51
sheep poison 74
shine bush 27
shining bush 27
shoal grass 15
shushel 42
shut-your-house-man-a-come 43
Sida acuta 63
Sideroxylon foetidissimum 72
silver bush 27
simen kontwa 32, 112
sinapis 72, 112
sissel 37
six-sixty-six 30
siyo 97, 112
skipping rope 61
slipper plant 56
small red trubba 88
small wiss 35
SMILACACEAE 19
Smilax oblongata 19
snakewood 60
SNAPDRAGON FAMILY 88
snowberry 93
snuff tree 63
SOLANACEAE 12, 86
Solanum americanum 87
Solanum torvum 88
soldier bush 81
soldier's tassel 100
sonnèt 46, 112
sorrell 3
soumaké 41, 112
sour prickle 67
Spanish oak 43
Spermacoce confusa 96
spider lily 20
spider whisp 39
SPIDERWORT FAMILY 8, 19
Spigelia anthelmia 73
Spilanthes urens 102

spinach 33, 87
Spiranthes lanceolatus 24
spirit weed 81
sprain bush 77
sprain leaf 75
St John's bush 91, 96
Stachytarpheta jamaicensis 84
star of Bethlehem 98
STEPHANOTIS FAMILY 74
STERCULIACEAE 64
sticky cherry 79
Stigmaphyllon ovatum 53
stinging nettle 29, 58
stink bush 39
stinking miss 39
strong man bush 35
strongback 78
Strumpfia maritima 96
Stylosanthes hamata 50
sucking bottle 59
Susanna 82
Susanna berry 82
susumba 88, 97
sweet briar 42
sweet broom 63
SWEET POTATO FAMILY 11, 75
sweet weed 50
sweetheart 46
syèj 67, 112
Syringodium filiforme 15

Tabebuia heterophylla 89
Tabebuia pallida 89
tamawen bata 43, 112
tan-tan 43
tapi (vè) 99, 112
té bò-lanmè 82, 112
té péyi 88, 112
Tecoma stans 90
teny wouj 30, 112
tèt à nèg 61, 112
Thalassia testudinum 15
THEOPHRASTACEAE 71
Thespesia populnea 63
thibbet 42
thistle 37
thorn apple 86
threft leaf 75
Thunbergia alata 92
Thunbergia fragrans 92
ti balyé 61, 112
ti bòm 54, 112
ti chik 81, 112
ti dayi 84, 107
ti kafé bata 96, 112
ti kafé bwa 30, 112
ti kafé mawon 96, 112
ti kwékwé 70, 112
ti kwèt a kòk 80, 112
ti léton 100, 112
ti lis jòn 21, 112
ti mawgwit 101, 112
ti Mawi 43, 112
ti pwa 45, 112
ti tanmawen 41, 112

ti teny 80, 112
ti teny won 29, 112
ti twèf 50, 112
ti vyòlèt 86, 112
TILIACEAE 61
tisane 88
tobbo broom 54
TOMATO FAMILY 12, 86
torchwood 71
tourist tree 52
Tournefortia filiflora 80
Tournefortia volubilis 81
town clammy cherry 79
Tragia volibilis 58
Trianthema portulacastrum 36
Trichostigma octandrum 35
Tridax procumbens 102
Trimezia martinicensis 23
Trinidad vine 101
Triumfetta semitriloba 61
trumpet bush 28
trumpet tree 28
tulip tree 63
turpentine tree 52
turtle grass 15
TURTLE GRASS FAMILY 15
turtle weed 36
twèf 30, 112
twèf jòn 50, 112

UMBELLIFERAE 70
Urena lobata 64
URTICACEAE 29

valéryàn 34, 112
vèdègwi 17, 112
velvet burr 84
venvenn (blé) 84, 112
venvenn kawayib 102, 112
venvenn latjé wat 84, 112
VERBENACEAE 11, 12, 81
verivine 84
vermifuge 32
vervain 84
VERVAIN FAMILY 11, 81
vèvenn ké a rat 84, 112
vèvenn kouwan 83, 112
véwonik 75, 88, 112
Vigna luteola 50
Vigna vexillata 51
vine nettle 58
VISCACEAE 30
VITACEAE 61
vonvon 45, 112
vyé fiy 42, 112

Waltheria indica 65
warri seed 40
water cress(ie) 27
water grass 19
water lettuce/lily 16
WATER LILY FAMILY 37
water mint 29
water thistle 44
water weed 73

watjèt (flè) jòn 67, 113
wazyé 108
Wedelia trilobata 102
WEST INDIAN ALMOND
 FAMILY 68
WEST INDIAN CHERRY
 FAMILY 53
West Indian elder 97
West Indian tea 88
wézen 32, 113
wézinyé 31, 113
wézinyé lanmè 32, 113
white cedar 89
white harklis 52
white hoop 35
white lily 20
white root 60
white vervain 84
white water lily 37
whitehead (bush) 101
whitewood 89
widdi widdi bush 61
wild anthurium 16
wild cherry 66
wild cinnamon 66
wild clary 80
wild clove 70
wild cress 38
wild cucumber 97
wild dolly 48
wild eggplant 88
wild geranium 99
wild honey tree 66
wild hops 47
wild ipecacuanha 74
wild iris 22
wild jasmine 72, 86
wild mahoe 61
wild okra 53, 62
wild olive 92
wild onion 21
wild parsley 58
wild pea(s) 41, 45, 48
wild pepper grass 38
wild physic nut 56
wild pine 17, 18
wild plantain 22
wild plumbago 72
wild poinsettia 55
wild sage 79
wild senna 41
wild spinach 33
wild sweet pea 46
wild tamarind 41, 43
wild tea 88
wind flower 21
winer 45
wire weed 63
woman stinging nettle 58
woman's tongue 42
womaren 78, 113
womaren bò-lanmè 96, 113
wonder-of-the-world 39
worm bush 32, 73
worm draft 32

worm grass 32, 73
worm weed 32
worm wood 32

yàn sèpan 61, 113
YAM FAMILY 22
yam wiss 19
yellow balsam 54
yellow blossom 90
yellow crocus 21
yellow elder 90
yellow hock 37
yellow hollyhock 37
yellow iris 22
yellow sweet pea 46

zakasya 42, 113
zanmouwèt 82, 113
Zanthoxylum caribaeum 52
zèb a albumin 33, 113
zèb a chans 16, 113
zèb a chik 80, 113
zèb a fanm 102, 113
zèb a fè 70, 113
zèb a kò 56, 113
zèb a koulèv 86, 113
zèb a lank 99, 113
zèb a lon kou 82, 113
zèb a pòk 87, 113
zèb a pyan 101, 113
zèb a vè 32, 113
zèb akwè 96, 113
zèb amè 87, 113
zèb blan 35, 113
zèb brenvilyé 73
zèb bwilan 29, 58, 113
zèb dwagon 37, 113
zèb gwa 19, 113
zèb gwo bouton 85, 113
zèb kouwès 27, 113
zèb makònèt 96, 113
zèb malonmé 54, 113
zèb malotèt 39, 113
zèb Man Bwaven 74, 113
zèb Man Lali 85, 113
zèb pwazon 73, 98, 113
zèb sek 47, 113
zèb sémityè 31, 113
zèb vochlè 51
zépina (péyi) 33, 113
Zephyranthes citrina 21
Zephyranthes puertoricensis 21
zikak 40, 113
zing-zing 43
zingting 41, 113
ziyanm bwa 22, 113
ziyanm kochon 22, 113
ziyanm mawon 22, 113
zouti 29, 58, 113
zouti bwa 29, 113
zouti bwilan 29, 113
zyé a chat 40, 113
zyé a kwab 58, 113
ZYGOPHYLLACEAE 10, 51